Writing PERSONAL STATEMENTS
AND SCHOLARSHIP APPLICATION ESSAYS

A STUDENT HANDBOOK

JOE SCHALL
Pennsylvania State University

THOMSON
BROOKS/COLE

Australia · Canada · Mexico · Singapore · Spain · United Kingdom · United States

THOMSON

BROOKS/COLE

Writing Personal Statements and Scholarship Application Essays
Joe Schall

Executive Acquisitions Editor:
Lucas Tomasso

Senior Editor:
Jeff Davies

Managing Development Editor:
Jennifer Wreisner

Developmental Editor:
Connie Dayton

Editor:
Stephanie Larson

Project Development Manager:
Linda de Stefano

Marketing Coordinators:
Lindsay Annett and Sara Mercurio

Production/Manufacturing Manager:
Donna M. Brown

Production Editorial Manager:
Dan Plofchan

Rights and Permissions Specialists:
Kalina Hintz and Bahman Naraghi

Cover Image:*
AGE footstock/SuperStock

The Adaptable Courseware Program consists of products and additions to existing Brooks/Cole products that are produced from camera-ready copy. Peer review, class testing, and accuracy are primarily the responsibility of the author(s).

ISBN 1-581-75653-4

International Divisions List

Asia (Including India):
Thomson Learning
(a division of Thomson Asia Pte Ltd)
5 Shenton Way #01-01
UIC Building
Singapore 068808
Tel: (65) 6410-1200
Fax: (65) 6410-1208

Australia/New Zealand:
Thomson Learning Australia
102 Dodds Street
Southbank, Victoria 3006
Australia

Latin America:
Thomson Learning
Seneca 53
Colonia Polano
11560 Mexico, D.F., Mexico
Tel (525) 281-2906
Fax (525) 281-2656

Canada:
Thomson Nelson
1120 Birchmount Road
Toronto, Ontario
Canada M1K 5G4
Tel (416) 752-9100
Fax (416) 752-8102

UK/Europe/Middle East/Africa:
Thomson Learning
High Holborn House
50-51 Bedford Row
London, WC1R 4L$
United Kingdom
Tel 44 (020) 7067-2500
Fax 44 (020) 7067-2600

Spain (Includes Portugal):
Thomson Paraninfo
Calle Magallanes 25
28015 Madrid
España
Tel 34 (0)91 446-3350
Fax 34 (0)91 445-6218

for my students

About the Author

Joe Schall is the Giles Writer-in-Residence in Penn State's College of Earth and Mineral Sciences. He received an M.A. in English from Penn State in 1988 and a B.S. in English Education from Juniata College in 1981. He has won numerous  awards for his writing and teaching, including a 2005 Creative Artists Fellowship in Fiction from the PA Council on the Arts and the Wilson Award for Outstanding Teaching from Penn State. He has published over 20 short stories and his first collection of fiction, *Indentation and Other Stories*, was published by the New York University Press. He has also published over 40 freelance articles and several style manuals, including *Style for Students: Effective Technical Writing in the Information Age*, Outernet Publishing. He is a regular contributor to the magazine *Graduating Engineer and Computer Careers* and a former editor for the National Institute for Occupational Safety and Health.

Comments on the Handbook

Comments on this handbook are welcomed by the author:

Joe Schall
Giles Writer-in-Residence
14 Deike Building
University Park, PA 16802

Phone: 814-863-6077
Fax: 814-863-3349
E-mail: schall@ems.psu.edu

Author's Acknowledgments

This handbook was inspired by the many supporters of its sister publication: *Writing Recommendation Letters: A Faculty Handbook*, Outernet Publishing. Faithful users of my faculty handbook, particularly members of the National Association of Fellowships Advisors (NAFA), helped me see the need for a parallel student handbook on personal statements and application essays, and I am grateful. Most importantly, I acknowledge the many students from across the country—identified here not by name but warmly remembered nevertheless—who contributed samples to this handbook so that other writers might benefit from their experience. The effectiveness of this guide is directly linked to the willingness of these students to share their personal stories and provide models for study. Thanks also to Jon Earl and Jennifer Wreisner of Outernet Publishing.

CONTENTS

CHAPTER 3 _____ 33
MATTERS OF STYLE

CHAPTER 1

ETHICAL MATTERS

> *Keep conscience clear, then never fear.*
> —*Benjamin Franklin*

To begin to demonstrate the ethical issues involved in writing personal statements and application essays, I put to you three cases:

Case 1) A student applies to graduate school simply because he's not sure what else to do with his life. As he naively writes in his personal statement for a long-term goal: "I'm open to limitless possibilities!"

Case 2) A student plagiarizes material in a graduate application essay, reasoning that the same rules of citation that applied in college papers are not relevant, and that no one would bother checking her source anyway.

Case 3) A 4.0 student competes for and wins a national scholarship, attends graduate school for one semester, then drops out. He relishes the spirit of competition in winning the scholarship, but finds graduate school to be more unfriendly and less fulfilling than he expects.

As a writing tutor who has worked with thousands of students on their graduate applications, I have witnessed variations of all three cases. Saddest and worst of all, at least to my lights, is the ethical conundrum posed by Case 3. Students who accept national scholarships are literally taking someone else's seat from them, and the idea that they would then drop a scholarship that could have gone to someone else could be viewed as unconscionable.

Unifying all these cases is one guiding principle and a key reason why graduate schools and scholarship committees ask students for personal essays in the first place: *self-definition*. What you're really asked to do in writing a personal essay is to define yourself: your motivations, your conscience, your aptitude, your history, your commitment, your confidence, your responsibility, your decision-making—

in other words, your personal ethic. Any discussion of writing in relation to a graduate or scholarship application begins best with a consideration of guided self-reflection and ethics.

> *Education has really one basic factor,*
> *a* sine qua non—*one must want it.*
> *—George Edward Woodberry*

Self-Reflection and Graduate School

Before even beginning the application process, you must consider your reasoning for attending graduate school. Here are some commonly cited reasons, good and bad:

- Grad school is a great way to put off having to deal with the real world.
- The job market is bad right now, but by the time I finish my degree it will be better.
- Others have been telling me I should go to grad school because I had good grades as an undergrad.
- My parents went to grad school, so I should too.
- If I don't go to grad school, I'll have to move back home.
- A graduate degree will guarantee me more money in a future job.
- I have no job offers, but a decent GPA.
- I enjoy teaching and research, and grad school is an opportunity to do both.
- Grad school is a great way to start my emotional life over, especially since I just got dumped.
- Having a PhD would give me greater status and more self-worth.
- My work experience so far has been uninspiring, and I want to explore new opportunities that would come with a higher degree.
- I've applied for and received a scholarship, so I owe it to others to accept and use it.
- It's a sanctioned and convenient way to defer my student loans.
- Quite simply, I love learning.

It's easier to pass judgment on some of these reasons than others, but all are used regularly, and the most important realization about them is this: even the worst of reasons doesn't guarantee failure in grad school, just as even the best of reasons doesn't guarantee success. Those who succeed in graduate school tend to have a dogged work ethic matched to an ambitious vision and a strong sense of obligation to self, while those who do not succeed tend to spend much of their emotional time questioning their own sense of value and purpose. Because of the personal and professional challenges that come hand in hand with graduate education, all grad students experience concentrated periods of self-assessment, and responsible students begin that assessment even before they apply.

The Culture of Graduate Study

Every graduate department probably has one—someone you hear about and maybe even witness in your first year of study. Someone who lives on coffee and cigarettes and socializes vigorously, perhaps even earning a nickname such as "the Professor" or "Rasputin." Or someone who is reclusive and rarely seen, spiriting around the hallways or labs mostly at night, writing secret little notes that are crumbled and quickly stuffed into trouser pockets as you walk by. What these someones have in common is that they are graduate students (perhaps only allegedly) who are endlessly working on their dissertations.

There's an old joke about a student being admonished by his professor: "No, I'm afraid students can't get tenure." Some grad students hang around long enough that they don't seem to have had that conversation. They receive several extensions on their dissertations, perhaps even get part-time university-supported

> There's an old joke about a student being admonished by his professor: "No, I'm afraid students can't get tenure."

work teaching or doing lab research, and yet they never seem to finish what they claim is a legitimate and active dissertation, and instead become the stuff of puzzled ridicule and whispered legend.

How can such a thing happen? Quite simple: In graduate school, you are responsible for your own education. Hence, you can manage it well or you can squander it. Although graduate programs certainly do push their students along and support them, they also include a great number of hurdles than can be difficult to clear. Some sobering realities about graduate education follow:

- It typically takes 2-3 years to complete a master's degree and 5-6 to complete a PhD, and for some students it takes longer.
- During your graduate study, your sources of funding from the school may change from year to year and sometimes might even be in jeopardy.
- By comparison to undergraduate study, there is far less attention to grades and far more emphasis on a long-term, meaningful, publishable project. Despite less emphasis on grades, some grad students do fail their comprehensive exams and are ejected from their programs.
- Your relationship with your advisor is one of the most important in your life, with all the paradoxical trappings that can come with complex relationships: mentorship, competition, collegiality, distrust, empathy, partnership, unfairness, kindness, acquiescence, and even break-up.
- Your teaching assistantship may throw you to the lions and expect you to teach your own class with virtually no supervision, or you may spend much of your assistantship fighting with the Xerox machine and processing grades from a class of hundreds of students.
- Often, your advisor is struggling to get tenure just as you are struggling to probe relevant literature or gather data. The two struggles don't necessarily coalesce, and yours is readily viewed as the less meaningful one.
- If you're attending grad school on a university or national scholarship, you may be looked at with some suspicion by your peers and the faculty, or you may be held in higher regard than others, with elevated expectations.
- When you reach the dissertation stage, you may spend a year or two gathering data about a bad hypothesis, or you may write a chapter or two and be told by your committee that you must throw them out.
- Your living circumstances may be very different from what you experienced as an undergraduate, involving a sprawling city or a lonely little Podunk built around the university.
- Your peers in graduate school may range in age from 21 to 50+, with diverse experiences that include marriages, divorces, children, multiple degrees, work in industry, publications, international travel, or a series of failures beyond any you've ever experienced. These peers become your social world and often your only support network.

Certainly, the picture is not always as grim as this, and many students relish their time in graduate school—in fact, some call it the best time of their lives, especially those who attend graduate school after some unsatisfying time away from education. However, there is also plenty of evidence to back up the argument that things go poorly for many. One 2004 article from *The Chronicle of Higher Education* suggests that 40-50 percent of students who enter PhD programs do not finish (1). To explain these numbers, despite the absence of national studies on the problem, research from institution-specific studies still reveals some noteworthy trends:

> Women drop out at a higher rate than men. Minority students leave at a higher rate than white students do. Americans drop out more often than international students. And students leave humanities and social-science programs at a higher rate than those in the sciences.

Considering these disappointing trends, one would think that graduate scholarship winners don't fall into these patterns. But even scholars who are awarded graduate research fellowships from the National Science Foundation finish their PhD programs at about a rate of 75 percent, which is only slightly higher than for other science students in doctoral programs (1).

Finally, if you'd like an account of one particular case outlining some of the challenges of graduate school, read the sample four-page personal statement in Chapter 4 (pages 110-113) by the grad student seeking a transfer from one PhD program to another. As revealed in her personal statement, the student had four different advisors in her first PhD program, suffering a series of missteps that reflect the circumstances of many graduate students. Happily, despite the student's obvious hop-along graduate educational path, at the time of this writing she was thriving in her new graduate program.

> Women drop out at a higher rate than men. Minority students leave at a higher rate than white students do. Americans drop out more often than international students.

The purpose behind presenting these realities, of course, is both to help inform your decision-making process and to help you consider, if after serious self-reflection you decide graduate education is for you, the most effective way to compose your personal statements and other application materials. Ideas on how to apply your research and self-reflection to your written materials are detailed in chapters 2 and 3 of this handbook.

The Ethics of Those Helping You Seek Graduate Study

Obviously, as you apply for graduate school and for national scholarships you are not alone in the process, with your primary help coming from your mentors, references, and designated academic and scholarships advisors at your school. However, in working with these individuals, you must understand the ethics that they uphold in the process of helping you.

Mentors and References

First of all, please understand that your references and mentors feel an obligation not only to you but to the program or scholarship to which you are applying. Many in academia feel that they should be guardians of their discipline, upholding high standards for those who work within it. Even supportive mentors sometimes say no to students seeking a letter of reference, in that they may feel they are too busy to write a letter, may not be fully supportive of you in relation to what you're applying for, or may not have been approached by you in a way that makes them comfortable writing a fully positive letter. More often, though, you will not be turned down by anyone you ask to write a letter of recommendation, but your references will probably have these ethical expectations of you:

- That you give ample time for the letter to be written before the deadline—typically 3-4 weeks if possible. Often, those most willing to write letters are also simultaneously writing them for others, under similar deadline constraints.
- That you clearly understand and communicate the application protocol regarding the letter of recommendation. Some programs ask references to mail the letter directly to them, some ask references to give the letter back to the applicant in a sealed envelope, and some don't specify any protocol and it is up to the student to sort it out.
- That you waive your rights to see the contents of the letter, thus allowing it to be confidential. Selection committees typically expect you to give up your access rights by signing a waiver on the application form. Some

references might nevertheless share the letter with you if they trust your maturity, but the choice is theirs to make.

- That you understand that the recommendation—especially if it is written to support your application for a national scholarship—might include some criticism as well as praise. Increasingly, selection committees are calling for honest and full assessment of a candidate's strengths and weaknesses both.
- That you follow-up with the recommender by keeping him or her informed of the progress of your application. Few students do this, which frustrates professors who have worked hard to be supportive.

Along with these expectations, which often make both you and your references equally uncomfortable, you may need to partner with your references in the reference letter and application process. Some professors will readily review and critique your personal statement and application materials, and in many cases, such as in the sciences where you are working on a team research project, you may require the help of a professor or graduate student to faithfully represent a full project description. Some professors ask to review your resume or a past essay you wrote to help them write a recommendation letter, and some will even ask you directly what kind of detail you would like to have included in the letter, suggesting that you write some of the text down for them in an e-mail. After that, it's up to the reference to reshape that material effectively in a letter.

Academic Advisors and Scholarships Directors

When you apply for a national scholarship, in particular a scholarship where the institution internally assesses and nominates its top candidates, your school will usually have a designated academic advisor or scholarships director to help you through the process. Understand that this person's role is to coax forth the best from you rather than write your application materials, and that schools are limited as to how many students they can put forth for each nominated scholarship. The role of the scholarships director is to be both cheerleader and judge—a precarious ethical tightrope indeed. Even if the director from your school personally "recruits" you for the scholarship because of your academic record, the director must ultimately view you in context of all the other potential scholarship candidates, both at your school and nationally, and must also be concerned with the reputation of the school you are representing. Just as one example, for the graduate scholarship

> The role of the scholarships director is to be both cheerleader and judge—a precarious ethical tightrope indeed.

awarded by the Jack Kent Cooke Foundation, each accredited college and university in the US may nominate up to two students only, and in 2005 the Foundation expected to award just 35 scholarships from a pool of over 1,000 applications (2). In making choices about which students to nominate for a national scholarship, your school's designated advisor must serve as a motivator and writing coach to you, while keeping in mind the odds against success, and maybe even deciding against putting you forth as a candidate in favor of one of your peers.

In short, you must understand the ethical and practical concerns of anyone helping you prepare your application, recognizing that the above concerns are typical rather than invented, and that your responsibility is to prepare an application of maximum efficacy, even in the face of the competing ethical dilemmas of others.

> *Traffic signals in New York are just rough guidelines.*
> —*David Letterman*

The Foundations of Ethical Guidelines for Writers

Before launching into a discussion of guidelines for student writers, it's useful to note that these guidelines carry well beyond your life as a student and into your life as a professional. Companies, schools, and other organizations often publish guidelines for ethical behavior right alongside their mission statements. Professional organizations publish guidelines for their members, and failure to follow these guidelines can result in a loss of membership.

As part of your graduate application materials, you may be asked to provide information about whether you were ever the subject of academic discipline or whether you have a criminal record. Disclosing such information certainly could hurt your chances of admission and require an explanation from you, but it would not necessarily disqualify you from acceptance. However, failure to disclose such information, if later found out, would almost guarantee expulsion or even the retroactive stripping of your degree.

In all these cases, a large reason that ethical guidelines are imposed is because they help ensure some standard of quality and equity for all members of a group. And the guidelines cut both ways: Just as a selection committee expects students to be honest in their graduate applications and contribute to a culture of credibility, candidates expect selectors to be fair and equitable in their reading of applications so that every individual can be assured of a fair shake.

One of the best examples I have seen of ethical guidelines for writing is that published by the American Chemical Society (ACS). In the book, *The ACS Style Guide* (3), one chapter is devoted to ethical guidelines for publishing chemical research. Broadly rendered, the guidelines apply well to anyone writing within an academic setting, and they emphasize the importance of ethical standards being upheld by every party involved in the process of writing and publication, including journal editors, authors, and manuscript reviewers. Browsing through just the 12 ethical obligations for authors, which consume several pages, writers find repeated emphasis on accurate accounting of information, objective discussion of the significance of evidence, and scrupulous documentation of resources. To be considered worthy of membership in graduate school, writers of personal essays must be careful to uphold these same standards.

> *I was kicked out of college for cheating on my metaphysics final;*
> *I looked within the soul of the boy sitting next to me.*
> —*Woody Allen*

The Ethics of Student Writers

Imagine having to type and sign your name under this sentence at the end of your personal statement:

> I certify that this essay is original work prepared by me, the author.

Well, you need not imagine it—many scholarship and grad school applications include just such a statement for you to sign. Though it may seem almost absurd, by definition, that a student's personal statement would need to be endorsed as being personal and original, growing concerns about academic integrity have made such a testimony necessary in the eyes of many.

The evidence that many students cheat in college is overwhelming. There are popular handbooks published on the subject, with titles like *The Cheater's Handbook* and *Cheating 101*, and a growing number of classes in high school and college where teachers ban cell phones so that students can't text message test answers to each other (there are other good reasons to ban cells in classes, too). One survey of 70,000 students conducted by the Center for Academic Integrity at Duke University found that 95 percent of high school and college students "admit to some form of academic cheating" (4). Other surveys report far less shocking but equally troubling results, usually settling on figures of about 50 percent of students who note that they have participated at least once in academic cheating.

Given the temptation and habit built into a culture where many students do cheat, and given the high stakes involved when applying for a scholarship or to grad school, it is not unreasonable to think that some students practice some form of cheating even in their personal statements. In this context, unethical practices range from exaggeration to poor source citation to outright plagiarism.

Lies, Exaggerations, and "Creative Truths"

One of the most famous cases of lies in a personal essay, which eventually led to a lawsuit by the writer of the essay, was in the news in 1998. Princeton University alerted the medical schools one of its graduates had applied to that he had made false claims in his personal statement. The graduate and would-be doctor then sued Princeton, but the judge threw out the case after testimony was over and before the case had gone to jury. During the course of the trial, the graduate admitted to telling several lies and "creative truths" in his application. In his personal statement, he misidentified his race, lied about winning a prestigious scholarship, and falsely claimed that "a family of lepers had donated half their beggings" to support his dream. (This last claim is particularly creative, in that it is highly difficult and unsavory to check up on its veracity.) Dean Nancy Malkiel at Princeton testified that the school had an obligation to inform the student's target medical programs: "It's up to us to see to it that the people entering the medical profession are competent, confident and trustworthy" (5).

> In his personal statement, he misidentified his race, lied about winning a prestigious scholarship, and falsely claimed that "a family of lepers had donated half their beggings" to support his dream.

And then there are "optimistic exaggerations" with just a whiff of truth. I once worked with a student on his personal essay, pausing with interest over a comment that he had "started a foundation" to help the unfortunate in a particular third world country meet their technological needs. Impressive, certainly, but also so exact and unusual that I questioned him about it. Because this student was applying for a prestigious national scholarship, where humanitarian service is especially valued, I knew this essay detail would certainly capture the attention of the selection committee if the student reached the interview stage. Well, it turns out that he had indeed spent a semester in the third world country he had cited—again, impressive—but the "foundation" he spoke of was really just him kindly sending a rebuilt computer to his former supervisor in that country upon his return to the States. He had plans to send more hardware and start an organized effort, but in fact it was much more of a noble dream than a reality.

My example isn't meant to belittle the student—in fact, his application otherwise was impressive and he quickly retracted his original statement after some discussion—but to represent how tempting it can be to exaggerate with the hope of impressing, and to note just how harmful a trumped up claim can be to one's credibility. I've seen this on resumes submitted as part of an application as well: "I served as an institutional sanitation engineer" really translated to "I was a school janitor"; "I was President of the Nancy Club" really meant "I traded old Nancy and Sluggo comics with some of the people in my web facebook." I genuinely believe that students who write like this don't necessarily mean to lie; they just aren't sure if the truth sounds impressive enough. And in the case of the Nancy Club, well, there's simply no way to dress it up, and it just doesn't belong.

> "I was President of the Nancy Club" really meant "I traded old Nancy and Sluggo comics with some of the people in my web facebook."

Clearly, students making exaggerated claims and telling "creative truths" in their personal essays only hurt their ethos and raise their audience's doubts. Usually these kinds of claims are highly transparent as well, and the only person who is in a position to defend or explain them is the writer. Seasoned readers easily sniff out the exaggeration or, worse, may even ask the student about the claim in an interview, only to receive a fumbling response or a downright, regrettable lie.

To state the obvious, then, tell the truth about yourself. A good rule of thumb is to assume that anything you write in a personal essay or on an application resume could come back to haunt you in a follow-up interview. Be prepared to back up any claim you make with verbal evidence, even beyond that provided in your essay, and don't put yourself in a position of having to retract something just because you hoped to make it look more impressive than it actually was.

Source Citation

As a writing tutor who helps students wrestle with issues of source citation on a daily basis, I know that well-meaning students are sometimes genuinely puzzled about ethical source citation practices. The nuances of this issue are many, especially when one cites internet sources; however, the underlying ethic should be clear—when you use someone else's original ideas or words directly, you cite your source. Unfortunately, so many students are habitually guilty of "sloppy thinking" in this area that professors have to give the issue special attention, even though they'd much rather not. I once had a student copy an entire page from another student's paper during a rough draft session without her knowledge, then hand the paper in as his own. When I compared the two papers and pointed out that he had actually plagiarized much of the material, he tried to claim that he had simply failed to cite the other student's paper. I've also had students innocently claim that if material appears on the web it need not be cited because, by definition, it's common knowledge. Such appalling reasoning induces premature aging and weary hearts in teachers.

In regards to citation practices within personal essays, the first principle you must understand is that citation within a personal essay is indeed a common practice.

> I once had a student copy an entire page from another student's paper during a rough draft session without her knowledge, then hand the paper in as his own.

You need not worry that it will look odd to cite sources within your essay, especially when you apply for, say, a Goldwater Scholarship or a National Science Foundation Fellowship. In these instances, parts of the application are akin to a scientific literature review, so failure to cite your sources professionally could actually be a kiss of death.

The second principle is that the same rules for citation are relevant as applied in your college papers—i.e., you must cite sources in the following circumstances:

- When you use statistics or data generated by other authors;
- When your quote verbatim or paraphrase in a way that your wording closely resembles the original source;
- When you borrow another author's interpretation, argument, theory, or hypothesis;
- When you wish to enhance your credibility or argument by comparing it to the published work of another.

In such circumstances, always cite your source, following the maxim that it is better to be safe than sorry. Further standards and mechanics to follow when citing sources in personal essays are detailed in Chapter 2 of this handbook.

Avoiding Plagiarism and Using Samples in This Handbook Responsibly

Finally, if you're not convinced that plagiarism is practiced by students applying to graduate school, just visit one of the many websites where papers are sold to students, such as lazystudents.com or 123helpme.com. In 2005, one professor who has extensively studied the subject estimated that about 150 websites were available with downloadable papers (6). At schoolsucks.com, one of the oldest websites devoted to this mission, a search for the keywords "personal statements" turns up hits including personal essays written for students seeking graduate study in nursing, business, teaching, and philosophy. For about $30-40 a pop, foolish writers can purchase one of these personal statements and potentially plagiarize from it, fundamentally cheating both themselves and their readers. Success in such a venture is, of course, both unlikely and unethical, and the idea that material from someone else's personal essay can simply be transplanted into your own reflects badly on the quality of the original and even more badly on your own self-image.

At the same time, I do offer many sample personal statements in this handbook for your considered study, and that is exactly how you should use them—for *study*. Chapter 4 offers both examples and critiques of those examples, while Chapter 5 includes both essays that won national scholarships and those that did not win but are nevertheless effective. These essays were written by students from across the country, and I adapted them for print with the permission of the essay writers, aiming for a diversity of samples and voices. When studying these examples responsibly, you'll realize that strong personal essays are so good that they, quite simply, cannot be copied; they succeed by persuading as argument, by achieving individuality, and—most importantly—by being personal.

CHAPTER 2

PRACTICAL MATTERS

> *I am writing for myself and strangers.*
> *That is the only way that I can do it.*
> *—Gertrude Stein*

I remember writing my first resume. It was a few years before the days of the personal computer, and my typewriter had just one unattractive font but also had a fancy function key that allowed for italic type. So I decided my resume would stand out if I did it in *all* italic type. Then I reasoned that a particular section would stand out even more if I typed everything in all capital letters *and* all italic type (thankfully, my typewriter didn't have boldface). In composing my "Experience" section, I'd had so many part-time menial jobs in high school and college that I couldn't figure out how to format the section without losing detail, so I came up with the self-styled strategy of just making my "Experience" section one long narrative sentence in one bulky paragraph (in all italics, of course), with each job description separated by ellipsis dots.

Obviously, it was pretty pathetic. Here's a mercifully short excerpt from "Experience," just as I originally wrote it and in its original font:

> *worked for a concrete block company moving concrete blocks . . . painted*
> *inside/outside of house . . . worked for YMCA at unskilled labor positions . . .*
> *worked weekends for the All American Cleaning Company . . . did evening*
> *restaurant work. . . various cleaning jobs for private home owners . . .*

In writing my resume, I had unwittingly made up my own rules of form and content, ignoring all the tried and true models available, and I naively told myself that I was just being creative and unique. I ignored my own ability to be selective and sidestepped practical conventions. For my poor reader, I'm sure that reading my resume involved both abundant confusion and significant eye strain.

Ignoring the practical details of writing—particularly when composing a personal statement or application essay, where the conventions are well established and the needs of the readers are well known—just doesn't make sense. Further, the consequences of not studying and following the practical conventions of personal essay writing are substantial, potentially changing the course of your life.

So use this chapter to answer the common questions many students have about writing personal essays, and realize that such an essay is a professional and public document to be viewed critically by the eyes of strangers, not a private and personal exercise in creative self-indulgence.

> *That's not writing, that's typing.*
> *—Truman Capote, on Jack Kerouac*

Defining the Personal Statement

Because a personal statement is unlike most documents you write in college, many students struggle with understanding the fundamentals of its definition. One of the best extended definitions I've seen is offered on the Fellowships website at Bryn Mawr (7). Below I offer a condensed version adapted from that website.

A personal statement is:

- A picture. Provide a snapshot of who you are as a person.
- An invitation. Your job is to "bridge the assumed distance of strangers." Invite your reader to know you.
- An indication of your priorities and judgment. Your selection of material reveals your priorities and ability to discern effectively.
- A story, or more precisely, your story. The personal statement allows room for creative, meaningful self-reflection.

A personal statement is not:

- An academic paper with you as the subject. The objective distance of academic writing disengages the reader from you in a personal statement.

- A resume in narrative form. Other parts of your application, which might include a resume, already tell readers about your accomplishments. A personal statement must reveal and interpret beyond a resume.
- A journal entry. A common mistake is allowing your personal statement to read like a diary. Share only relevant material selectively, in a voice that remains both individual and professional.
- A plea or justification. Don't beg and don't defend the (incorrect) assertion that you are more worthy than other candidates—it only backfires.

Of course, nuances to this definition may be added based on the circumstances. For instance, at times an application might require three different essays with highly specific parameters. Always look to the application itself to determine the degree to which the definitions above apply, and know that when there is a series of questions one of them is usually designed to elicit a personal essay from you.

> *Englishwomen's shoes look as if they had been made by someone who had often heard shoes described, but had never seen any.*
> —*Margaret Halsey*

Issues of Length and Form

Normally, the length of a personal essay will be dictated by the application—500 words or 800 words are typical limits, as are one-page or two-page limits. If you're given, say, a count of 1,500 words, you need not write to the maximum length, but to compose only one-half of the word count might be an opportunity missed. In any case, what matters most is that the material you present conforms to these word or space restrictions—parts of your application might literally not be read if you violate the rules—and that your presentation is aesthetically pleasing and easy to read. To achieve these goals, I recommend the following:

- If your personal statement is a stand-alone document within your application, open it with a simple heading such as "Personal Statement for Janet Lerner." Thus, if your documents would get separated somehow, they could more easily be reassembled.

- If there are any pages to your essay beyond one, number them, and perhaps include your name on those pages as well.
- Choose a publishing font that is highly readable, such as Times or Bookman. Some fonts allow for more tightness to the text, which is fine as long as the essay remains readable. Ideally, use no more than a 12-point size and no less than a 10-point size, favoring the larger.
- Allow for ample enough margins that the reader isn't distracted by cramped-looking text. Margins of at least one inch are standard.
- Single space your text, skipping a line between paragraphs. You can indent paragraph beginnings or not, as long as you're consistent.

At times, especially when you fill out an application electronically or have to cut and paste, word limits will be defined by physical space. In such a case, keep enough white space between your text and the application text that the material isn't crowded, and choose a font different from that used in the application.

> *We think in generalities, but we live in detail.*
> *—Alfred North Whitehead*

Generating Detail

For most writers, one of the first struggles in personal essays is selecting detail, then the second struggle is figuring out what material to *de*-select. Obviously, especially if you have just 500 words, only one or two meaty examples per paragraph will be possible. To generate and select relevant detail, the following guidelines will almost always apply.

Read the Question or Prompt Carefully to Extract Definitive Criteria

Always begin by discerning the criteria of the question itself. Sometimes you'll just be given a broad sweeping statement such as "Discuss those personal qualities you think will aid the committee in making its decision." Such a statement is highly open to interpretation, yet there is definitely a wrong way to go about answering it as well—for instance, discussing your charm, financial hardship, or ability as a magician would be completely off target. More often, you'll be given a more concrete, clear prompt with criteria imbedded. For the sake of context, here's a typical sort of prompt:

In no more than 800 words, discuss your personal motivations, academic interests, relevant research or experience, long-term objectives, and your specific interest in attending Mythic University.

In this case, a typical response would be to follow with one paragraph devoted to each of the discussion points, with a savvy writer using the diction of each criterion within topic sentences for focus and context. Some writers would opt to be more creative in their approach, but even so a reader should not feel that any part of the question has been dodged.

Articulate a Personal or Professional Inspiration

Some writers open their statement with an inspiring quote or a narrative (discussed further in Chapter 3), while others make a comment about their academic discipline. What matters is that readers have clear context through your opening, and that we understand immediately that you are talking about something of motivational meaning to you. Briefly sketch out a positive influence: a memorable self-defining experience, a high school or college project that ignited deeper interest, an inspiring teacher or role model, a relative who followed a career path that you emulate—even a core theme that will carry through the rest of your essay. Always remember the usual fundamental goal of the opening: to provide a quick, meaningful snapshot of who you are as a person.

Discuss your Academic Background or Research as a Set of Learned Skills

Again, some writers might desire to be creative throughout their personal statement, but a more traditional route is to open the second or third paragraph with a discussion of academic background or research in relation to skills you have acquired. Certainly, work experience could be relevant as well, especially if you were a teaching assistant for a class and you plan on holding an assistantship in graduate school, but you must be careful not to rehearse resume-like details about any jobs you've held. Readers will be most interested in specific, skills-oriented detail: lab techniques acquired; analytical tools gained; participation in team decision-making; journal research and publication experience; oral presentation skills. Think in relation to those skills most valued in your discipline, and describe your background in a way that highlights those attributes.

Many writers approach a discussion of their background by forecasting ahead to what they wish to study in graduate school, employing their past experiences to project future aptitude. For example, in Chapter 4 of this handbook, one writer uses these sentences to describe his thesis research:

> My project involves the taphonomy, stratigraphy, and identification of a middle-Ordovician coral bioherm as well as its bryozoan constituents. The research is now well under way, involving many aspects of a sound paleontological study: sampling, analysis, identification, and finalization into a report.

Clearly, the writer's intention here is to wed his present and the future—to project ahead to graduate research within his field of paleontology. By focusing on the techniques and skills relevant to his academic field while describing his thesis project, he lays the foundation for his intended future area of research.

In many cases, especially if you apply for a national scholarship or to a sciences program, you may be expected to discuss your research interests and background thoroughly as the heart of your personal essay. Specific details that might be included in these cases are the hypothesis of your undergraduate research, the exact nature of a research question you would like to focus on in graduate school, and even the name of a professor you would like to work with in graduate school and a rationale for how you made that choice.

Establish Some Long-Term Objectives

Some students hesitate greatly over this criterion, feeling as though they're committing to an unbreakable covenant, while others reach too high or actually get too specific—"I plan to win a Nobel Peace Prize," they claim, or "I intend to write four textbooks." Keep in mind the needs of your readers here: They simply wish to confirm that you have a seriousness of purpose, and that you have the ability to envision some concrete plans (else why would you be applying for graduate study?). Your long-term objectives can usually be rendered briefly rather than expansively, perhaps woven into the beginning or end of your final paragraph. Good options here include articulating a plan to continue work in a particular research area, a desire to earn a PhD or teach at the university level, or

> Some students hesitate greatly over this criterion, feeling as though they're committing to an unbreakable covenant, while others reach too high or actually get too specific—"I plan to win a Nobel Peace Prize," they claim, or "I intend to write four textbooks."

future plans to work as an independent or corporate consultant. Also, depending on the context you've created in the essay, personal goals may be just as relevant as professional ones: to serve the public through grass-roots activism; to be the first member of a large family to earn a graduate degree; to write and publish.

Close with Specifics About the Target Program

Learning all you can about the target program, which usually begins with a visit to the school website, will give you concrete closing material for your essay. Most students go a step further, e-mailing professors at their target program, reading publications of the faculty, or making it a point to meet grad students and faculty connected with the program at a conference. Such material, of course, could be integrated to give natural closure to your personal essay, thus affiliating you with the program of choice. Your goal is to create a personal and professional link between yourself and the graduate school. Go beyond simply inserting the school name into the final paragraph; prove you have done your homework.

Finally, as a practical matter, many students visit their target programs on their own, sometimes even before they apply. Not only does this give them the opportunity to get a feel for the area and meet other grad students or faculty, it also helps them generate relevant material to include in their personal essay.

> *The skill of writing is to create a context in which other people can think.*
> *—Edwin Schlossberg*

Citing Sources

Chapter 1 discusses the ethical concerns associated with source citation as you write personal essays. Below are ways to address common challenges in relation to the more practical problem of citation mechanics:

- In generic terms, the two basic citation styles appropriate for personal essays can be referred to as the *number system* and *author-year system*. In the number system, a number is provided in the text corresponding to a numbered source cited fully at the essay's end. In the author-year system, the writer provides the author and year of the source in parentheses after the corresponding text, then cites the source fully at the end of the essay in a references list alphabetized by authors' last names.

- For the references section at the essay's end, provide full bibliographic information for your sources—e.g., author, article title, book or journal title, relevant page numbers, and website address if relevant. Because the mechanics of citation vary slightly from one journal to the next, most writers model their references page on that of a respected journal in their field.

- For convenience in a personal essay, it is acceptable to cite sources—especially if you use just one or two—in numbered footnote form at the bottom of the page. If you have more than a few sources, a separate section entitled "References" at the end of the essay is best.

- Sometimes, rather than a formal footnote or end citation, a contextual narrative citation will be sufficient if you are using a well-known quote or paraphrase ("Einstein said that imagination is more important than knowledge") or attributing authorship and context directly ("As stated in a funding proposal authored by our research group, the hypothesis for my thesis research is . . .").

- If you include figures or tables taken or adapted from a published source, cite the source in the figure or table caption, using the same citation style employed throughout the essay.

To see the above tips in action, browse through the sample essays in chapters 4 and 5, where you will find ample evidence of how other writers met their source citation challenges.

> *Equations are just the boring part of mathematics.*
> *I attempt to see things in terms of geometry.*
> *—Stephen Hawking*

Figures, Tables, and Equations

Especially when lengthy application essays are permitted and desirable, and especially in the sciences, you might wish to include figures, tables, and equations within your personal essay, or they might be necessary to include in a part of the application where you describe an area of research or write a literature review. Obviously, the presentation of figures, tables, and equations must be both mechanically sound and necessary to rapid understanding of the material. Both aesthetically and contextually, you should apply the same standards that you would if submitting material for publication.

Some commonly overlooked fundamentals of figures and tables follow:

- Figures are drawn or photographed pictures; tables are lists of numbers and words. Be sure to define them appropriately—many writers call a graphic a figure when it is really a table, or vice versa.
- Use line graphs to plot continuous variables (e.g., unbroken time measures); use charts or bar graphs to plot discontinuous variables (e.g., percentages that occurred in intervals).
- The caption for a figure appears below the graphic; for a table, above.
- Leave ample white space around the graphic that it doesn't interfere with the reading of the text, but when considering space constraints keep in mind that modern word processing allows you to imbed graphics directly within paragraphs.
- While producing a figure or table and its caption, follow the old maxim that the graphic could be ripped from the paper and still make sense.
- If using multiple graphics in your essay, refer to them consecutively by number, both within a relevant paragraph of text and in the caption.
- If the graphic comes directly from or is adapted from a source, it is critical that you cite the source after the caption, then include full bibliographic information for the graphic at the end of the essay.

For equations, follow these principles of aesthetics and grammar:

- Grammatically, treat an equation as a single noun that is a member of a sentence.
- Commonly, "we" is used to introduce equations, promoting the active voice and fluid readability.
- Short equations can be included as part of a sentence without any special spacing, as long as the equation flows within the sentence as a readable unit. Otherwise, equations are normally centered on the page, with a line skipped before and after. If an equation is too long for a single line, break it just before a "verb" or "conjunction."

- When appropriate, define members of the equation just after presenting it, normally introducing those members with the word "where."
- Equations may include punctuation marks after them, but your practice must be consistent within the essay.

For an excellent example of how to effectively integrate both graphics and equations into an essay, see the sample extensive scholarship essay by a student in biological science in Chapter 4 (pages 101-107). Several examples also reside in Chapter 5, though the graphics there are not always presented in their original full size for reasons of space.

> *One thorn of experience is worth a whole wilderness of warning.*
> *—James Russell Lowell*

Tailoring Material to Special Circumstances

Rarely, but occasionally, while working with a student on a personal essay, I can't help but wince. It's a concerned, gut response to the student taking an unnecessary and unwise risk. The most ready example I recall is the day that one of my students spent an entire paragraph discussing a suicide attempt. And this student was no dummy—in fact, held a 3.9 GPA. What I'm sure happened was that the student misconstrued the context for the personal essay and interpreted it almost as a confessional opportunity. I've witnessed other students use the personal statement to stumble sloppily through discussions of the death of a pet, a protest rally that turned into a small riot, a bad case of lactose intolerance, a religious conversion, and ten years away from school "bumming around with a rock band."

Writers who do this are often focusing on one small part of their application (such as a poor semester of grades) or something they view as so self-defining (such as a political cause) that they feel almost obliged to discuss the topic. Audience and context are key here, with the astute writer only taking chances when the risk is clearly worth it. As the following discussions make clear, though, there are often good practical reasons for bringing up something unusual, highly personal, fundamental to your background, or even something controversial.

Managing Controversial Topics

On university campuses, not a week goes by without spirited debate or sponsored speakers addressing such controversial issues as sexuality, religion, racial intimidation, crime, politics, drinking, animal rights, the use of firearms, environmental ethics, and other issues specific to a particular campus. Therefore, admissions and scholarship committee members are not strangers to these topics, and some are even an integral part of the debates. Effective attention to controversial issues in one's personal statement requires a writer who can handle nuance and audience in a sophisticated way. So much depends on the context for the discussion, and the writer who takes a stance on such issues in an application should have a good reason to do so.

As one example, note how one writer in Chapter 5 addresses the issue of civil rights regardless of sexuality in her policy proposal for a Truman Scholarship (pages 188-189). The Truman Scholarship seeks students who will be "agents of change" and requires applicants to write a mock proposal to a government official. Thus, by definition, students must take a stance on a potentially controversial topic. This student does so by first establishing that sexuality-based discrimination occurs, tying this practice directly to public opinion and policy. She cites sources ranging from the *Journal of Counseling Psychology* to recent testimony in a government hearing, showing that her convictions are grounded in research and awareness. In her boldest and most direct appeal to her target audience—a particular Republican senator—she states: "Your recent support of the Employment Non-Discrimination Act is commendable, but this bill is not sufficient." Here, she shows herself to be both informed and opinionated. She purposely pushes.

> Effective attention to controversial issues in one's personal statement requires a writer who can handle nuance and audience in a sophisticated way.

In this case, the student has chosen to express her views on a topic of controversy in a context where sound argument defending her views is clearly welcomed, no matter the direction towards which the views lean. In fact, selection committee members are *always* looking for writers who can argue about difficult topics effectively—not for writers who necessarily share their personal views.

In cases where you create the context for the controversial topic yourself, perhaps because you genuinely see the issue as a driving force in your life, you simply need to be sure that you present yourself as informed, involved, and insightful.

Wherever your personal and political views fall, show yourself as one invested in the struggle for such principles as fairness, justice, dignity, morality, truth, spirituality, safety, and tolerance, and trust that your readers will respect the struggle as long as you argue about it effectively. Show yourself as one whose views are shaped by experiences and information, and consider highlighting the benefits to others or to your profession if your views are accepted. Also, if you bring up controversial issues in a personal essay, you should certainly be ready to discuss them further in a follow-up interview.

Issues of Diversity, Under-representation, and Open-ended Questions

In recent decades, academic programs and scholarship awards alike have taken a specific interest in increasing their diversity pool among candidates, paying special attention to fields where certain populations have been under-represented, such as women in engineering or African-Americans in medicine. Often, this specific interest is reflected right in the application, either in the form of a statement of commitment or a question inviting some discussion of how you as a candidate would contribute diversity to a particular program or discipline.

In considering this issue, especially if the question response allows only one paragraph for a reply, note how other parts of the application will help to address issues of diversity or under-representation as well. Checkbox data including gender, ethic background, and citizenship will reveal relevant background information about you, along with lists of your chosen activities and membership in organizations. Select information for such lists accordingly.

Also, examine the wording of open-ended questions and determine whether they are trying to tease out information in a particular area. As a demonstration, note the variety in these questions adapted from different applications:

> Write a short essay about a topic of importance to you.

> What other personal information would you like to share with the scholarship review board?

> The graduate program at Mythic College is especially interested in enhancing diversity among our students. Describe experiences in your background that would contribute to such diversity.

To determine the best answer to such questions, writers need to consider what information they have shared in other parts of the application, avoiding redundancy and favoring either emphasis or a fresh response that will draw favorable attention. Depending on context and your personal taste, all three of the questions might legitimately get the same written response. What would be especially hurtful to the application, however, is if you chose to make *no* response to such a question and wrongly deemed it irrelevant, sending the message that you self-define as both lazy and uninteresting.

In defining such areas as diversity, it is also important to think beyond categories of ethnic identity and gender. I've seen savvy students answer diversity questions by discussing themselves as a returning adult student, an engineer interested in law, a poet among scientists, one who daily manages a physical disability, a woman who has survived a life-threatening illness, a conservative Republican attending a highly liberal school, a horticulturalist living in the city, a speaker of three languages, a world traveler, an ROTC student, a man who aims to devote his life to service. Such responses not only draw our attention, they also show that the writer understands and embraces diversity in a way that is not narrowly defined—where diversity draws positive attention to both the individual and the collective.

Most importantly, share something individual in any diversity or open-ended question. Note how the following answer—excerpted from a Udall Scholarship application in Chapter 5 from a writer invited to share additional information—showcases how the writer perceives herself as a strong, driven individual.

> I was raised by two strong women—my mother and my grandmother. Three generations of women living under one roof provided me with a unique experience while growing up. My mother was the first woman in my family to pursue higher education and continued her pursuit even after having a child. As I was growing up I watched her finish her nursing degree at Oakland University and begin a career in Neonatal Nursing. My interest in the sciences and the environment most definitely stemmed initially from my mother's interest and passion for the subject. While my mother was attending classes and studying, my grandmother was my primary caregiver and she too encouraged my exploration and growth. Throughout my life, my mother and grandmother have continued to be my source of inspiration and encouragement.

Finally, recognize that some writers choose to give no specific space to issues of diversity or under-representation even when invited, either because they would prefer not to, they know that a reference of theirs will address the issue in a recommendation letter, or because they feel other issues are more worthy of their limited space. The option of silence may suit you well, as long as you've made a strong, complete application otherwise.

Describing Interesting Personal or Educational Experiences

As reported in the book *How to Write a Winning Personal Statement for Graduate and Professional School* (8), the Stern School of Business at New York University does something a bit unusual in its application questions to applicants. As many programs do, the school uses a series of questions rather than just one, but the third question asks students to describe themselves to their classmates, allowing for some creative elbow room. The answers to this third question, says the Director of Admissions and Aid, are her favorite. Though most applicants simply write creative essays, others send in poems, games, puzzles—even cassette recordings or videotapes (8). Obviously, in most graduate applications, students don't have such options when it comes to delivering the material. However, those with particularly interesting personal tales or educational paths might look for ways to highlight them in writing.

Many schools pride themselves not only on their programs but on something flexible or specialized about they education they offer. My alma mater, Juniata College, has students build a "program of emphasis" rather than declare a major, allowing students to customize their program of study. St. John's College engages all its students in a classics-grounded course of study "based in the great books of the Western tradition," which includes four years of math and one year of music for all

> St. John's College engages all its students in a classics-grounded course of study "based in the great books of the Western tradition," which includes four years of math and one year of music for all students.

students. Mount Holyoke, an all-women's college, has a program in speaking, writing, and arguing, and sponsors an annual intercollegiate poetry competition. Not all readers will know the details about these programs, and the personal statement provides a perfect opportunity for graduates of such programs to take advantage of interesting experiences built right into their education. Writers who flesh out such detail in their personal statements both educate their readers about their background and affiliate themselves with programs of earned reputation.

Other educational background worthy of consideration for your personal statement includes:

- Participation in a first-year or senior seminar, assuming the seminar was academic and required you to produce meaningful work and some deliverable product.
- Past academic scholarships and the criteria by which you won them, especially if they are competitive national awards.
- Any co-op or work experiences directly relevant to graduate study, especially if the work you did was integrated into senior thesis research.
- Study at more than one school or study abroad, in particular if you are fluent in multiple languages.
- Honors education classes or an honors thesis.
- The completion of an integrated bachelor's/master's program, with discussion of program particulars.
- Completion of a senior thesis, especially if some facet of the thesis research can be continued at graduate school.
- Educational training through the military or professional certification programs, with an emphasis on relevance to graduate study.
- A transfer of schools or a return to school after time away, emphasizing positive lessons learned from the experience and giving evidence of accomplishments and motivation.

Finally, sometimes writers have such interesting personal stories that they capture their audience just by sharing something meaningful about their lives. Interesting stories I've read about in personal statements include a woman who grew up in four different countries while her parents worked for the Peace Corps, a blind student from South Korea who was adopted into an American family and completed an internship involving service to disabled high school students, a student who completed a bachelor's degree over an eight-year period while battling multiple sclerosis, a student who had placed a novel with a major publishing house at the age of 19. Such personal stories and accomplishments are too interesting, and in some cases too moving, *not* to share.

Discussing Shortcomings and Challenges

Many applications, especially those for law school and business school, ask students to explain some challenge they've overcome or even to discuss a failure in their lives. The best writers tend to handle this issue directly but creatively, discussing a challenge that doesn't undermine their abilities or character and emphasizing positive lessons learned from the experience. An excellent example of how one writer handled this issue is in Chapter 4 (pages 71-73), within two essays written by a student in business. The writer frames his challenges within ultimately positive experiences—the completion of a 3500-mile bike trip and a successful team business project—so that he both answers the questions but keeps favorable attention on his accomplishments.

Even unprompted, many students—especially if they had a bad semester of grades, a prolonged illness, a personal crisis, a switch of majors, or took some time off from school—feel compelled to provide an explanation in their personal statement or elsewhere in their application. This can be risky, of course, because it may draw a disproportional amount of attention to something negative, and it may be unnecessary anyway. Consider whether an explanation is already taken care of by the circumstances (such as one poor semester during sophomore year followed by two years of high grades in your major) or whether the matter might be best handled by a sympathetic advisor writing you a letter of recommendation (who can be encouraged to explain the issue for you if privy to the necessary information). Weigh carefully the decision to reveal anything negative unprompted, and discuss it with a trusted advisor.

> The writer frames his challenges within ultimately positive experiences—the completion of a 3500-mile bike trip and a successful team business project—so that he both answers the questions but keeps favorable attention on his accomplishments.

An interesting window into the kinds of challenges students discuss in writing is provided in examples from the book *Graduate Admissions Essays* (9). Here, students reveal the following tales in their personal essays:

- Working 35 hours per week for five years to finance community college without taking out a student loan.
- Taking a job as a court interpreter before applying to law school to gain some relevant experience.

- Working in a West African village and experiencing language barriers, distrust, and cross-cultural embarrassment.
- Juggling the simultaneous experiences of being a student athlete, a resident assistant, and a class president.
- Starting a service program for disadvantaged high school students only to find that some of those students didn't show up for their appointed meetings.
- An acknowledgment of good study skills lacking in the first two years of college study, followed by a gradually rising GPA.

In all these cases, of course, the writers focused on the value of these experiences and stressed eventual success even among some admitted mishaps. Such willingness to discuss one's personal challenges—and in the process admit a propensity to take on too much, or confess a naiveté about the world, or realize that lofty goals must sometimes be adjusted to reality—can go a long way in gaining a selection committee's trust.

Addressing Application Details Beyond your Understanding

At times, you'll be faced with uncertainty about how to complete parts of an application or about whether you've followed the proper protocol for processing. This is especially true for students who must submit material online or in pdf form (sometimes without acknowledgment of successful transfer of material), and for those who, even after considering the relevant material elsewhere in this chapter, choose to leave something blank or incomplete. Here, the help of an academic advisor, scholarships director, or a staff member at the target program is in order. Assuming you've done your best to follow directions and research your options, there is never harm in a focused e-mail or phone call to a staff member to decide how to handle an uncertainty or check on a submitted application's status.

As a final assurance regarding this topic, I've known students who have been accepted to grad school even when their application did not include the required number of reference letters, when they sent an application in a word processing program forbidden by the target program, and when they took the chance of leaving some questions unanswered. In all these cases, the students either felt that the risk they took was unavoidable or they checked with an authority about how to handle the circumstances. By taking small risks or admitting uncertainty, we sometimes gain exception.

CHAPTER 3

MATTERS OF STYLE

> *I love smooth words, like gold-enameled fish*
> *Which circle slowly with a silken swish.*
> —*Elinor Wylie*

Of the thousands of personal essays I've read over the past 15 years, one of my favorite introductions is from an application to law school, and it opens thus:

> My interest in the law began with donuts. As a child, I developed early persuasive skills during family disagreements on how to divide boxes of the treats. My parents belonged to the "biggest people deserve the most donuts" school of thought; while as the youngest family member, I was a devout believer in the "one person, one donut" principle. The debates were often cutthroat, but when it came to donut distribution, I sought justice at any cost.

This opening, taking from a sample essay in the book, *Perfect Personal Statements* (10), isn't just effective because of its cleverness. It's also efficient in detail, humorous and surprising in delivery, focused in theme, universal in appeal, and even moralistic in meaning. This writer is concerned with justice, even at an early age when decisions of right and wrong could be reduced to the distribution of donuts. Obviously, the paragraph that follows the opening discusses justice at a more advanced level, and gradually this law school applicant addresses social issues such as poverty, nationalism, and prejudice, and he emphasizes his passion to address them through law. As he later sums up near the close of his essay: "My identity rests on these convictions" (10).

This example shows just how much can be accomplished in even a short personal essay by the introduction alone. It also demonstrates that stylistic creativity is not always about flashy word choice or complex sentencing—sometimes the best style is the most artfully simplistic, the most pithy. Whatever else readers think of the content of a personal essay, if they can take delight in the style, they are more likely to assess the writer as worthy of being read and re-read, and thus more likely to plop the application into the acceptance pile.

This chapter is about helping you write stylish personal essays, with an understanding that style is revealed through everything from mechanical correctness to efficiency of presentation to nuances of tone. Put simply, to write with style is to invite and earn your reader's respect.

> *Art thou a pen, whose task shall be*
> *To drown in ink, what writers think?*
> *Oh, wisely write, that pages white*
> *Be not the worse for ink and thee!*
> —*Ethel Lynn Beers*

Common Stylistic Concerns

Like the resume, the personal statement has evolved to the point where there are both built-in and commonly used stylistic devices as well as room for individuality and creativity. And as with the resume, there are appropriate ways to word certain material and there are certain risks not worth taking. The very language you use and the rhetorical approach you take can be guided by the informed practices of others.

Using Formalities and Generic Phrases

Many writers feel the need to use excessive formalities and niceties within personal statements, partly because they've seen others do so and partly because they worry that the weight of the occasion calls for refined or austere language. Thus, we find statements such as the following in personal essays, often in the opening or closing:

> It is with great pride and deep respect that I hereby do apply for the honor of the Rhodes Scholarship. Herewith you will find my complete application materials.

I sincerely hope that the graduate committee of Mythic University deems my application worthy of full consideration so that I may contribute to a program already deserving of its national reputation.

The problem with these examples should be painfully obvious. In the first case, the committee already knows what applicants are seeking so the generic sentences become useless; in the second case, an elliptical construct, the writer unintentionally insults readers, as though they might not give every application equal consideration or as if they are unaware of their program's own reputation.

Avoid such mannerly drivel. Instead, assume a respectful, individual tone throughout your writing, and trust that you will be treated both respectfully and individually. When tempted towards formalities, take a cue from some of the writers showcased in Chapter 5, whose formal comments on their fit for their respective scholarships are both meaningful and self-reflective, as follows:

I look forward to the challenges that this project presents as well as the opportunities for further maturation as a practicing scientist.

Ensconcing myself in British culture, intellectual environment, and vigorous research at Oxford is the chance of a lifetime. I hope to be able to seize it.

Effective Jargon and Informality

In general, jargon is underrated. Jargon—the specialized language of a discipline—is so often overused or used poorly that it gets a bad rap. However, to use jargon economically and effectively is to show that you are an "insider," comfortable with the vocabulary and discourse of your field of study. To create written context where jargon is the natural choice also promotes an efficiency of understanding and a direct connection with the reader. For instance, in the sample essay from biological science in Chapter 4 (pages 101-107), note the economy of using the term "invasives" instead of "pest species that invade an area." In a later essay from a military pilot in the same chapter (pages 108-109), note how terms such as "biplanes" and acronyms such as NGA and GIS almost suggest that the writer is having an informed, relaxed conversation within a specialized community—thus there is no need to define simple specialized terms that the audience can readily understand. These writers use jargon to save their readers time and to communicate directly and professionally.

At the same time, it's possible to converse informally in order to 1) facilitate clear narrative, 2) to involve yourself as a character in the action, or 3) to provide contrast to the denser surrounding material. In the essay just cited written by a military pilot, the writer refers to "challenges [he] faced as an undergrad," notes that he "can do little to affect Congressional funding," and wryly comments, "I don't expect the military to begin training squadrons of GIS wizards." Here, the writer shows the courage to be plain speaking and informal, sending the message that he can comfortably shoot from the hip.

Of course, both jargon and informalities can be overused and be inappropriate for your target audience, and if readers feel that jargon is used only to impress or that informalities turn too colloquial, they will only be annoyed by your style. But manage both jargon and informalities sparingly and with purpose and your audience will barely notice—they'll be too busy reading comfortably.

Using Narrative and Anecdotes

Compact stories and nifty narratives, especially in the opening of a personal statement, can communicate efficiently and creatively with your readers, while potentially providing welcome relief during the reading of hundreds of application essays that strongly resemble each other. Some stories put us right in the moment alongside the writer: "When I received my first microscope set at the age of eight, I couldn't wait to swab the inside of my cheek and smear my cells on a slide." Others invite us directly into the writer's mind: "I remember thinking about the long, cold nights that Edwin Hubble spent staring into the telescope at the Mt. Wilson Observatory." Still others surprise us and create a bit of suspense: "Some protestors around me carried large flashlights; I clutched a bullhorn."

> When I received my first microscope set at the age of eight, I couldn't wait to swab the inside of my cheek and smear my cells on a slide.

These examples, all imbedded within personal essays written by students, represent how writers used narrative snippets to engage and inform the reader. Note how these examples do more than just narrate—they also underscore the writer's passion for a field of study or a commitment to a cause. When you use small tales to capture our attention, be sure they are both relevant and revealing, so that we're impressed not just with your ability to tell a quick story, but also your desire to tell a meaningful one.

Avoiding Cuteness and Gimmicks

Especially when using narrative or setting your sights on originality, it can be easy to lapse into a mode that is merely trite and cute. Such a lapse is critiqued by the Dean of Admissions at the UCLA School of Law as follows:

> Humor is fine; it's a welcome break, as long as it is actually humorous. I hate seeing essays that begin with something like: "In the matter before the court of UCLA, regarding the admission of . . ." Everyone who uses this approach thinks it's unique, but it's not (10).

Other misguided gimmicks that a surprising number of writers attempt when writing personal essays:

- Listing the impressive icons—probably long since dead—who have graduated from your school, blatantly placing yourself amongst their ranks. This may be good PR for your institution, but it's bad PR for you.
- Sprinkling your essay with 50-cent vocabulary, obviously aided by a thesaurus. Choose the best word for the circumstances, not the fanciest.
- Bleeding your heart all over the page, as though your compassion or sensibilities or literary muscles have simply overtaken the writing process. I've seen students write about "dripping in agony" over an exam, or "languishing with deep-infested guilt" while watching a hungry child eat a meal.
- Referring to yourself throughout the essay in the third person and telling some tragic or heroic tale, then revealing that the essay's humble protagonist is (surprise) indeed you.

There are also gimmicks of form, as discussed in the book *Perfect Personal Statements* (10): medical school applicants submitting essays in the form of a diagnosis; applicants who submit essays in leather binding, on parchment scrolls, or written in calligraphy; business school applicants with essays structured like a corporate prospectus.

Such gimmicks are meant to be cute, obviously, but it is doubtful that a selection committee would find them to be anything but odd. In fact, readers would likely question your suitability for graduate study if you stoop to gimmickry. To put it bluntly but truthfully: children and puppies are cute; grad students are not.

Creative Beginnings and Calculated Risks

Without question, the most common place for writers to exercise their freedom in personal statements, as well as the most common place where writers feel uncertain about what they've done, is in their beginnings. Even personal statements that are scientific in tone and content might have creative beginnings. Although there's nothing wrong with a straightforward opening simply stating your purpose, especially if you have just one page for your essay, most writers take a bolder tack. Readers of personal statements are used to openings that tell stories or borrow quotations, essays that discuss relevant current events, and even daring writers who risk a bit of well-conceived humor or surprise.

Personal Stories

The most common creative beginning, a personal story tells a tale by briefly setting a scene, often capturing some formative moment of your past when your interest in your course of study blossomed. Whether setting the scene in a classroom or on a mountaintop, remember that your goal is make readers feel they are there with you, and remember that the setting itself can be a character in your "short story"—influencing both the action and a response to that action.

Here is a perfect example of a lengthy creative beginning that winds its way into a formal thesis statement, excerpted from a Rhodes Scholarship essay in Chapter 5 (pages 174-175):

> Soaked in sweat, I sat deep in thought on the small mound of sand and broken rocks in northern Kenya, where 1.7 million years ago a desperately ill Homo erectus woman had died. Her death had entranced me for years. KNM-ER 1808 had died of Hypervitaminosis A, wherein an overdose of Vitamin A causes extensive hemorrhaging throughout the skeleton and excruciating pain. Yet a thick rind of diseased bone all over her skeleton— ossified blood clots—tells that 1808 lived for weeks, even months, immobilized by pain and in the middle of the African bush. As noted in *The Wisdom of the Bones*, by Walker and Shipman, that means that

someone had cared for her, brought her water, food, and kept away predators. At 1.7 million years of age, 1808's mere pile of bones is a breathtaking, poignant glimpse of how people have struggled with disease over the ages. Since that moment two summers ago, I've been fascinated by humans' relationship with disease. I want to research paleopathology, the study of ancient diseases, in relation to human culture, specifically sex and gender.

Note how this opening confidently integrates technical detail and even slips in an informal citation on the journey to the thesis. Here, setting itself acts as a character, moving our story's protagonist to imagine a woman's long-ago death, and we also recognize the writer's seriousness of purpose about her work as she as a character in the tale contemplates the woman's fate from a "small mound of sand and broken rocks in northern Kenya." Just as she was taken to this important place and moment in her life, we are taken with her through narrative.

Other essays open with much briefer and less fiction-like personal stories, sometimes relying on just one line to set the context, with the writer heading to a purpose statement shortly thereafter. Here are some straightforward but artful beginnings to personal statements in the book *Graduate Admissions Essays* (9):

> I attended seventeen different schools before high school.

> I spent the morning of my eighteenth birthday in an auditorium with two hundred strangers.

> Radio has been my passion for as long as I can remember.

Clearly, the style of an opening that shares a personal story can range from the flashy to the plain—what matters most is that the opening truly is *personal*.

Compelling Quotations

Like many writers and readers, I'm a sucker for a good meaty quotable quote, which is part of why quotations are used to open each major section of this handbook. We tape handwritten quotes on our bathroom mirrors, clip them onto the visors in our cars, and paste them into our e-mail signature lines. In a personal essay, not only do quotes set context for the reader, they also allow you to ride on the broad shoulders of another who actually managed to say or write something that was *worth* quoting. Quotations might be used at the start of the essay, in the closing, or they might appear at a key moment within the body as a way to set context or emphasize a point. In Chapter 5 of this handbook, a quotation is used as an opening to a science-related essay by an applicant for a National Science Foundation Fellowship. In the same chapter, another writer uses a narrative opening in her essay to repeat a favorite quote that her mother used to say: "To find out where you're going, you need to know where home is."

> Some find Forrest Gump's "Life is like a box of chocolates" hilarious; others just groan when they hear it.

Keep in mind that some quotations are highly overused and that quotations can also come off as merely trite and silly, depending on the taste of the reader. Some find Forrest Gump's "Life is like a box of chocolates" hilarious; others just groan when they hear it. If using a quotation, be sure that you're not just propping yourself up on it as an apology for a lack of substance to your text. Comment on the quotation's relevance to your life rather than just let it sit there, and choose the most meaningful quote for the circumstances rather than one that simply tickles your fancy.

The Use of Surprise or Humor

Indeed, the weapon of surprise is a key ingredient in a Monty Python skit about the Spanish Inquisition (no one expects it, just in case you forgot). But in a personal statement humor and surprise can fall flat in the hands of a fumbling writer. Nevertheless, some writers take these calculated risks, and do so with style. Witness this passage from a sample essay in Chapter 4 (pages 98-100), as a film student explains how he spent his freshman year in a different major:

> With a high school education grounded rigorously in math and science, I entered Mythic University on an academic scholarship with Polymer Science and Engineering as my intended major. I like to joke that, after seeing Mike Nichols' film *The Graduate* and hearing that terrific line, "plastics," delivered poolside to a wayward Benjamin Braddock (Dustin Hoffman), I was inadvertently led into the hands of the great polymer Satan. But, by sophomore year, I quickly escaped the plastic devil's clasp and found a new home in the film department.

Here, this student uses self-deprecating humor as many do in the personal statement: to explain what might otherwise look like a curiosity in his background. Readers need not question his devotion to film despite his beginning in the sciences—he even blends the two interests together by being influenced into his initial major *by* a film, aligning himself briefly and humorously with the hapless character of Benjamin Braddock.

Others use humor or surprise less expansively, but again with the purpose of revealing something personal and intentional self-commentary. One writer quips that his high school classmates voted him "Most likely to have a publishable resume" (10), which shows that this writer can simultaneously poke fun at and uplift himself. Another writer opens her essay unconventionally with a surprising admission—"Skeletons. Like everyone else I have some hanging in my closet" (9)—then later reveals herself as a "survivor of sexual assault." Here, the writer's tone is surprisingly frank, which under the circumstances could help her be viewed as mature and courageous.

Perhaps what unifies these disparate approaches is that the writers clearly *know* they are taking a risk with their rhetoric—there's nothing accidental or highly cutesy about it. All of them reveal a passion for their chosen fields, and the humor and surprise are attention-getting without being too distracting.

Perhaps a good rule of thumb is this: If using humor or surprise, aim it squarely at yourself without making yourself look silly or undermining your character, and dispense with it quickly rather than push it over the top. No matter how well you tell a joke, some readers may not care for it. And hard as it may be to believe, not everyone likes, or even *gets*, Monty Python.

Topical Context

It's often said that one of the best ways to prepare for an interview for a national scholarship is to read *The New York Times* and be ready to discuss current events. If you make it to the interview selection, it's already clear that you have an excellent academic record and look good on paper. What's unclear is how you present in person. By showing yourself to be not just

> It's often said that one of the best ways to prepare for an interview for a national scholarship is to read *The New York Times* and be ready to discuss current events.

committed to your field but also knowledgeable about the world, you paint yourself as a mature thinker, an informed citizen, a responsible student of life.

In a personal statement, writers typically create topical context by narrating a recent event of some consequence, citing a respected source, or simply establishing an arena for discussion. "Martial arts and medicine," opens one personal essay (8), using an intentional sentence fragment to grab our attention and crisply define two intertwined themes in the writer's life. Other essays create a sense of weightiness to their subject matter through topical references:

> As I write this statement, Governor Mario Cuomo makes preparations to vacate the Executive Mansion in Albany, New York, after New Yorkers rejected his appeal for another term (10).

> As the United States launched yet another small war in a distant corner of the globe, Senator Everett McKinley Dirksen returned to life and captivated a hometown audience in Pekin, Illinois, with the folksy eloquence that made him nationally famous (9).

As these politically savvy allusions show, writers who use topical references impress upon their readers that they are both informed and concerned. Here, the color of one's political stripes is irrelevant—what matters is that they are painted clearly. Whether employing a political reference or citing a current event, when you create topical context you represent yourself as a keen observer of the world.

> *If you wish to converse with me, define your terms.*
> —*Voltaire*

Definitions, Metaphors, Similes, and Analogies

Take a tip from Einstein. In one of his famous papers published in 1905 when he was 25 years old, he completely transformed our understanding of physical laws and introduced his theory of relativity. In order to do this, he first proposed that the laws of physics are absolute, then he made both time and distance relative. Equations aside, to help us accept what was then an unthinkably brash concept, he wrote about how we merely understand time as a condition of simultaneity:

We have to take into account that all our judgments in which time plays a part are always judgments of *simultaneous events*. If, for instance, I say, "That train arrives here at 7 o'clock," I mean something like this: "The pointing of the small hand of my watch to 7 and the arrival of the train are simultaneous events" (11).

If trying to understand Einstein's writing (even translated to English) fizzles your brain, you're not alone. But note what he turns to as he aims to help us re-invent our notion of time: *trains* and *clocks*. In other words, he uses comparisons to things that we see as everyday. In particular when we contemplate science, we turn to comparisons—often by using similes, metaphors, or analogies—to simplify and to define. Such comparisons, when deployed well, can have the impact of the proverbial "light bulb" illumination for our readers—they understand suddenly, and hopefully they agree. And even if they disagree with our ideas—and Einstein's paper on relativity was first rejected in its dissertation form, so take comfort—they have to consider them carefully.

Well-made comparisons, then, make us *think*, and the rhetorical tools by which we compare, such as metaphor, are handy, well-established, and universal. In fact, to explain what happened to him in 1905 with the explosion of his seminal papers and the birth of the world's most famous equation, Einstein even used a metaphor: "A storm broke loose in my mind," he famously said.

Providing Definitions

An important consideration in writing personal statements is when to provide definitions of key terms and concepts. The decision can be driven largely by audience and context, based on your audience's likely level of understanding of the subject matter and the importance of the definition to the context of your essay.

At times, the material itself will be technical enough and important enough to context that you will need to supply a quick definition, as in this excerpt from a personal essay about neuroscience appearing in Chapter 4:

> One of the projects I worked on during that summer was developing a diagnostic procedure for HIV encephalitis using PK11195, a ligand for the peripheral benzodiazepine receptor present on the mitochondria of macrophages.

Here, the definition of PK11195 is important to audience and context—both of which are clearly scientific—and the efficient wording demonstrates that the writer is both comfortable with the language of science and understands her project. In this same essay, however, the writer did *not* specifically define "HIV encephalitis," "ligand," and "pathogenesis," fully aware that her audience members would already be familiar with these terms.

A further example from Chapter 4, written by a student studying medieval literature, is a more conversational and expansive definition:

> Ogam is not a spoken language, rather, a code of inscriptions that gave the Irish language an alphabet and supplied the Irish people with a means of writing on stone, wood, and other natural elements with relative ease.

In this essay, the writer's goal is to study Ogam in graduate school, so she supplies a contextual and historical explanation of its meaning in plain, direct language.

For help in supplying definitions, don't hesitate to turn to authoritative sources, including your advisors and dictionaries specific to your field, citing your sources if needed (discussed in Chapter 2 on pages 21-22).

Making Fundamental Comparisons

In addition to definition as a stylistic device, one of the best ways to make fundamental comparisons in writing is by using analogies, similes, and metaphors. Analogies, similes, and metaphors can be used to compare unlike but arguably similar things, either by implicit or explicit comparison. Such comparisons help aid our understanding and can be used to clarify or strengthen an argument, and they do so with efficiency. As with definitions, issues of audience and context help guide us in deciding when to employ these devices.

> Analogies, similes, and metaphors can be used to compare unlike but arguably similar things, either by implicit or explicit comparison.

Here, we need not worry about exact distinctions among similes, metaphors, and analogies, other than a reminder that when we use them we often rely on phrasings such as "like" or "as," and that when we make a fairly loose comparison we might use quotation marks around the words whose meaning we're "stretching" (as I just did). Here are just a few commonly used similes, metaphors, and analogies from various disciplines:

- In discussions of grammar, we might refer to a colon as acting like a flare in the road—a symbolic promise that something important is coming. A semicolon in a sentence's middle acts like a caesura does in music or verse—as a timely pause linking two related parts.

- In biology, mitochondria are often referred to metaphorically as the powerhouse of the cell, while the liver is loosely referred to as the body's "garbage can."

- In discussing fungi, there's a bright yellow fungus that grows on wet logs in the northwestern US, and it can be compared visually to a pat of melting butter. Underground, the roots of some mushrooms resemble the legs of a toe-standing ballet dancer.

- In information technology discussions, we often speak of cyberspace as a metaphorically parallel world, with clipboards for saving information, surfing as virtual travel, and gophers allowing us to tunnel through to some desired goal.

As examples from personal essays written by students, what follows are a few fundamental comparisons that writers made through analogy, simile, and metaphor, with their surrounding material further explaining the comparisons. Notice how none of the comparisons are difficult to grasp, but all are illuminating.

> These ripples of space-time curvature, called gravity waves, are radiated outward much like ripples in a pond.

> The model uses the compartmentalized cascade to treat the intrinsic pathway as a "black box" leading to the output of thrombin in the common pathway.

> I established a home for myself in a metaphysical and emotional space: the space where my family, passions, and goals all intersect.

As these writers did, when composing personal essays you should consider the similes, metaphors, and analogies available—even if they are commonly used—as efficient ways to demonstrate stylistic creativity, represent your understanding of a topic, describe related phenomena, and discuss fundamental concepts important to your field.

> *Writing is an act of faith, not a trick of grammar.*
> *—E.B. White*

Useful Verbs

The E.B. White quote above is especially meaningful here, as I am about to provide a list of useful verbs, in that it reminds us that good writers seem almost to compose by faith and intuition, confident that their instincts rather than their knowledge of grammar will guide them towards the best diction and syntax. When we write well, we learn to "feel" our way through an essay rather than pull up a rote system of rules and regulations to guide us.

That said, many find it helpful to turn to lists when they write, either because they find the word they're looking for on the list or because the act inspires them to think in relation to a class of words they're looking for. In fact, as writers become more specialized within a field, they turn again and again to mental or physical word lists to write effectively. Read a good weather forecast and you'll find the weather patterns described with such active verbs as "hammered," "trounced," "sliced," and "eased." Read a good sportscast and you'll find gleeful discussions of how a losing team was "throttled," "bashed," "whipped," or "humiliated."

Active verbs in particular are useful tools for writers of personal essays, because they help us to 1) efficiently summarize our achievements, and 2) describe relevant phenomena. On the next page is a list of commonly used active verbs in these two categories, organized randomly to emphasize that these lists are not to be used in the way that many blindly use a thesaurus—as though one verb can be swapped for another. In fact, in assembling these lists I chose verbs that are unlike each other in meaning, to emphasize that writers should always be aware of both the denotations and connotations of their chosen words. When unsure of a verb's usage and meaning, always look it up in a well-thumbed dictionary.

Verbs to Summarize Achievements

Achieved
Determined
Observed
Managed
Inspired
Checked
Empowered
Allocated
Lectured
Encouraged
Analyzed
Validated
Enforced
Provided
Measured
Engineered
Conveyed
Appraised
Denounced
Led
Diagnosed
Communicated
Computed
Translated
Mediated
Supervised
Systematized
Persuaded
Calculated
Prioritized
Navigated
Screened
Simplified
Originated
Counseled
Indexed

Integrated
Presented
Witnessed
Recorded
Demonstrated
Catalogued
Implemented
Controlled
Generated
Improved
Taught
Converted
Improvised
Pioneered
Improved
Invented
Effected
Grouped
Experimented
Judged
Defined
Modeled
Researched
Facilitated
Transcribed
Accomplished
Maintained
Advised
Interviewed
Undertook
Noted
Verified
Sorted
Wrote
Founded
Tabulated

Verbs to Describe Phenomena

Discharged
Exchanged
Emitted
Converged
Invaded
Bonded
Deposited
Oriented
Accelerated
Interacted
Transmitted
Mixed
Quickened
Originated
Enriched
Saturated
Restored
Superimposed
Crystallized
Transferred
Halted
Behaved
Plunged
Fused
Evolved
Ascended
Bisected
Disintegrated
Mutated
Accessed
Stood
Overlapped
Competed
Forced
Led
Separated

Curbed
Collapsed
Coalesced
Isolated
Fractured
Elongated
Absorbed
Scattered
Propelled
Radiated
Bombarded
Deteriorated
Permeated
Ceased
Lagged
Circulated
Divided
Ruptured
Propelled
Disseminated
Surrounded
Constrained
Slowed
Traversed
Rotated
Fell
Cut
Penetrated
Linked
Froze
Exerted
Fought
Exuded
Guided
Inverted
Exchanged

Transitions

In personal essays, often the best transitions are simply contextual. For instance, to discuss graduate research plans, you might open a sentence with "For my graduate research, I plan to . . . ." In broader circumstances, to transition from one idea to another, writers turn to the list below—handy because the transitions are sorted by function, emphasizing the work they do. When choosing a transition from this list, focus on providing connective tissue that moves us through time, provides example or interpretation, or advances argument.

Interpretation
Fortunately
Interestingly
Significantly
Surprisingly

Closure
Finally
In sum
On the whole

Causality
Accordingly
Consequently
For this reason
Hence
Therefore
Thus

Similarity
In the same way
Likewise
Similarly

Amplification
Again
Also
Equally important
First, Second, etc.
Further
In addition
Moreover

Emphasis
Above all
Certainly
Clearly
Indeed
In fact
In short
Obviously
Of course

Example
For example
For instance
To illustrate

Time
Afterward
Earlier
Next
Simultaneously
Soon

Contrast
However
In contrast
Nevertheless
On the contrary
On the other hand
Still

Detail
In essence
In particular
In relation to
Impressively
Namely
Specifically
To enumerate

> *It's never too late—in fiction or in life—to revise.*
> *—Nancy Thayer*

Smart Revision Strategies

In general, good writers love to revise. It gives them a sense of accomplishment, and they find it easier or more satisfying than composing a first draft. I once revised a short story that I wrote over a two-year period, whittling it down from 35 pages to 13, dropping a character, changing the central theme, and ultimately producing one of my most well-published pieces. Some writers even revise their work after it's been published, just for themselves, nagged by some imperfection they perceive or based on how their readers have reacted.

Of course, when you write a personal statement or application essay, you don't have the luxury (or curse) of endless opportunities to revise. Nevertheless, you do have to expect that your first draft of the material might require multiple re-readings and revisions to be ready for submission. My best student writers tend to report that they re-read and revise their personal essays at least seven times, even if they change only one word or two each time, and they seek feedback from professors, advisors, Writing Center tutors, friends, and even their parents. As they revise, they consider how to effectively use their space, tailor their content, perfect their grammar and mechanics, and improve their tone. As the discussions that follow will show, these principles are often tightly related to one another.

Revising for Space

When revising to save space or meet a word count, the first tactic is to think in physical terms. If your essay runs just a few lines over a boundary, look carefully at your paragraphs. Often, an entire line might be taken up by just a word or two, and shortening that paragraph accordingly can save a line. Of course, in physical terms, you can also experiment slightly with font and form (discussed in Chapter 2, pages 17-18), but keep in mind that astute readers will be critical of anything that is physically difficult to read because of how you managed space.

More important in revising for space is for you to look at your material holistically and ask yourself if any essay part is taking up more proportional space than it should or is simply too long to justify its value. I once worked with a student who was having trouble conforming to her word count, so we looked at her first draft carefully for any weak areas, deciding that her introduction wasn't really worth the space it took up. Here was her original introduction:

> There are moments in my day when students buzz by like bees do, I take a confused pause and ask myself: oh no, where am I going? The pause is almost unnoticeable, nevertheless daunting. Of course, the quick answers are: the student union, class, work, and a never ending list of meetings. However the larger question looms over my body as I hustle to register students to vote and plan more ways to increase political awareness on campus. I used to dread the exploration of my future possibilities; this looming entity was a cloud ready to break apart and drown me in a rainstorm. Despite my love of running around in rainstorms, I found more comfort in my mother's words: *to find out where you're going, you need to know where home is.*

Upon reflection, the writer realized that not only was the opening lengthy, it was also redundant with other parts of the application. Readers would learn plenty about her energy and political activism in her resume and list of activities. And as far as the introduction's creativity, the writer realized she was just using it to show off a bit, and in the process using clichés ("students buzz by like bees") and providing irrelevant detail (her "love of running around in rainstorms").

Fortunately, this writer spared her readers and hacked her introduction down to the material that was the most original—her mother's comforting words, which were a central theme in her essay. Her revised introduction read thus:

> I have always found comfort in my mother's words*: to find out where you're going, you need to know where home is.*

Much nicer—crisp, interesting, and meaningful. By revising six sentences down to one, the writer emphasized what she cared about most in her original introduction, which also turned out to be the material that was the most personal.

Revising for Content

Recognizing the audience's need for content, especially guided by the application question criteria you're addressing in a personal essay, you should always consider ways to revise that will provide further substance. For instance, knowing from the application question that his readers were interested in specific details about his planned master's research, one writer changed this:

> As part of my master's research at Mythic College I am interested in the information overload issue—it can cause anxiety, poor decision-making, and reduced attention span.

. . . to this:

> For my master's thesis at Mythic College I plan to focus on cognitive architectures that allow us to make simulations of and predictions about human performance in situations such as driving vehicles or piloting fighter aircraft.

In this revision, we learn much more meaningful information about the planned research, including the practical applications of the work. Thus, we are more likely to assess that this student is indeed ready to begin his research.

As this example demonstrates, revising for content is usually about providing more concrete detail based on audience needs, keeping in mind that the content you choose reveals you as a person, as a thinker, and as a student. The more these three parts can be blended together through your content revisions, the better.

Revising for Grammar and Mechanics

Like many teachers, I sometimes urge my students to read their work aloud as a proofing tactic and so that they can literally hear how their writing might sound to others. This can be very effective, in that it helps you listen to your own sentence rhythms, sense gaps in logic, intuit where punctuation is needed, and identify words that you're misusing or overusing. However, a curious problem surfaces with this practice. Writers who read their work aloud tend to insert words that aren't really there on the page, or substitute correct words for incorrect ones, not even realizing they're doing it. Cognitively, what's happening is that they're revising, effectively and automatically, even if someone else looking over their shoulder at the printed work has to point it out to them.

Matters of Style • 51

The key to revising our work for grammar (both word choice and wording) and mechanics (small but important matters such as punctuation) is to, in effect, listen to our work anew. The best writers adopt an objective "listening ear," learning to detect their problems of grammar and mechanics both intuitively and methodically, pretending they're encountering the work for the first time no matter how many times they've re-read it.

Meanwhile, you can count on two things: 1) we tend to repeat the same errors over and over in our writing, and 2) other writers make the same errors we do. If we have one comma error in an essay, we're likely to have others; if we have a particular usage problem such as the distinction between "affect" and "effect," we can be sure other writers have it too. Therefore, by studying the most common errors and revising accordingly, we're likely to improve our work substantially. And when we make particularly common errors in our personal essays (such as confusing "it's" with "its"), our audience is justified in viewing us as lazy and unthinking, in that such errors are so easy to reason through and correct.

Grammatically, writers tend to make their most obvious errors in these areas:

- Subject/verb agreement, which can usually be addressed by identifying each subject and verb in your sentences, ignoring the other words mentally, and making certain that they match in number and sound. Also, remember that the word "and" linking two subjects makes them plural ("Grammar and mechanics are related"), and that when subjects are connected by the word "or" the subject closer to the verb determines the verb's number ("Either the punctuation marks or the usage is flawed").

- Verb tense, which must be considered both for consistency and context. Writers can switch verb tenses within a paragraph as long as the context calls for it, but unnatural shifts in verb tense stand out loudly ("The sample was heated and then cool before storage"). As a general principle, the simplest verb tense should be chosen for the circumstances (avoid "has," "have," and "had" as helpers except when necessary), and favor the present tense when possible (it brings the material "closer" to the reader).

- Runs-ons and fragments, which can again be addressed by identifying your subjects and verbs, and in some cases by assessing sentence length.

- Commonly confused terms, which are easy to look up in any style handbook, and therefore a potential source of great irritation to your educated readers. Just to rehearse and briefly describe a few, "affect" is usually a verb meaning *to influence*, while "effect" is usually a noun meaning *outcome* or *result*. "It's," of course, always means *it is*, while "its" always *shows possession*. The abbreviation "e.g." is Latin for *exempli gratia* and means *for example*, while "i.e." is Latin for *id est* and means *that is*. The word "imply" means *to suggest* or *to indicate*, while "infer" involves *a person actively applying deduction*. The word "that" is used *to define and limit the meaning* of a noun, while "which" is used *to provide descriptive information* not central to the noun's definition.

From a mechanics standpoint, writers do themselves a great favor by learning to understand punctuation conceptually and fundamentally, as follows:

- A comma is a separator. Therefore, when you use one you should identify why the material is worthy of separation. Common reasons include that you used a transition word that creates a natural pause, you wrote a lengthy, complex sentence with multiple subjects and verbs, and that you supplied a list of three or more related items or phrases in a row. All three of these reasons helped me punctuate this paragraph with commas.

- A colon is an arrow pointing forward. It tells us that new information, which is promised by the wording before it, is about to arrive. The colon is especially handy for introducing an announced piece of evidence, a focused example, or a list. Contrary to popular belief, the colon can be used to point us forward to a single word or to an entire sentence. My favorite example of the former is an old George Carlin joke: *Weather forecast for tonight: dark.*

- A semicolon is a mark of co-dependency. This mark is so often mentally confused with the colon that I am often forced to repeat to my students: *the colon is two dots; the semicolon is a comma below a dot.* Though it's sad to have to say it, at least the explanation actually *involves* a semicolon. As my italicized explanation demonstrates, the semicolon is usually used to join phrases or sentences having grammatical equivalency, and it emphasizes that the joined parts are related, even co-dependent, in context.

- <u>A dash redefines what was just said</u>. I'm amazed at how many writers simply don't use the dash at all—except excessively in e-mails—because they're afraid of it. But the dash is a powerful way to make an important aside, as I did above, and to tack on an additional comment of consequence—a comment that redefines. When typing the dash, be certain that you don't type a hyphen, but *two* hyphens in a row or a long bar (which Word is perfectly happy to provide automatically as you juxtapose two typed hyphens or via its pull-down symbol map).

Speaking of Word, by all means do use the grammar checker to test grammar and mechanics in your personal essay, but don't trust it blindly. To state the obvious, the grammar checker *does not think*, and it doesn't know the contextual difference between, say, "mescaline" (an illegal hallucinogen) and the word "miscellaneous." I choose this particular example because one of my students once accidentally claimed on her resume that she was in charge of "mescaline responsibilities" at her summer job. With that one slip, she could have worried and alienated both her former employer and her future one.

Revising for Tone

Put simply, tone is the writer's attitude towards the subject. We discern the writer's tone by both the words chosen and the content selected, and in personal essays many writers unknowingly send the wrong message about themselves because of their tone. They often do this because they feel they should explain some blemish on their record ("It took me a long time to decide on the right major") or because they think that arrogance might be taken as confidence ("I invented a totally new method of scientific research"). Instead, such writers are likely to be perceived as indecisive and lacking in confidence in the first case, and hubristic and naive in the second.

> We discern the writer's tone by both the words chosen and the content selected, and in personal essays many writers unknowingly send the wrong message about themselves because of their tone.

If I had to boil the issue of tone in personal statements down to one word, it would be this: *affirmation*. Your job is to affirm—what is true, what you've accomplished, what you value, how you think, what your plans are, what your research means, what program you'd like to attend, and so on. Too many writers focus on the negative, stressing their uncertainties, their doubts, and even their failures. There's always a positive way to spin a point—watch the spin doctors and politicians on television news shows if you need a primer—and in a personal statement a positive, affirmative tone is critical.

As examples, here are some sentences taken from personal essays that I've read, altered so that they're spun as negatives:

> I only completed a generalist degree in a field called earth sciences, which gives you a little bit of everything without any real specializations.

> Unfortunately, government red tape and bureaucracy are intertwined with how we learn about our environment in school.

> My long-term goals remain uncertain, but I feel very sure that I don't want to be a professor.

Though these are altered to make a point, many personal statements contain such negative attitudes, with writers unwisely expressing dark feelings about themselves and towards the very fields in which they plan to study. Here are the positive versions of the same sentences, as they originally appeared:

> As a scientist, my training began in earth sciences—a bachelor's degree combination of geography, meteorology, and geoscience.

> Many of our existing federal ecosystem management protocols are based on a rich tradition of physiographic study.

> My future plans lean more towards industry and research than academia.

As you revise personal essays, concentrate on exuding an affirmative, positive tone. Be upbeat but not overbearing. Explain but don't equivocate. Be realistic but not pessimistic. Speak confidently but don't brag. Be idealistic but not naive. Tell the truth about yourself and your background but don't apologize for either.

Do all this in your tone, and your readers may pay you the compliment most commonly coveted by writers: "I like your style."

CHAPTER 4

SAMPLE PERSONAL STATEMENTS, APPLICATION ESSAYS, AND RESUMES

> *Easy writing makes hard reading.*
> *—Ernest Hemingway*

As a graduate student taking fiction writing workshops many moons ago, I recall what was most motivating to me as a creative writer. It wasn't the reading of published or award-winning work, and it wasn't the classroom critique given on high from the professor nor the scribble from my classmates on my manuscripts— all these things were helpful and valuable, but nothing motivated me more than comparing my fiction to the work of my peers. As I read their work carefully, both objectively and subjectively, I found myself thinking that I was sure I could write better than the others around me at the seminar table—then I'd read an artful, poignant story that made me wonder whether I could ever even compete.

Perhaps somewhere between these two attitudes is the most profitable approach when studying the work of your peers. In critiquing the work of others who essentially represent your competition, you should take a respectful stance both critical and kind, just as selection committee members are likely to do. The samples in this chapter are opportunities for you to study, admire, question, emulate, reject, and—most importantly—consider how to present the best, truest, most effective picture of yourself in the eyes of others. These samples were chosen from a field of about 100 students because they represent personal stories that are intriguing, diverse, complex, honest, and humanizing.

For even further samples and advice, especially if you're interested in law, business, or medical school, I recommend *How to Write a Winning Personal Statement for Graduate and Professional School*, by Richard J. Stelzer (8), *Perfect Personal Statements*, by Mark Alan Stewart (10), and *Graduate Admissions Essays*, by Donald Asher (9).

> *If one word does not succeed, ten thousand are of no avail.*
> —*Chinese proverb*

Critiques of Short Personal Essay Samples

In the first half of this chapter are personal statements and application essays representing strong efforts by students applying for both undergraduate and graduate opportunities. These efforts are not meant as templates, but as material worthy of your study and critique. To help guide your assessment of this material, I offer a few comments—even objective criticisms at times—in the pages that follow.

The first 10 essays in this chapter have one thing in common: They were all written by students under the constraint of the essay being 1-2 pages due to the target program's explicit instructions. In such circumstances, writers must attend carefully to the essay prompt (sometimes as simple as "Write a one-page summary of your reasons for wanting to pursue graduate study") and recognize that evaluators tend to judge these essays on the same fundamental principles, as follows:

- First, you are typically expected to provide a window into your personal motivations, offer a summary of your field, your research, or your background, set some long-term goals, and note specific interest in the program to which you are applying.

- Second, you are expected to provide some personal detail and to communicate effectively and efficiently. Failure to do so can greatly limit your chances of acceptance.

Good writers accomplish these tasks by immediately establishing each paragraph's topic and maintaining paragraph unity, by using concrete, personal examples to demonstrate their points, and by not prolonging the ending of the essay needlessly. Also, good writers study the target opportunity as carefully as they can, seeking to become an "insider," perhaps even communicating with a professor they would like to work with at the target program, and tailoring the material accordingly so that evaluators can gauge the sincerity of their interest.

Short Personal Statement: Geology and
Short Personal Statement: Paleontology (page 66 and page 67)
The two one-page statements written by students in the geosciences are interesting to compare to each other. In both essays, the opening phrasing in each paragraph clearly establishes focus. A simple demonstration can be seen in these excerpts:

Growing up in Canada . . .
Geographic information systems . . .
For my graduate research project . . .
My long-term goals . . .
In applying to the University of Alberta . . .

From an early age I was fascinated . . .
. . .when the time to choose a thesis . . .
My aspirations for study in . . .
The program at the University of . . .

Such focused, audience-centered paragraph openings immediately engage our attention, and they are backed up by highly concrete examples. For the student aiming to study Canadian geography, she showcases her knowledge of the John Evans Glacier, comfortably uses the acronyms and vocabulary of one studying geographic information systems (GIS), and discusses her research plans to improve "current GIS data models to better incorporate time as a variable in studying climate change." For the student working in the paleontology field, he establishes his scientific fluency as he summarizes his thesis project, which involves "the taphonomy, stratigraphy, and identification of a middle-Ordovician coral bioherm as well as its bryozoan constituents." He is equally detailed in his discussion of graduate research interests to employ morphology in phylogenetic analysis. Both students end their essays with concrete reference to the suitability of their target programs. The second essay is especially impressive here, with the writer noting a specific discussion and a particular affinity with a professor in his program of choice.

Short Internship Essay: Geography (page 68)
The first essay, applying to an intern program, opens with the writer admitting that she previously had a limited view of geography, then describing how a course changed her way of thinking so that she came to understand geography as a "balance of physical, social, and cultural studies." She continues her discussion by noting the theme for her honors thesis, with the intention to travel to various cities related to her thesis topic. Her third paragraph mentions aspirations of joining the Peace Corps or obtaining a law degree, and her final paragraph links her interests directly to the intern program offered by the National Geographic Society.

Reading this essay critically, some readers might find it too broad and speculative at times, but more generous readers might interpret that this student simply needs time and experience to focus. Certainly this student does need to become more certain about her future and to grow, and the internship program she seeks might provide the perfect opportunity.

Short Application Essay: Environmental Law (page 69)
The one-page essay from a student applying to law school traces the student's motivation to study environmental law to his experience working for 11 years at his father's gas station, where he first encountered the legal issues connected to compliance laws for underground fuel storage tanks. He ties this formative experience to a desire to use his science background "to make it easier on other small business owners to comply with environmental laws."

In other parts of this writer's application, we would note a somewhat spotty educational record, so he directly addresses the fact that he is not a traditional student in that he worked two years after high school before continuing his education, then transferred to a four-year school after attending a community college. This also quietly helps to explain to the selection committee any grade inconsistencies or seeming gaps in education.

The writer's final two paragraphs cite his work with a government agency and his senior thesis research on using geophysical methods to decide where to install hydrogeologic equipment. These experiences, he argues, equip him well to become "a dynamic participant in the University of Pittsburgh Law School," and he reminds us—despite his somewhat piecemeal education—that he is "motivated by personal experience, a highly evolved work ethic, and a strong education." Thus, his overall argument is affirmative and persuasive.

Short Fellowship Essay: Materials Engineering (page 70)
Being directed at an internal fellowship, this one-page essay has an especially difficult task: The writer must persuade those who already know him (and thus know both his strengths and his limitations) that he is worthy of internal funds to help him continue his graduate education. He attempts this by first citing the goal of his research group to "design microwave-active materials to facilitate the procurement of a low-powered miniaturized solid-state antenna." He follows this with a brief summary of the literature related to this topic, noting his broad goal of further developing the necessary technology.

His second paragraph summarizes his research experience with the Navy, while his third points out how comfortable he would be working in two labs (one in materials and one in electrical engineering), "with graduate students often using equipment in both labs freely." He ends the essay noting how "a ceramist should also be versed in electrical engineering."

Despite this essay's strengths, it should be noted that the argument may not be fully persuasive to hard-nosed committee members. The writer's *personal* research goals are painted with a broad brush, and his hope to merge two disciplines will likely have to be much more exact to make him an attractive fellowship candidate in a competitive field. Also, he is likely to be competing with students who provide far more detail about their graduate research progress.

Two Application Essays: Business (pages 71-73)
The two business application essays, written by the same applicant, are in response to questions posed by an MBA program, which is especially interested in how candidates take risks and overcome challenges. The writer handles the first question, which allows for one page to describe a personal risk and its impact, by describing a life-changing 3500-mile bike trip he took across the US with his brother at the age of 21. Some vivid moments of narrative detail are included, as he describes the possessions carried along on the bikes and the 150 rocky miles across the Mojave Desert, which caused him to land in the emergency room with exhaustion and dehydration. Also, remembering that part of his rhetorical aim is to impress upon his readers that he is business-minded and self-reflective, he makes two mentions of the co-op experience he completed in Colorado, which opened up "a world of business opportunities" and "revealed my passion for adventure." He ends the first essay effectively in a narrative stance, commenting on the humbling and uplifting experience of the cross country ride as "part of a master plan of personal growth and achievement."

The second essay gives applicants two pages to describe a challenging team experience and their contributions to its success. Here, the writer has the advantage of having already worked in business for a few years after completing his bachelor's degree, so he wisely turns to his most successful team experience at his company, where he was a project leader. He shows his comfort with the language of the business world, using terms such as "go live" and "supply chain," and he repeatedly stresses his own role in promoting positive team effort, even to the point that his team went during a critical week to the warehouse "to share the load of training 100 employees across multiple shifts."

Finally, recognizing from the question prompt and from the nature of MBA programs that he is expected to discuss challenges and even failures, the writer repeatedly cites a need to improve on his "ability to communicate at a high level with upper management" and a motivation to "continue to improve my managerial skills." He also notes his ethic of communicating with the client when the project was behind schedule. Even if we tire somewhat of this writer's persistent "rah-rah business" tone, we are encouraged to trust him because of his honesty.

Personal Statement: Neuroscience (pages 74-75)
Having a bit of room to work with (a 700-word limit, which the writer noses under by three words), this essay opens with narrative technique, telling an affecting story about working in a lab at the University of Pittsburgh. The writer depicts herself poring over records about HIV-infected brains from which she has tissue samples. Repeatedly recording the age of the subjects in the appropriate column, she realizes that many of those subjects had died of AIDS when they were near her age or even younger. Thus we are introduced to one of the motivating forces behind her interest in neuroscience.

In the third paragraph, the writer presents more detail about her drive to conduct research on the molecular basis of disease, citing three undergraduate research experiences and her interest in the linked sciences of disease: immunology, biochemistry, genetics, and pathology. The third paragraph ends with the writer matching her interests to the interdisciplinary program at the University of Pennsylvania, a match strengthened in the next paragraph when she knowledgably cites a researcher at that program working on the pathogenesis of Alzheimer's disease. Finally, as many students do, she ends on a personal note, expressing a desire to live in Philadelphia, which is near her home base.

A highly critical reader might note that this writer doesn't actually present a specific research plan for graduate study, and her tone can sometimes be informal ("They would never be able to have the career of their dreams . . ."). However, given the facility with which she speaks about science, her three previous research experiences, and the fact that a personal statement does allow room for one to be, well, *personal*, the writing is persuasive and powerful.

Personal Statement: Medieval Literature (pages 76-77)
This personal statement immerses us in detail about medieval literature throughout the essay, eventually citing the Irish medieval manuscripts *The Gospels of St. Willibrord, The Book of Kells,* and *The Book of Durrow.* With these examples and others, we are convinced that this student truly does see medieval literature as a "passion," as she claims in her first sentence. Further examples of this passion in practice emerge throughout the first page, with the writer quoting Gregory of Tours and providing a discussion of Ogam—a code of inscriptions that gave the Irish language an alphabet. In the middle of the essay she ties this discussion to a desire to study and decipher the inscriptions of Ogam stones.

Most noteworthy in the essay is how the second half is devoted so thoroughly to individual professors and programs that the writer envisions as part of her graduate plans. She repeatedly cites two professors and "mentors" whom she has already met, noting how they have shaped her highly specific academic goals, and tying her almost headlong approach directly to the National University of Ireland at Maynooth, where she will have flexibility in designing her own program.

Doubts that readers might have about the student's ability to carry out this plan in Ireland are likely assuaged by her obvious passion, her evidenced appreciation for historical context, and her recognition that she will need to become versed in the fundamentals of Old and Middle Irish language to succeed. Indeed, she ends her essay with the Gaelic expression *Is d'Éire mé* ("I am of Ireland").

An interesting way to study this essay is to compare it to a personal statement for the Rhodes Scholarship (pages 176-177) in Chapter 5. This essay is written by the same writer but with a highly different focus—further testimony to her depth and ability.

Scholarship Application Essay: Education (pages 78-79)
A junior faced with stiff competition for the Beinecke Scholarship program, which awards $32,000 towards senior year and graduate school, this student writes an interesting theme-based essay and projects forward toward graduate school. Given that Beinecke applicants are nominated by their institution for the scholarship, with each school permitted to make only a single nomination each year, the essay must be compelling and worthy of such singular nomination.

This writer's sense of self-definition is particularly strong, and her personal story compelling. As she establishes in her creative opening ("Passion drips from the lips of the preacher at the pulpit. . . ."), passion is an inspirational theme in her life. In the second paragraph we learn of the writer's personal background, which included growing up in the unsafe streets of one of Chicago's worst neighborhoods, driving her to the safe harbor of reading and to academic success that led her to a magnet elementary school and a gifted high school program.

When writers offer such a level of detail about their personal background, it is important that they tie this background to personal motivations—else readers have a potentially compelling story but one without a point or central theme. In this case, the themes that emerge for this student are about inequities and injustice. She witnessed these themes in the way some of her peers, "poor pupils from the area's housing projects," were treated in her high school at the hands of others and even by the system itself, and she witnessed it again in how she was sometimes treated socially and institutionally at her rural university. The writer describes in her final paragraphs how these experiences have led to her proposed senior thesis research exploring how a select population of students transitions from community college to four-year schools, and how her long-term goal, through graduate degrees, is to become a policy analyst for the government's Department of Education. Put simply, this student aims to be an agent of change.

Just as importantly, we hear detailed discussion of the theme of how the writer's identity and experiences as an African-American woman have shaped her plans. She cites African-American heroes and activists such as Thurgood Marshall and W.E.B. Dubois, and even makes reference to Steptoe's "Black Cinderella" story (*Mufaro's Beautiful Daughters*). We hear of her experiencing comments and attitudes during college that demean her because of her race, but at the same time, because of the examples offered, we see how this student has uplifted and integrated herself successfully into her community. Further, she even chooses to remove herself from her found "comfort zones," committing to her upcoming student teaching requirement by electing to teach in England, "amidst a culture of people I have never been exposed to, thousands of miles from home."

As expressed in her essay, this student's strong sense of identity and affirmative accomplishment amidst personal challenges combine to make her an excellent candidate for the desired scholarship.

> *To avoid criticism do nothing, say nothing, be nothing.*
> —*Elbert Hubbard*

Critiques of Sample Resumes

Frequently, graduate school or scholarship applications provide an option or requirement for you to submit a resume to complement your other written material. The two sample resumes here provide good examples of what graduate schools and scholarship committees look for in a resume (or "curriculum vitae").

Short Resume: Geoscience (page 80)
The writer of the short resume wisely excludes the usual "Objective" section (needless for a graduate application) and focuses instead on his education. Note how he briefly discusses his thesis research and lists his key courses—information he hopes will be of special interest to the selection committee. With little meaningful work experience in the field, the writer simply summarizes his experience briefly and lists activities, some of which relate to his field of study. Admittedly, standing alone, this resume will not help the student rise above other applicants, some of whom are bound to have paid work experience in the field. However, though necessarily limited in its offerings, this resume is professionally presented and may be helpful to the application, particularly when joined with the corresponding personal statement written by the same student (page 67), where the writer fleshes out his impressive thesis work thoroughly.

Extensive Curriculum Vitae: Political Science (pages 81-83)
With curriculum vitae tailored to graduate school or scholarships, the category headings can be determined both by the writer's strengths and by the selectors' needs. Thus, the sample three-page curriculum vitae focuses on languages, international experience, and leadership positions. Note how the writer effectively uses subcategories to underscore a diversity of experience, ranging from political involvement to research. She describes volunteer positions as thoroughly as one would describe a job. Also, she uses various formatting strategies, including ample white space, selective indentation, and boldface of parallel headings to allow for easy visual scanning of her credentials. Clearly, this student has a lot of offer in her chosen field of political science, especially when we also read her Mitchell Scholarship personal statement in Chapter 5 (pages 196-197).

SHORT PERSONAL STATEMENT: GEOLOGY
(This material is critiqued on page 59.)

Growing up in Canada with a life-long fascination for Canadian geography, I have always been interested in returning to the country. Although my family moved to the US before I entered high school, I have always kept my eyes turned north, especially in recent years as I began to read journal articles about research conducted on John Evans Glacier, located about 80ϒ N latitude. Graduating next semester with a B.S. in computer science and engineering and a minor in geographic information systems, I am interested in attending the University of Alberta for graduate study.

Geographic information systems (GIS) is a field especially suited to investigating spatial patterns, modeling diverse scenarios, and overlaying spatial data. This semester, in my advanced GIS course, Spatial Data Structures and Algorithms, I am part of a team developing a temporal database and program for tracing historical trading data. My computer science skills have also been put to use in two summer internship projects, where I acquired proficiency with using LIDAR (light detection and ranging) technology, now favored by NASA in its current 10-year study of Greenland and changes in the ice cap extent. Through my coursework and project experience, I have also accrued skills in using Arc/Info, ArcView, Microstation, and RDBMS software packages, and I am equally comfortable programming in Visual Basic, C++, and Java.

For my graduate research project, I would like to investigate methods for improving current GIS data models to better incorporate time as a variable in studying climate change. Changes in glaciers and polar environments occur rapidly, and these changes become important indicators of broader, potentially catastrophic, global changes. By developing and applying temporal GIS methods to glaciology, I can contribute to improved spatio-temporal analysis techniques for studying the polar environment and glaciers. Also, I can discern which temporal methods serve as the best predictors and provide benefits to the GIS research community that apply to areas other than glaciology.

My long-term goals are to enter the GIS field as a consultant or to extend my research and earn my Ph.D. at a program of international reputation. Having advanced experience with temporal GIS technology would make me a valuable consultant to a company, especially in the twin burgeoning fields of computer science and GIS.

In applying to the University of Alberta, I recognize your strengths in both computer science and glaciology, and the recent application of these areas to field research at Ellesmere Island in Nunavut, Canada, is especially appealing to me. With my deep-rooted interest in Canadian geology and recognition of the quality of your university programs, I hope you will give my application every consideration.

SHORT PERSONAL STATEMENT: PALEONTOLOGY

(This material is critiqued on page 59.)

From an early age I was fascinated with fossils. My respect for ancient life has always included an admitted partiality for the study of vertebrates. Upon taking my first college-level paleontology class I knew without a doubt that I had chosen the right path. The study of fossils has never felt like unwarranted labor, but an opportunity to learn about these creatures that lived so long before our time. Throughout my geology coursework my ears have always pricked up at the mention of the word fossil. My college education has been a means to entering the study of vertebrate paleontology.

Naturally when the time to choose a thesis project came, I made sure that I would do mine in the field of paleontology, working directly with fossil specimens. My project involves the taphonomy, stratigraphy, and identification of a middle-Ordovician coral bioherm as well as its bryozoan constituents. The research is now well under way, involving many aspects of a sound paleontological study: sampling, analysis, identification, and finalization into a report. Fossiliferous rock samples were acquired from the field, cut at proper orientations, polished, and peel section slides produced from them. My analysis of these slides led to identification of the specimens utilizing the established literature. Fossil specimen photography will soon follow. The abstract from this research project has been submitted in time for the Northeastern Section Meeting of the Geological Society of America in March. From this project I will take away an understanding of how to conduct a proper paleontological study and I will write a thesis.

My aspirations for study in vertebrate paleontology are primarily in understanding what fossil specimens can tell us about how ancient vertebrates lived, interacted with their environment, and evolved through time. More specifically, my research interests within the field include employing morphology in the phylogenetic analysis of major evolutionary bifurcations such as that involving theropods and birds, exploiting biogeography to better understand vertebrate expansion and speciation, and the use of functional morphology and biomechanics to understand vertebrate movement. My long-term goals are to educate others and spur interest in vertebrate paleontology while conducting research. The position of professor would encompass these goals as well as allow me to publish and maintain a successful presence in the field.

The program at the University of Chicago would prepare me extremely well for what I ultimately intend to do in life. The works of professors within the Division of Biological Sciences, the Department of Geophysical Sciences, as well as the Field Museum are impressive. I appreciated meeting Dr. Paul C. Sereno during his visit at Mythic University in December 2004, and I find his approach toward exploration and his application of cladistics in phylogenetic studies indispensable to the field of vertebrate paleontological study. From this correspondence I feel the research that I would conduct at the university would not only be interesting and rewarding, but give me experience in the field to then apply toward my ultimate goal of becoming an academic professor.

SHORT INTERNSHIP ESSAY: GEOGRAPHY
(This material is critiqued on pages 59-60.)

Prior to coming to Mythic College, I had a very skewed view of what geography was. When I thought about geography, visions of memorizing all fifty state capitals and exercises of filling in the world map came to mind. Freshman year, I enrolled in Geography 20 (human geography) simply because it was the only honors class that fit in my schedule. Instead of being bored, I was stimulated to think of the world through a different focus, through the lens of a geographer: to view people and places and examine how each relates to the other. Suddenly, I was thinking of everything in this fashion. When walking to class, I would ponder why the paths were designed the way they were and how this affected the different flows of traffic. I found that geography addresses my varied academic interests well. It offers me a balance of physical, social, and cultural studies. Therefore, it was a natural progression for me to pursue geography as a major.

Throughout my geography experience at Mythic College, I have gained skill in Geographic Information Sciences, which has given me great insight in many fields. For one, I obtained a greater understanding of how the US Census is calculated and this enabled me to be a more informed enumerator. Now, I find myself completely captivated by the various elements of geography and how they all are interwoven in a nexus of relations with historical, economic, physical, social, and cultural nodes. For my Honors Thesis next year, I will be exploring the Rothschild family to see how they fit within these various geographic realms. I am fascinated by how this family began as foreigners and within a few years was able to build a banking empire and become leaders in the economic world. As part of my thesis research, I intend to travel to the various cities where they lived and make observations on both economic and social grounds.

After I complete my undergraduate education in geography, I hope to work for an organization that incorporates geographical education and exploration. I hope to be able to write articles and essays that would be used to increase geographical awareness as well as educate people about lesser-known cultures in the world. I also intend on participating in the Peace Corps and speculate about earning a law degree.

I wish to participate in the Geography Intern Program with the National Geographic Society because, in short, it would be the fulfillment of my dream. It would enable me to work in an environment with people who share similar interests, providing me with an opportunity to contribute to a product that reaches a broad audience of people who subscribe to the magazine, visit Explorer's Hall, or glance through a National Geographic book. It would provide me with the practical experience that would aid me tremendously in pursuing my future goals, and reveal paths I might otherwise never discover.

SHORT APPLICATION ESSAY: ENVIRONMENTAL LAW

(This material is critiqued on page 60.)

My first personal introduction to the profusion of environmental laws in our country came while working for my father. I worked for over eleven years at my father's business, an Exxon Service Center. While there, I performed every job, task, and duty associated with the operation of a service station. One duty involved the maintenance of records for the underground storage tank field on the site. I was amazed at the amount of paperwork required to comply with the laws governing underground tanks.

My two years of full-time work after high school taught me much about myself, but I realized that I needed a different environment to continue growing. Therefore, from 20xx to 20xx, I attended classes at Mythic County Community College while continuing to work at my father's Exxon station. I was certain I would eventually choose a science-related major, but an event in 20xx showed me that geology was what I wanted to pursue. In 20xx, during the installation of a new, larger underground field tank at the station, an environmental consulting firm tested our soil and found hydrocarbon levels well above the allowable limits. Seventy tons of soil had to be removed from the site and incinerated, at great expense to my father's business. These environmental regulation problems that my father had as a small business owner made me realize that eventually I wanted to use my science background to make it easier on other small business owners to comply with environmental laws.

I transferred to Mythic College as an undergraduate in geology in 20xx, tailoring my courses to environmental geology and hydrogeology. My senior thesis directly reflects my career goals. I am working with the United States Department of Agriculture on a study of riparian zones and their favorable effects on elevated nitrate levels in groundwater due to farm fertilization practices. Meanwhile, I am developing a shallow subsurface geologic map of a riparian zone using seismic refraction techniques. This map will allow a first-order approximation of groundwater flow at the field site and also guide the installation of hydrogeologic equipment by the USDA. I now understand more fully how geophysical methods serve an important role in environmental work, and my senior thesis is a good introduction to this field.

I had initially intended to acquire a position with an environmental consulting firm upon graduation, but discussions with several of my professors confirmed my interest in studying environmental law, which will help me combine my dual interests in science and law and better prepare me for a position with a consulting firm. Thus, I am ready to become a dynamic participant in the University of Pittsburgh Law School this fall, motivated by personal experience, a highly evolved work ethic, and a strong education. Please do give my application every consideration.

SHORT FELLOWSHIP ESSAY: MATERIALS ENGINEERING

(This material is critiqued on pages 60-61.)

As a master's student, I am currently working in the Materials Research Laboratory (MRL) in the Ferroelectrics group spearheaded by Dr. John Teacher. In my research group, we are attempting to design microwave-active materials to facilitate the procurement of a low-powered miniaturized solid-state antenna. I am personally interested in what role highly polarizable ions in the prototypical Perovskite-type crystal structures can play in tunable microwave antennas. Barium Strontium Titanium Oxide (BSTO) in tandem with non-electrical oxides has recently been used in phase array antennas. The addition of non-electrical oxides, for example, magnesium oxide (MgO), has improved the tunability and adjustable electrical properties of the BSTO over wider ranges, as well as improved the impedance matching of the antenna/air interface. Empirical studies suggest that doping BSTO with MgO lowers the impedance by lowering the permittivity of the composite, in turn lowering the insertion losses over appreciable ranges of microwave frequencies. With the aid of the materials science graduate fellowship, I would like to develop this technology and apply it to the miniaturization of solid-state low-powered antennas in my Ph.D. graduate study.

In my previous work experience at the Space and Naval Warfare System Centers San Diego (SSC-SD), I worked side by side with engineers to design innovative communication devices for the Navy. In particular, requirements relating to interoperability, transmission security, and multifunctionality were approached in several ways as teams brainstormed concepts. Based on this experience, my interest in telecommunications and data transmission, coupled with my background in engineering, will provide me with the tools necessary to address tomorrow's communications issues.

Mythic University is a strong research institution with talented faculty and state-of-the-art facilities. My familiarity with Mythic University's faculty and facilities allows me to avoid many of the pitfalls commonly associated with getting a Ph.D. My current lab and the Department of Electrical Engineering have several professors who have overlapping interests, with graduate students often using equipment in both labs freely. This is exactly the type of environment where I can easily merge the two disciplines.

In the long run, I want to be as versed in electrical engineering as I am in materials science so that I can contribute to a research and manufacturing facility in the areas of communication and related fields. This desire comes with precedence: I can remember junior year attending one of my first major courses taught by my current mentor, where he suggested that a ceramist should also be versed in electrical engineering in order to be effective. The seeds planted then are now ready to bloom.

TWO APPLICATION ESSAYS: BUSINESS
(This material is critiqued on pages 61-62.)

Question #1: In no more than 500 words, discuss the most significant personal or professional risk you've taken and its outcome. How did this change you as a person?

My life has been an amazing journey of physical, mental, and spiritual growth. The most significant event of personal development occurred at age 21, when my brother and I ventured to California to independently bike 3500 miles across the country. Even though my bike trip began in the summer of 20xx, my dream of achieving such a feat had started the previous summer in the foothills of the Rocky Mountains. Not only did my student co-op in Colorado open up a world of business opportunities, it also revealed my passion for adventure. The following summer, my brother and I headed west armed only with a two-man tent, sleeping bags, two used touring bikes and accessories, 10 state maps, a calling card, an ATM card with limited cash, and an unending supply of enthusiasm.

Since my student co-op was the only time I had traveled outside of the midwest, I had never witnessed the magnitude of the southwest. From the map, the Mojave Desert appeared simply as 150 flat miles between Barstow, CA, and Needles, AZ. However, on old route 66 from a bicycle in 115 degree heat, it was a rocky, unforgiving road of massive hills in which only sheer determination and mutual encouragement brought us to the next town by sunrise.

Two weeks later, in the Santa Fe National Forest, I was reminded of the goodness of human nature. That evening, as it rained for the first time in our three-week-old trip, I awoke with severe stomach pains. After I crawled out of the two-man tent and threw up for 20 minutes, my brother agreed to bike back into town for help. I laid for over an hour with a flashlight, as my brother raced 15 miles out of the forest and to the nearest town to call for an ambulance. At the hospital, I was administered six liters of saline solution in the Emergency Room. After understanding our predicament for both lodging and finances, the on-call ER doctor allowed my brother and me to stay at his home for three days as I slowly recovered from severe exhaustion and dehydration. He was just one of a dozen, previously unfamiliar families who offered unconditional assistance on our successful 46-day adventure. Few experiences can so clearly demonstrate that life's challenges are only part of a master plan of personal growth and achievement.

Now, during difficult times, I am able to confidently sit back and set short-term goals, allowing me to continue the course of accomplishing my ambitions. I have learned the power of determination and teamwork, while enhancing my self-discipline and self-motivation. When challenges face me today, I can reach back to that experience and be both humbled and uplifted, recognizing how important it was to my personal growth.

Question #2: In no more than 1,000 words, tell us about the most challenging team experience you've had to date. What role did you play? What factors made it a challenge for you? How did you and the group address these issues? What did you learn?

After my third year as a staff consultant in the Warehouse Management Practice of Mythic Partners, I was tasked with the challenge of independently managing the second warehouse implementation project at our largest client to date. The $1.5 million engagement followed an extensive go-live in which two previous project managers were removed from their roles one month earlier. According to the client sponsors, they had failed to deliver quality results during the support of the live production system.

This situation created my first opportunity to work directly for the Fortune 100 Vice Presidents of Mythic Manufacturing. Previously with this client, I had managed the successful delivery of all interfaces to the new warehousing software, but I had limited contact with any of the project sponsors. The office supply retailer had also recently hired a senior manager and multiple staff who were deeply skilled in warehousing processes. I needed to work diligently to establish both Mythic Partners and myself as the preferred integrator to replace the client's three northeast Distribution Centers into one new 350,000 sq. ft. facility servicing up to 200 retail stores.

I had less than one week to prepare the entire project plan. The project partner assigned me a 10-member team, all of whom were in new roles and with less than two years of consulting experience. I organized the group into three logical teams and worked with each team lead to develop a mutually agreed-upon project plan. After multiple late nights of preparation, I presented the plan to the client managers and project sponsors.

I had established myself as a capable project manager in all areas of the project, with a team of knowledgeable consultants. As a team, we had won the work and were excited about the challenge of our new roles. Also, I had successfully led sub-teams for the previous two years with Mythic Partners in all areas but technical infrastructure. Consequently, I spent most of the first month with my infrastructure team lead understanding our new responsibilities to build the warehouse computer center, as well as organize the layout of all hardware, conveyors, radio frequency terminals, and printers in the warehouse. For the first time, I had to work with a hardware reseller, identifying exact requirements for the computer center. I realized my lack of knowledge in the area, and worked with my practice's lead infrastructure consultant to purchase the necessary hardware components. Thereafter, I was well prepared for all detailed activities of the project, providing the client with one contact for all project-related questions.

After three years of experience with Mythic Partners, I had learned to delegate and trust the work of my staff. Despite all team members taking on new responsibilities, everyone responded extremely well and worked hard to meet the deadlines we had defined as a team. When the functional training team needed extra help during a critical week, the entire team went to the warehouse to share the load of training 100 employees across multiple shifts. We created a database on the client's network to efficiently communicate issues and project status across the multiple locations. This enabled me to work openly with the client on resolving potential problems; I also established weekly meetings with the client upper management, sharing all progress, whether we were behind or on-schedule. At first these meetings were coordinated with my project partner, but after I improved on my ability to communicate at a high level with upper management, the client was comfortable with only limited participation from the project partner.

Near the end of testing, I learned there were delays in the final construction of the new facility. I worked with my team and client to incorporate further testing and enhanced functionality into the work plans. With the client's assistance, we were able to improve the picking process and product placement within the warehouse during the delay.

After the first week of go-live, one of the major setup programs was incorrectly slotting materials according to height instead of width. Because the team was confident to raise the issue directly to me, a major setback was quickly avoided during the receiving of product from the three discontinued warehouses. While we fixed and tested the program, the client stopped receiving product and corrected the slotted inventory.

The project was extremely successful, implementing on-time and within budget. To further emphasize the success of the project, the Warehouse Management Practice vendor used the project as their top achievement for the year, the client project sponsor was selected as one of two keynote speakers at the year-end Mythic Partners Regional Meeting, and the client was featured in multiple supply chain periodicals.

This experience motivated me to continue to improve my managerial skills. I coordinated a third-party review of the project, interviewing the key client participants and providing a questionnaire for the Mythic Partners staff members. The client praised our team approach, along with my ability to move into the new project management role.

From a challenges standpoint, I learned that I needed to continue to improve on my confidence to communicate with upper management, but there was significant improvement over the course of the project. Finally, my team appreciated my willingness to involve them in major project decisions and allow them to manage with limited supervision. After becoming certified in SAP, I successfully led Mythic Partners largest Warehouse Management Practice implementation that interfaced directly with a major SAP go-live. Capping off this experience, this past summer I felt very proud as all three of my team leads were promoted to Principal Consultants within the firm.

PERSONAL STATEMENT: NEUROSCIENCE
(This material is critiqued on page 62.)

Personal Statement
Janet Lerner

I sat in Dr. Wiley's lab at the University of Pittsburgh, poring over files of records about HIV-infected human brains from which we had tissue samples. I had just learned how to read the autopsy reports, looking for key words and descriptive phrases the doctors had written that might disqualify the samples as potential candidates for our study. We were looking for HIV-positive human brain tissue samples that either had been diagnosed as having HIV encephalitis or not having encephalitis (to be used as a control). My objective was to find samples that had HIV encephalitis, but no other complicating disorders such as cytomegalovirus, bacterial infection, or meningitis. This was a more difficult task than one would perceive because the HIV infection often leads to the development of opportunistic infections that would not normally be of concern in patients without HIV.

As I sifted through one manila folder after another, entering data into an Excel spreadsheet, I became aware of the fact that many of the brains we had were from patients who were only a few years older than I. I was twenty years old at the time, and after having to repeatedly enter "19" or "23" into the Age column, I began to realize that AIDS had literally taken these peoples' lives. I could not even imagine what it would be like to be 17 years old knowing that I had a fatal disease. They would never be able to have the career of their dreams, go on a trip to Italy, or graduate from college. Life was taken from them before they fully experienced it.

The above summer internship inspired me to want to help people with fatal diseases such as AIDS. More specifically, I knew I wanted to conduct research on the molecular basis of disease. One of the projects I worked on during that summer was developing a diagnostic procedure for HIV encephalitis using PK11195, a ligand for the peripheral benzodiazepine receptor present on the mitochondria of macrophages. The fundamental design of the experiment and its applicability to human disease left me intrigued. From then on, I wanted to attend graduate school so I could have the opportunity to better peoples' lives through research as a biomedical scientist. After consideration, I realized that I am interested in taking more than one approach to answer scientific questions. Many fields of science interest me, including immunology, biochemistry, genetics, and pathology. I have always been extremely fascinated by the nervous system and its vital link to human disease. Having had three research experiences as an undergraduate, I feel prepared and excited to begin my path of research and study. Thus, I am applying to the Graduate Training Program in Neuroscience at the University of Pennsylvania because it is an interdisciplinary program that would allow me to serve people through biomedical research and help me achieve my goals.

Penn's graduate program in neuroscience is one of the most prestigious in the world. As the home to many of the greatest researchers in the field, Penn's educational opportunities would meet my greatest expectations. The research done by Dr. Robert Doms, who is currently investigating the cellular biology of membrane proteins involved in Alzheimer's disease pathogenesis, is of particular interest to me. My experiences using molecular biological techniques to study intracellular protein localization make his approach very appealing. I am specifically interested in studying the γ-secretase complex and its effects on the amyloid precursor protein (APP). Dr. Doms' research has the potential to help millions of people with Alzheimer's disease, and I would welcome the opportunity to work with him.

Beyond my desire to attend Penn for academic reasons, Penn also appeals to me on a personal level. After spending four years in the rural setting of Mythic College, I am ready to live in a new, urban setting. Living in Philadelphia would be perfect for me because it would allow me to experience life in a major city while still in reach of my family's home in Reading. I would be very excited to be surrounded by the academically and culturally rich environment at UPenn, and I hope to have the opportunity to do so.

PERSONAL STATEMENT: MEDIEVAL LITERATURE

(This material is critiqued on page 63.)

Medieval literature is a passion that has enveloped me since I read Chrétien de Troyes' *Lancelot* during my freshman year. In this Arthurian romance, Chrétien represents Lancelot as conflicted—a chivalrous knight whom one expects to find only in myth, yet in violation of the code of honor, desirous of his lord's queen. I began thinking of the tales of the Arthurian knights as more than legendary—as potentially credible historical accounts. Soon, I wrote a paper on Gawain's rhetoric as a means to elicit specific responses in *Sir Gawain and the Green Knight*. Gawain's rhetorical strategies and their manipulations ultimately lead him to a deeper personal recognition and self-acceptance. This early exercise alerted me to the pleasures of working with languages of the Middle Ages.

My academic interest in Celtic Studies was piqued when I learned of Ogam stones in my Literature in the Natural World class. Ogam is not a spoken language, rather, a code of inscriptions that gave the Irish language an alphabet and supplied the Irish people with a means of writing on stone, wood, and other natural elements with relative ease. Ogam is also found in many manuscripts, where it is both written and read in a manner different from that employed when it is found on stones. As an aspiring academic in Medieval Literature, I recognize that knowledge of the literature of medieval cultures is vitally important. Irish literature, including Ogam inscriptions and manuscripts, is therefore essential to a medieval scholar. The Frenchman Gregory of Tours said of the humanities in medieval Europe, "Culture and education are dying out in every city in Gaul . . . People often complain 'Alas for our times, literacy is dying among us.'" While Gregory's testimony may have been true for much of Europe, where culture floundered in the midst of war, he neglected to speak of Ireland, the country where literature and language flourished during this era and later became known as the "Land of Saints and Scholars." Three of the most impressive medieval manuscripts were created in Ireland: *The Gospels of St. Willibrord*, which is on display in the Bibliothèque Nationale in Paris, *The Book of Kells*, and *The Book of Durrow*, both of which are displayed in Trinity University's Library.

Last May I had the pleasure of meeting with Professor Damian McManus, head of Trinity University's School of Irish, who presented me with a copy of his book *A Guide to Ogam*. I met with him to discuss the graduate opportunities available in Old and Middle Irish Language and Literature at Trinity University. Dr. McManus has many research initiatives, although these are open only to students who have previously worked with Early Irish studies. During our meeting, he suggested that I first conduct my studies with Dr. Kim McCone at the National University of Ireland at Maynooth, and then return to Trinity where I can further pursue a research degree under his guidance. After obtaining the necessary fundamentals of Old and Middle Irish language, I will be better equipped to study Ogam stones and to read the inscriptions, which would enable me to study another field of academia: epigraphy.

The National University of Ireland at Maynooth provides the opportunity to create one's own program. This would best prepare me for future graduate research in Ogam stones and would allow me to enhance my knowledge of medieval writings by including both Irish literature and the English, French, and Latin literature that compose much of the western medieval canon. Professor McCone, whom Dr. McManus regards as one of the "finest scholars in the field of Early Irish," is the head of NUI Maynooth's Department of Old and Middle Irish, and personally helps international students to construct a program to suit their needs during their study in Ireland.

In order to prepare myself for Ogam studies with Dr. McManus, I plan to complete a one-year program of study leading to an M.A. in Old and Middle Irish Studies, which would consist of the standard canon of Medieval Irish Literature, Old and Middle Irish language, and a class devoted to the women of Medieval Ireland. This class specifically catches my interest because a study of medieval women is integral to a full understanding of the Middle Ages, as many Irish scholars were monks, living in monastic settlements such as Clonmacnois and Glendalough, where women were forbidden. That NUI Maynooth offers a class devoted to medieval women—often prohibited from studying at these monastic centers of education—exhibits the department's intent in providing students with a balanced history of Ireland's Middle Ages. There is no doubt that Ireland's wealth of medieval literature boasts women writers comparable to Marie de France, whose "Lanval" was the first piece of medieval literature written by a woman that I studied.

While attending university in Maynooth and learning the early Irish language, I would also have the invaluable opportunity of learning from my distant cousin, who resides in Maynooth. She has taught modern Irish in schools for years and would tutor me in modern Irish language while I study Old and Middle Irish with Dr. McCone. This unique prospect would allow me to study the development of Irish from its beginnings to its modern form, a development which I am currently studying in an Honors English seminar on the history of the English language. Because I am now tracing the development of English, I will already have many of the skills necessary to study the evolution of the Irish language.

Clearly the journey of a young scholar is more complete with an understanding of other cultures, specifically those relevant to the student's chosen field of study. I look forward, therefore, to studying the ancient, medieval, and modern ideas and languages of Ireland in situ. *Is d'Éirinn mé.*

SCHOLARSHIP APPLICATION ESSAY: EDUCATION

(This material is critiqued on pages 63-64.)

Beinecke Scholarship Personal Essay

Passion drips from the lips of the preacher at the pulpit. Passion shakes on the shoulders of the general during war. Passion clings to the moist brow of the attorney during a heated courtroom debate. The passions of others, like lawyer and activist Thurgood Marshall, have opened doors for me as an African-American woman. I am grateful for Marshall's work over 50 years after the Brown vs. Board of Education decision, which pushed racial integration in schools and defended the concept that "separate was inherently unequal." The devotion of others has inspired and humbled me, and it is with this same passion that I honor education and service to others today.

My passion for education is steeped in the notion that I believe it literally saved my life in the form of opportunities that took me out of an unsafe environment. Growing up on the south side of Chicago in one of the city's worst neighborhoods was difficult, and I understand now it could have been much worse. Gangs had a wealth of power, drugs permeated the streets, and young girls were cautioned to watch for "Stranger Danger." I could not play outside, so instead I read. I made friends with Alice in Wonderland, or Huck on the Mississippi, Pip in England, and John Steptoe's "Black Cinderella"—Nyasha in Zimbabwe. My mother, seeing the passion for knowledge in me as a young child, enrolled me in a magnet elementary school on the other side of Chicago, to which I would ride the bus for two hours a day. There I flourished and soon I was recruited to test for entrance into the Pre-International Baccalaureate Program, a curriculum that prepared gifted and talented students for the International Baccalaureate Program in high school. I had been given an opportunity to pursue a high quality education in a public school, a chance some African-Americans, in their devotion, had died for to guarantee.

The passion I have to serve others has its roots in my high school experience, during which I noticed some pivotal points of interest. At my high school, African-American students composed a small percentage of those placed in gifted education, with most students being labeled "regular education students," who were poor pupils from the area's housing projects. They had fewer resources and opportunities to pursue college preparatory work when compared to their white or wealthier counterparts, and it was no secret that the "regular" kids were at the bottom of the totem pole. It became clear to me as I listened to others berate them that they were not expected to go on to college. As an African-American student in a gifted program, I had access to a wealth of resources. I felt angered that my peers were excluded from the smorgasbord of knowledge, which many others were encouraged to partake in freely. It was the first time I was mature enough to see the inequities of education, my prized and valued yellow brick road. Passion to enact change welled in my stomach and stayed there.

As a beginning college student at rural Mythic University I continued to experience injustice. Professors seemed surprised at my academic abilities, students questioned my worth by muttering "affirmative action" under their breaths, and white people openly stared at my brown skin on the street. My passion for change had no choice but to evolve into action. I joined professional organizations like the College of Education Student Council to voice my concerns, and I formed a new organization, the Multicultural Education Student Association, when they were not addressed. Through this organization I was able to form support groups with other students and mentor first-year students of color in the college.

As my education progressed, I decided to fight injustice intellectually in the study of the politics, economics, and sociology of education, which revealed the reasons why and how disparities occurred in education and society. In my senior year, I will explore these disparities in my honors thesis research, which focuses on the ability of students of color and low socio-economic backgrounds to transition from community college to four-year institutions. Research-based evidence is a powerful tool to enact change, and I look forward to gathering this evidence during an upcoming summer internship, during which I will interview students of color about their experiences.

Currently I challenge myself socially by removing myself from comfort zones. An example of such is my study abroad experience to occur in the fall semester, 20xx. I have committed to completing my student teaching requirement at Bognor-Regis University, on the southern coast of England, amidst a culture of people I have never been exposed to, thousands of miles from home. Despite some admitted nervousness over the challenge of this experience, my passion for success drives me to overcome any obstacle and achieve success in every area I venture.

My graduate school experience will be used to seek out knowledge (for which my thirst can never be quenched) and for research. My research interests include studying factors that affect equal access to educational resources for students of color in grades K-12 and equality of student access to higher education. These interests will guide the creation of projects that will lead to real-life applications. I will also pursue a master's degree, then a doctorate in Public Policy with a concentration in education and urban planning. My long-term goal of becoming a policy analyst for the government's Department of Education would give me the opportunity to help develop effective public policy in these areas of interest.

W.E.B. Dubois said that a "talented tenth" of educated African-Americans could go forth to enact social change for the oppressed. I believe I am a living example of Dubois' passion-filled dream. My passion has given me the power to propel that social change in an often unjust society. For all of those denied opportunity I want many more to receive it. If awarded the Beinecke Scholarship I would use this support to explore, research, and contribute treasures to the field, valuable not only for their intellectual depth, but also because of their social implications for a better society and America.

SHORT RESUME: GEOSCIENCE

(This material is critiqued on page 65.)

JOHN LERNER
jlerner@hotmail.com

Education   <u>Mythic University</u>, Mythic, XX 99999
Bachelor of Science in Geosciences
Expected Graduation: May 20xx

<u>Senior Thesis Research</u>, 20xx-present
Study of a potential bryozoan reef near Mythic Creek, XX
Production and analysis of peel block sections
Comparison of specimens with established literature for identification

Curriculum
Physical Geology   Paleobiology Seminar
Intro to Environmental Geology   Structural Geology
Earth Materials   Earth History
Biostatistics   Micropaleontology
Geochemical Processes   Principles of Stratigraphy
Geophysical Processes   Coral Reef Ecosystems
Paleontology and Fossils   Geology Field School

Experience   <u>Librarian</u> for Mythic Laptop Computer Library, 20xx-present
Answered technical questions regarding programming and connections
Circulated, re-imaged, and conducted inventory on laptops

<u>Lab Assistant</u> under Dr. Janet Lerner, 20xx-20xx
Consulted with professors and professional researchers
Used chemical acid baths to clean equipment in an Earth Systems Lab

Activities/
Honors
Scuba Certification, 20xx
        Geosciences Club, 20xx-present
        Field Trip Coordinator, 20xx-20xx
        Secretary, 20xx-20xx
        Vice President, 20xx-present
Mythic University Pan-Hellenic Dance Marathon, 20xx-present
        Operations committee member, 20xx-present
Dean's Freshman Scholarship, Mythic University, 20xx
Mythic University Alumni Chapter Scholarship, 20xx

EXTENSIVE CURRICULUM VITAE: POLITICAL SCIENCE

(This material is critiqued on page 65.)

JANET LERNER

123 Ivy Road
Mythic, XX 99999
Phone: 555-123-4567
E-mail: jlerner@mythicu.edu

EDUCATION: **MYTHIC UNIVERSITY,** Mythic, XX 99999
B.A in Political Science with Honors
Minors in Japanese and Economics
Cumulative GPA : 3.85/4.00
Dean's List: All Semesters

Relevant Coursework:

Geography of Political Extremism
Latin American Intl. Relations
Geography of Developing World
Understanding Tyranny and Oppression

Comparative Urban Politics
Research and Methodology
Development Economics

International Experience:

Experience living and traveling in different countries including Japan, China, Peru, Greece and Brazil.

Languages:

Fluent in Spanish, Proficient in Japanese, and Working Knowledge of Portuguese. Experience with Microsoft Access, Microsoft Excel, and Dreamweaver.

LEADERSHIP INVOLVEMENT:

President, The Political Science Association, Mythic University
   President 20xx, Vice President 20xx, Secretary 20xx-20xx
Oversaw and managed the restructuring of the only non-partisan organization on campus. Now with over 250 members, the organization provides opportunities for political involvement. Sponsored major domestic and international speakers such as journalists and elected officials. Coordinated campus-wide voter registration events and created a tuition advocacy group to educate students on tuition issues under the organization. Strengthened ties between students and faculty of the Political Science Department by facilitating luncheons. Developed relationships with Mythic University Alumni through the reinstitution of the annual Alumni Dinner.

LEADERSHIP INVOLVEMENT (continued):

Founding Member, Rescue Childhood, (UNICEF campus initiative, Service
 Organization) *20xx-20xx*
Established student campus organization, aided in fundraising over 10,000 dollars for the
construction of a children's shelter in the Dominican Republic. Actively supported the
coordination of advocacy events promoting children's rights including organizing
petition signings and efforts to finance speakers.

Participant, Global Aids Initiative, Mythic University, *20xx*
Actively engaged in the planning process of World Aids Day 20xx in addition to
advertising and volunteering throughout the day.

Group Leader, Mythic University Literary Initiative, *Fall 20xx-present*
Coordinate and participate in weekly discussions of challenging texts with other Mythic
University scholars.

EXPERIENCE:

Economics Grader, Mythic University Economics Department, *Fall 20xx*
Helped in grading Introductory Microeconomics lecture course with over 300 students.

Hotline Intern, Project Vote Smart, *Summer 20xx*
Searched and collected evaluations of the U.S. Congress and State Legislatures compiled
by political interest groups. Entered interest groups data in order to make them available
to the voting public. Also maintained the hotline service by answering specific political
questions and conducing special research requests for callers, including the national news
media.

Scholar Assistant, Mythic University, *20xx-20xx*
Coordinated major speakers and educational events to promote SHC vision. Counseled
students with academic questions, provided welcoming atmosphere in residence halls,
and conducted administrative duties.

Field Intern, Mark Kennedy Shriver U.S. Congressional Campaign,
 Summer 20xx
Trained in "Get out the Vote" strategies and database systems for use in coordinated
grassroots efforts. Executed campaign strategies to maximize votes.

RESEARCH EXPERIENCE:

Undergraduate Research Assistant, Mythic University Political Science
Department: Advocacy and Public Policymaking Project, *Fall 20xx-present*
Collected and compiled relevant information on advocacy tactics using Internet research
guidelines. Coded arguments made in primary interviews for further analysis on effective
lobbying methods and influence of lobbyists on policymaking in Washington D.C.
Currently training other undergraduates and supervising research on recently coded data.

Undergraduate Research Assistant, Mythic University Political Science
Department:
Project: Collaborative Research on Agenda-Setting: Attention to Disease in
the Public Arena, *Spring 20xx-present*
Identifying relevant congressional hearings on specific diseases in order to discover the
extent to which diseases receive attention by the media and Congress. Entering data on
hearings into Microsoft Access.

Researcher, Kokusaika and Japanese National Policy Initiative, *Summer 20xx*
Conducted interviews and compiled data for independent project on the
internationalization policy of Japan during the 1980s in Osaka and Kobe, Japan

Researcher/Volunteer, Mythic City Field Project, *May-June 20xx*
Investigated property acquisition practices through field research with Habitat for
Humanity in Mythic City. Lived in the area, supervised construction volunteers, built
homes, and structured filing system for acquired properties.

Student Researcher, Correlates of War 2, *Spring 20xx*
Translated Spanish sources and collected data for chronology of wars in Latin America

AWARDS:

The Pi Sigma Alpha Honor Society
Golden Key Honor Society
Jesse Arnelle Liberal Arts Scholarship

INTERESTS:

Reading, Running, Tennis, Playing Piano, Ceramics

> *All good writing is swimming under water and holding your breath.*
> —*F. Scott Fitzgerald*

Critiques of Lengthy Personal Statements and Application Essays

The second half of this chapter showcases writers who, to varying degrees, took chances or simply reached higher. Not only did these writers compose lengthy essays (still within prescribed word-count limits), but in many cases they did something bold with content, form, or personality. To help guide your reading of these samples, I offer some critique in the following pages.

In the samples that follow, length can readily be justified by the fact that these are writers who don't necessarily fall into "typical" student categories but nevertheless are applying to graduate programs or for scholarships. To be competitive, these writers decided to stand out by telling their stories in a way that they hoped would set them apart from, and above, the crowd. A common thread linking these diverse writers is their obvious belief that 1) their essays *matter* to the selection committee, and 2) their essays will be both noticeable and *noticed*.

Extensive Application Essay: Mechanical Engineering (pages 90-94)
What stands out immediately about this essay is its length and the photographs. In this case, the student was applying for an engineering scholarship, so he was given room to flesh out technical material as well as address issues such as personal motivations one would expect to read in a personal statement. Thus, on the first page, there are some humanizing moments about the man behind the scientist, such as when his father asks him about the physics of a curving baseball. Much of the essay is given to a discussion of his thesis work, which involves the examination of "the propagation of a flame in a small glass tube." Along with his labmates, this student helped to build a portable experiment station (Figure 1) that can be used for combustion and propulsion experiments, and a glass tube assembly (Figure 2) which allows one to determine velocities and accelerations of the flame within the tube. Figure 3 depicts the success of preliminary thesis results, visually indicating the likely point at which the flame reached detonation. Though the explanatory material here is lengthy and highly specific to the experiment, clearly the writer has a solid understanding of the work he is doing.

The connection the writer makes in his final paragraphs between his thesis work and his graduate plans to improve fuel cells may be a bit sketchy, but he also makes it a point to discuss his knowledge of fuel cell limitations, notes a professor (Dr. Prinz) with whom he would like to work at Stanford, and says his "communications with Dr. Prinz thus far have been promising." We are left with the impression that this mechanical engineer who once tinkered with alarm clocks and helped build an experimental apparatus in college has the ability and the drive to succeed.

Extensive Personal Statement: Liberal Arts (pages 95-97)
The three-page personal statement by this liberal arts student is interesting in that it is often intentionally abstract and a bit philosophical. This student attended a small liberal arts school that promotes a "Think, Evolve, Act" theme to its students, and this student reflects on this theme and embraces it in his own life from the beginning of the essay. His reflection leads him to question how much he really understood upon entering college, and near the end of the essay he notes: "that which I know may be based on false suppositions." Throughout his essay he expresses ideals that shape his actions, including a "hope for a better future," a desire to "play an active role in" globalization, and a goal of promoting principles "common to all of humankind." The loftiness of this student's tone cannot be missed, and admittedly it could even be a bit over-the-top for some readers; such readers, one would hope, would look carefully at the student's actions as demonstrations of his ideals rather than judge him as naive.

In considering content and actions by this writer, we find that he has made choices showing that he lives his ideals. In his curriculum, he has taken a course on Gandhi and Nonviolence, studied abroad in Belgium, and self-designed a program of "Peace and Conflict Studies with an emphasis in Technological Revolution." He has also taken a ten-day service learning trip to Costa Rica, studied at the Institute of Gandhian Studies in India, served part-time as an assistant to a member of the European Parliament, and written a paper entitled "A Knowledge-Based Society and the Digital Divide." He links these experiences to a goal of finding a graduate program that will allow him to combine fields such as Peace Studies and Global Governance and one that "would not hesitate to send a student abroad to conduct research inquiries." Based on this evidence, this writer has worked to demonstrate how he applies the "Think, Evolve, Act" theme to his life and education. Meanwhile, he plans to graduate with distinction in both of his majors. In jazz terms, he certainly does seem to have the chops.

Extensive Personal Statement: Film (pages 98-100)

One way to get a sense of the daring of this personal statement, written by a student who aims to study film at Columbia University, is simply to consider the allusions he makes throughout his statement. With neither apology nor obvious humility, this writer makes references to Steven Spielberg, Woody Allen, Jean-Luc Godard, Jean Vigo, Terrence Malick, and David Gordon Green. Such an approach could seem immediately pretentious if handled poorly. Further, this writer takes the unusual step of using section headings in his personal statement, including, on his first page "Poetry," "Plastics," and "Children." While these headings could (and do, I think) entice us to read, they could also make us wonder if this guy is so self-styled as to be, well, just plain *strange*.

What we find quickly in reading this essay is that the writer's tone is both confident and relaxed. He's relaxed enough with narrative to discuss discovering *Annie Hall* in a dirty little corner of his local "Video Stars" and renting it for forty-seven cents, but confident and genuine enough to define the experience as seminal: "For me, I had found a new poetry and a new poet in Woody Allen, and he revealed to me other poets, including Godard." He's equally comfortable discussing potential red flags to a selection committee such as his choice to switch his major from Polymer Science to Film during his sophomore year ("I was inadvertently led into the hands of the great polymer Satan") and his choice to complete a second major in Geography, much to the puzzlement of his friends ("So, do you wanna, um . . . create chloropleth maps of celebrity sightings?"). What we find is a confident writer simply telling his story in a natural, creative, and entertaining way.

Ultimately, of course, we must also judge this writer on his evidenced ability as a filmmaker. In that regard, he showcases his ease with talking about films and directors, posits an analogy about student filmmaking ("directing your own material is like parenting"), and discusses the success of his nineteen-minute senior project, *Burying Dvorak*—a film he promoted by taking a year off after graduation, successfully landing it in more than 20 film festivals. As he closes his essay, he makes a specific pitch for Columbia University, where he hopes to continue "to discover my own voice, my own poetry." Such creativity and confidence is needed in a field such as film, in that during his graduate school interviews (which earned him, along with his personal statement, acceptance into several programs), this student was challenged with such prompts as "In sixty seconds, describe how you would direct a film about your own life story. Go!"

Extensive Scholarship Essay: Biological Science (pages 101-107)
An important detail to know about this essay is that its length and scientific depth
are necessary because the student is applying for the highly competitive STAR
Fellowship. The STAR (Science to Achieve Results) program offers graduate
fellowships through the US Environmental Protection Agency (EPA), funding
several years of study. Given the competitiveness of the process and the EPA's
mission of environmental protection, it is vital that this student presents a viable,
environmentally important project in a persuasive, professional manner.

To achieve this, the writer successfully approaches the essay as she would a thesis
proposal, using science-related section heads, providing original figures and data,
focusing heavily on future research goals, and essentially performing a literature
review, citing 19 sources ranging from basic textbooks to refereed journals. She
correctly assumes both that her audience may know little about her specific topic
of gypsy moth invasion in North America (offering interesting historical tidbits
such as the accidental release of the gypsy moth in Boston in 1869) and that
audience members also have a high degree of scientific literacy (using Latin
names for species, discussing numerical research models, offering an equation,
and applying her work to the broader problem of invasive species management).

From an environmental protection standpoint, the writer broadly discusses
ecosystem threats from biological invasions of pest species, demonstrating that
her numerical model has successfully been used as an environmental management
tool in areas ranging from wildfire control to effective crop rotation, and citing
figures such as the $34 million spent on managing just the Asian strain of the
gypsy moth in North America during 1991 and 1993. Dominating the essay is
detail about the exact model being used in the student's research, and she is
careful to define her assumptions and parameters, defend her model algorithm,
and describe the model's various strategies designed to optimize management.

In other parts of the application, where we note this student's success in tackling
both the bachelor's and master's degree in a single program, we recognize her as
having the ambition and ability to be a successful STAR scholarship candidate,
reinforced by her stated goal at the essay's end to complete "experimental and
mathematical work in the areas of biological invasion and conservation biology."

As an exercise, it is interesting to compare this essay to the second set of Udall
Scholarship materials in Chapter 5 (pages 124-129), written by the same writer.

Application Essay for Online Education: Military (pages 108-109)
Written during a peak of US involvement in Iraq, this essay manages the intriguing challenge of how a member of the military can make an effective case for on-line graduate study. The obvious need here, especially for an Air Force pilot of seven years, is to keep the focus on academic interests rather than, say, battle successes and the number of missions flown. An additional challenge is to use military experience and vocabulary in a way that is not obscure nor off-putting to academic selection committee members.

To address these challenges, this writer intertwines his literacy in matters both military and academic, keeping focus on applications of Geographic Information Systems (GIS), his chosen field of graduate study. He broadly embraces principles such as "the ability to collect and analyze information" and the need to exploit spatial data and technical expertise. He also uses concrete examples to demonstrate "the power of well-applied spatial data in battle," focusing on how satellite data give the pilot the virtual experience of having flown in an unfamiliar area before, and how an onboard laptop can be used to overlay data sets to help pilots avoid danger zones.

Most importantly, this writer views himself as much as a geographer and learner as he does a pilot. He speaks of the desire to make decision-makers more aware "of the speed and flexibility the geographer can bring to problem solving," and imagines a "geoinfo-awareness course" for officers hosted by an on-line geography department. He ends his essay seeking entrance into the offered on-line graduate program "excited to find this opportunity to become a more expert geographer while continuing my active duty military service."

Finally, despite this writer's obvious dedication to US military service, he maintains a tone that should keep resistant readers from feeling they are being force-fed the flag. His comments are often a bit surprising and self-reflective, including how he can do little personally to affect Congressional funding, how he wishes to "encourage collaboration across the military's often rigid organizational and functional lines," and how despite his enthusiasm he doesn't "expect the military to begin training squadrons of GIS wizards." In a word, this writer has perspective. Meanwhile, his writing style is crisp, articulate, and compelling. Unsurprisingly, he was admitted into the graduate program based on his academic record and this essay.

Extensive Application for Graduate Transfer: Toxicology (pages 110-113)
This student, seeking to transfer from one graduate program to another mid-stream through her PhD, has an especially daunting challenge. A simple demonstration: Counting up the advisors she has had during her graduate career, the number comes to four. She also took a few years off to work in the middle of her master's degree. These factors, coupled with the fact that this student is making the unusual move of jumping ship from one program to another, could give readers the impression that they are dealing with a grad student hot potato.

The writer's management of this issue is done with both directness and subtlety. She notes how she delayed the writing of her master's thesis for two years while working in the clinical pharmacology department of a pharmaceutical company, then returned to school missing the intellectual rigor of research and with a passion for teaching. She directly explains her transitions from one advisor to the next, noting factors such as one of her advisors taking the position of Acting Dean of Research and thus no longer working in the lab, a lack of project funding available in her next lab after a year of disappointing research, and her pro-active insistence that she spend the remainder of her final academic year in the more established lab of another colleague. More subtle moments include the writer's wording of how she became her former mentor's "first graduate student in toxicology," suggesting that there was no proven track record of success for this advisor. Obviously, she hopes that her readers will interpret that she is a driven student (but not a career one) caught up in unfortunate circumstances.

Of course, ultimately this student's ability as a scientist and toxicologist has to be highly persuasive. In that regard, she opens immediately and stylishly with commentary that mechanistic toxicologists "are often mistaken for their forensic distant cousins," emphasizing her view of toxicants as tools "that inform our understanding of basic physiology or elucidate a disease process." Later, we discover that her master's research yielded her numerous abstracts and three publications in refereed journals. Even in misdirected research, she focuses on the reasoning behind her research hypotheses, and she shows a great deal of fluency with the language of science. In her final page, she affirms her decision to pursue a transfer as "a desire to improve and expand my skills, and a drive to produce and communicate results." Indeed, this student was accepted into her program of choice, receiving a fellowship with two years of funding. Part of this success can surely be attributed to the persuasive power of the application essay, smartly tailored to address an understandably skeptical audience.

EXTENSIVE APPLICATION ESSAY: MECHANICAL ENGINEERING

(This material is critiqued on pages 84-85.)

As long as I can remember I have always gravitated towards mathematics and science, tinkering with alarm clocks, launching model rockets, excelling in calculus and physics courses, and reading about great scientists and inventors like Albert Einstein and Thomas Edison. When I came to Mythic University, I knew that I wanted to pursue a major that involved science and mathematics, but I wanted to be able to apply these concepts to inventions and developments that would benefit society. Consequently, I decided to study mechanical engineering, taking classes in and engaging in research about combustion, fluid mechanics, and propulsion.

While I had enrolled in mechanical engineering in freshman year, it was not until the first semester of junior year that I realized I wanted to be a mechanical engineer. That semester, I took six engineering classes, and two of them especially drew me in: fluid mechanics and thermodynamics. Since then, I have taken an elective laboratory class in fluids, I have enrolled in a class on compressible flow next semester, and I am currently studying small-scale fluid mechanics for my senior honors thesis. Additionally, I was finally able to answer my dad, an avid baseball fan and reader of Robert Adair's *The Physics of Baseball*, when he pestered me, "John, you're the scientist in this family. Why does a curveball curve?"

When I began my research with Dr. John Teacher in the Propulsion Engineering Research Center, I was also given the opportunity to apply my knowledge to a laboratory setting. My first project was to design and assemble a portable gas flow system. I learned invaluable information about experimental methods by conceiving this system, finding the necessary parts and looking up specs sheets, and finally putting it all together. Now that I have almost finished constructing the system, I feel a strong sense of accomplishment knowing that this is my own creation.

At the beginning of this semester, I began engaging in my senior honors thesis project. My thesis satisfies the innate curiosity that I had when I was eight years old and taking apart alarm clocks. In my thesis, I am examining the propagation of a flame in a small glass tube. Right now, I am at a very exciting stage of the project, having just created my experimental apparatus and begun gathering data. Taking the first pictures of the flame and gathering the first velocity measurements with the photo diodes has been a thrilling experience. This stage of the research process has made me aware that I love doing research. For me, it's an opportunity for constant intellectual stimulation, satisfying my yearning for knowledge and serving as an outlet for my creativity. My thesis project experience has motivated me to continue in research in graduate school and hopefully afterwards as a college professor.

The most exciting aspect of my research experience thus far was helping to create an instrument to be used in my lab. I designed, ordered parts for, and helped assemble a portable experimentation station for our laboratory. It is a self-contained tabletop device (approximately 19" x 17" x 6") that produces regulated gas flows at precise flow rates to be inputted into an experimental apparatus. It also measures data from the experiment. The purpose of this device is to enclose all the necessary hardware for running combustion and propulsion experiments into one compact, portable apparatus. Figure 1 shows the portable system in the assembly stage.

Figure 1: Portable Experimentation System.

The device utilizes a choked nozzle of ~100- m-diameter to produce a known, constant flow rate, independent of downstream conditions. The flow rate can then be adjusted by regulating the pressure upstream of the orifice. The portable station houses three 300-mL gas supply tanks (to store the gases at ~1800psi), pressure transducers and thermocouples (to take the upstream pressure and temperature measurements used in the calculation of flow rate), and compact pressure regulators (to adjust the upstream pressure and, hence, the flow). An external digital data acquisition card and laptop computer with LabView will then be utilized to record the data and calculate other parameters, such as mass flow rate. The system is designed to produce flow rates ranging from 0.2 to 1.5 LPM. My fellow lab members and I intend to use this portable system to perform experiments in other laboratories, for technical demonstrations in college classrooms, and at scientific conferences. Now that I have almost completed that project, I am engaging in my senior honors thesis project. I am performing an experimental study to determine the prevalence and nature of frictional effects in narrow channels (on the scale of 1 mm), by studying the propagation of a flame.

Since conventional fluid mechanics is based on the assumption of a continuous fluid (i.e., not a substance composed of many individual particles), there is a lower limit at which the laws of traditional fluid mechanics break down. This is because of the increasing significance of the behavior of individual particles that no longer allow the fluid to be considered continuous. I am attempting to determine this lower limit in circular channels and analyze the behavior of fluids under those limits. Several papers have been dedicated to small-scale flame propagation, such as James D. Ott's "A Mechanism for Flame Acceleration in Narrow Tubes," but currently no experimental work has been done to establish the actual behavior of small-scale fluid mechanics and combustion. This project will shed new light on the concepts alluded to by Ott, by essentially mirroring this study with an experimental rather than computational approach.

Theory predicts an acceleration of the flame as it propagates for two main reasons. The first is that the burned mixture, at high temperatures and high local pressures, behind the flame, act as a piston propelling the unburned mixture, through which the flame is traveling. Since a subsonic flame travels at the laminar flame speed relative to the unburned mixture, propelling the unburned mixture will result in a faster flame speed relative to an outside observer. Additionally, frictional effects actually serve to accelerate the flame even further, due to the formation of a boundary layer in the unburned mixture. This boundary layer restricts the cross-sectional area available for the propelled unburned mixture and thus the area available for the flame to travel. Since mass flow rate remains constant due to conservation of mass, the velocity must increase. Thus, by studying the acceleration of a flame through a narrow channel, I can gain insight into the nature of frictional effects and other behavior of fluids on such small scales.

As noted above, I have created the experimental apparatus and have begun to perform experiments. My setup includes a 91-cm-long, 1-mm-diameter glass tube with a tungsten filament at the center to ignite the ethylene-oxygen mixture, photo diodes to record when the flame reaches certain points in the tube in order to determine velocities and accelerations, and a digital camera triggered by the photo diode signal to gather information about the flame profile. Figure 2 illustrates the glass tube assembly.

Figure 2: Glass Tube Assembly.

Preliminary results indicate that the flame reaches supersonic conditions. A picture of the flame integrated over its entire path reveals a bright spot followed by a luminous streak at ~25cm from the point of ignition as depicted in Figure 3. I suspect that the flame achieves detonation at this location. I performed a calculation in CEA (NASA computer program, Chemical Equilibrium with Applications) and determined the detonation speed to be ~2470 m/s, which coincides with the measured velocity of ~2400 m/s. Building on this small initial success, I need to do more work to gather a complete velocity profile though the tube and compare my results with those predicted computationally.

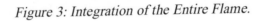

Figure 3: Integration of the Entire Flame.

For further study, I may employ smaller tubes to carry the flame, gather pictures of the flame with a high-speed camera to ascertain the flame shape, or obtain schlieren images to analyze shock formations. When I take the glass tube assembly to other specialized labs with such sophisticated instrumentation, such as a high-speed camera or schlieren imaging apparatus, I will utilize my portable experiment station to supply regulated concentrations of combustible mixtures to the tube.

My results will ultimately be used in designing MEMS (Micro Electromechanical Systems) devices as applied to micro-propulsion thrusters for station-keeping of small satellites, a major area of study in our group. Additionally, since this information has wide-ranging applications to numerous other fields, I plan to publish a technical paper in a scientific journal in order to share my findings with other engineers and scientists.

In graduate school and likewise in my career, I want to pursue research topics that have application in future energy use in the United States and other countries around the world. As a mechanical engineer, I can address those issues by exploring the fundamentals of and designing new methods of clean combustion and alternative fuels. One particular topic I am intrigued by is electrochemical fuel cells. These devices have the potential to be the future of our energy storage and conversion. Fuel cells are a possible method of providing power that is both clean and efficient. Potentially, they will have applications in powering laptop computers, cellular telephones, and automobiles. As of now, fuel cells are still a rising, albeit crude, concept that requires time and the attention of our country's great scientific minds to come to fruition. I want to do my part to help advance this budding and exciting idea, which I consider to be the future of energy.

Currently, however, there remain serious problems with the practicality and feasibility of this concept that need to be solved. First of all, hydrogen, in and of itself, is not actually an energy source. Consequently, an energy source such as coal power, which accounts for 51% of the United States power generation, or gas, which accounts for 16%, is needed to produce pure hydrogen, in which case we are still faced with harmful emissions and waning hydrocarbon resources. Additionally, since hydrogen is a gas at atmospheric pressures and reasonably achieved temperatures ($T>20K$), hydrogen must be stored in a high-pressure vessel, which has the potential to burst, or in the form of methane or methanol, which must be processed to obtain pure hydrogen by a reformer (a catalytic heated chamber that strips the hydrogen from methane) that releases carbon dioxide, a greenhouse gas, and reduces efficiency by about 30-40%. Another concern that requires attention is the efficiency of the fuel cell itself. Electrochemical fuel cells have ideal efficiencies of around 80%. However, efficiencies achieved now are much lower— around 40-70%.

As a mechanical engineer, I want to investigate this aspect of fuel cell design and development, as this is the area in which I have the background and desire to study. Dr. Fredrick Prinz of Stanford University has determined that higher efficiencies can be achieved by utilizing smaller channels. Such information might also be implemented in the design of higher-efficiency, large-scale fuel cells composed of these smaller channels. Considering my interest and background in small-scale fluid mechanics and MEMS (Micro Electro-Mechanical Systems) devices, I aim to explore topics related to the micro-fluidics and scaling effects of these fuel cells.

My current study of the frictional effects and fluid behavior in small channels will provide me with the proper knowledge and experience necessary to pursue this topic. In my graduate study at Stanford University, I intend to study under Professor Prinz to advance the development of electrochemical fuel cells, which have extensive capabilities in the future of energy, by improving their efficiency. My communications with Dr. Prinz thus far have been promising, and I hope to have the opportunity to realize this promise during the coming fall at Stanford University.

EXTENSIVE PERSONAL STATEMENT: LIBERAL ARTS

(This material is critiqued on page 85.)

Personal Statement—John Lerner

Mythic College has been my home for more than three years. Our relationship started very innocently with an advertisement campaign in which three separate postcards arrived at my house over the course of a month entitled simply *Think*, *Evolve*, and *Act*. At the time, I was like many other high school kids: I knew everything. I was in the top ten percent of my high school class—I knew academics. I lettered in track three years in a row—I knew athletics. I was actively involved in community service—I knew how to change the world. I served as the leader of my church youth group region, gave sermons, and led discussions—I knew Truth.

Of course, like a proper liberal arts institution, Mythic College was quick to tell me that I knew nothing. It created a vacuum into which new and original thoughts could be harnessed and developed, only to be questioned once again at a later time.

Looking back, I realize I once saw education simply as a means to the end of financial security. I completed numerous computer courses and certifications in high school since both promised a profitable career. Today, I understand education as an ongoing process in which my thoughts and actions are continuously being molded by every new experience. Each new experience generates a unique lens through which to view the world with a fresh set of priorities. But the most influential portion of my college experience has been my ability and good fortune to expand my education beyond the classroom through travels abroad. While the lessons learned in these journeys are too numerous to list, I will attempt to concisely encapsulate their essence.

During a ten-day service learning trip to Costa Rica, I was exposed to negative impacts of globalization as I walked through a teak forest that a foreign company would be turning into souvenir pencils. Since teak trees make rainforest soil so acidic that it cannot be reclaimed by the natural foliage for over 100 years, the impact of such an act is felt by several generations.

As part of a three-credit course focused on Gandhi and Nonviolence, I traveled to India to study at the Institute for Gandhian Studies. There, I lived the ritualistic lifestyle of the Mahatma and met individuals who did not abide by Western ideals of "the developed world." Nonetheless, I found their lives contained a certain spark, guided by love and a conception of Truth stronger than could ever be found in any material possession.

On a spring break service trip to Guatemala, I witnessed the results of brutal regimes that controlled their people through coercion and fear. At the same time, my hope for a better future was renewed as I looked upon smiles and the peace signs of the children at the Colegio de Miguel Angel Asturias.

In my most recent semester, I studied abroad in Belgium and served part-time as an assistant to a member of European Parliament. Through this opportunity, I was able to attend committee meetings and experience the process which has brought peace and integration to a continent that was once consumed by bitter hatred and war.

In all I have done, I discovered there is a chasm between the textbook analysis about the present global situation and the reality of personally experiencing it. These opportunities have helped my educational goals to coalesce into a unique program of study. Mythic College supports the idea of students designing their own study programs to suit their individual needs. My self-designed program of "Peace and Conflict Studies with an emphasis in Technical Revolution" combines elements of Peace Studies, Politics, Philosophy, and Information Technology.

With this diverse focus, I plan to study how the dissemination of communication technologies can foster the development of a common global humanity—centered on themes such as government accountability, the promotion of human rights, and transnational cooperation in dealing with collective problems of the global community.

My research in this field has already taken many forms. In one recent project, I considered the way political activists have utilized communication technologies to undermine or overthrow authoritarian regimes which had kept them in silence and slavery for so long. In another paper, I analyzed the way the transition from an oral culture to a literate culture led to the emergence of the nation-state and a national identity for which people could be mobilized to kill others; I then argued that today a transition is occurring from a literate culture to a digital culture, which will lead to the emergence of a global identity, cosmopolitanism, and a greater focus on collective goals.

In my dual role as a student at the Irish Institute in Leuven, Belgium, and an assistant to a member of the European Parliament, I produced a paper entitled "A Knowledge-based Society and the Digital Divide" in which I explored the perpetuation of information communication technologies in developing countries and how such developments could either provide economic growth or represent a new covert imperialism. The Director of the Irish Institute noted the work as "impressive" and suggested that I should keep her informed of future research plans.

I am currently working on a senior research thesis for Peace and Conflict Studies that will attempt to prove that the shift from a literate culture to a digital culture will undermine the nation-state based identity. Next semester, I will write a senior research thesis for Information Technology, addressing some aspect of technology-enhanced cooperation. In May of 20xx, I plan to graduate with distinction in both majors.

After completing my undergraduate work, I hope to find a graduate program that will allow me to combine fields such as Peace Studies or Global Governance with my previous studies regarding the impacts of communication technology dissemination. I wish to find a program that combines classroom theory with first-hand experience and would not hesitate to send a student abroad to conduct research inquiries. After graduate school, I plan to move beyond research to work for an organization such as The Carter Center which engages in need-based development work at a people-to-people level.

While all of these research plans may seem to imply that I hold all of the answers for solving the world's problems, Mythic College has certainly taught me at least one important thing: I do not know everything. In fact, in many instances, that which I know may be based upon false suppositions. However, knowledge and acceptance of such a mental void appropriately undermines the fanaticism of one's own convictions, provides for the time to make one listen instead of trying to prescribe, and allows for the constructive acceptance of critique to spawn new and truly creative approaches to common problems.

The last three years of my life have brought great transitions in both attitude and action. Along with the creation of a void comes the desire to fill that void with something. I now have more questions. I talk to more people. I engage in the world. I offer my viewpoint from my own experience and actively listen to those of others. Through it all, I hope that I can play an active role in this globalization process and promote those principles that I have found in my travels to be common to all of humankind—the desire for a safe and peaceful living environment, the passion for quality education, the hope of being able to decide one's fate. Such principles unite all of humanity by one common thread, and drive me forward as I reach towards graduate study.

EXTENSIVE PERSONAL STATEMENT: FILM

(This material is critiqued on page 86.)

Personal Statement by John Lerner

Poetry

Steven Spielberg has said that he makes the movies he loved to watch as a child. Woody Allen has expressed the same approach. I can say no such thing.

I remember hating the cinema as a child—at least those films that were prescribed to my gender and age group. While my father studied cinema in college (and my mother theater, no less), the medium had no appeal to me. My three adopted siblings frequented the local Ritz Theater on Saturday afternoons. I chose not to go.

In the fall of my senior year of high school, everything changed—I fell in love. My father recommended *Annie Hall* to me, and I rented it on a whim, finding it stuffed into a rack in a dirty little corner of "Video Stars" and priced conveniently at forty-seven cents. I watched the film at 2 AM that night and did not get a wink of sleep. I had discovered the cinema. Jean-Luc Godard, who had original intentions of being a novelist but was "crushed by the spectre of the great writers," likens his discovery of the cinema to discovering a new poetry, perhaps a new voice. "I saw a film of Jean Vigo, a film of Renoir, and then I said to myself, I think that I could do that too, me too." For me, I had found a new poetry and a new poet in Woody Allen, and he revealed to me other poets, including Godard.

Plastics

One year later, a jump into the study of film was not an immediate decision. With a high school education grounded rigorously in math and science, I entered Mythic University on an academic scholarship with Polymer Science and Engineering as my intended major. I like to joke that, after seeing Mike Nichols' film *The Graduate* and hearing that terrific line, "plastics," delivered poolside to a wayward Benjamin Braddock (Dustin Hoffman), I was inadvertently led into the hands of the great polymer Satan. But, by sophomore year, I quickly escaped the plastic devil's clasp and found a new home in the film department.

Children

I remember being told once as an undergraduate (and the actual source of this like so many other pieces of great advice has slipped away into some crevice in my mind) that directing your own material is like parenting—you don't have to know what you're doing so much as have an idea, and try very hard, and listen, and be honest, and your children will still turn out all right, and you will likely even have some insight into and influence on them. To be honest, I really have no idea if this advice will prevent me from raising a serial killer one day, but I have found it to be an accurate description of directing my own material as a student and usually a favorable approach to take with a cast and crew of peers. Despite this reassuring advice on directing and my degree in film production, I still feel that my writing abilities are far more developed and refined than my visual storytelling skills. This is a major reason for my interest in graduate-level study of directing.

The culmination of my student film work was a nineteen-minute child called *Burying Dvorak*—a coming-of-age comedy about a fourteen-year-old boy and his taxidermist-stuffed basset hound. The film, since its premiere at Mythic University's Annual Student Film Festival (which routinely sells out the 700+ seat Mythic University Auditorium), has now appeared in more than a score of festivals, including the Los Angeles International Short Film Festival and the New York Expo of Short Film and Video, and has won several awards. I dislike awards in art, however—as treasurer of Mythic University's Student Film Organization I strongly advocated the removal of awards from the student film festival—and am most happy through film festivals just to reach new people with the work and similarly meet other wonderful filmmakers. This was an opportunity only afforded to me because I took a year off after my undergraduate studies to save money, travel to arts and film festivals, and write.

Geography (Plastics Reprise)
I return to the subject of plastics because I never fully left them. Mythic University's Polymer Science Department is housed within the same college as the university's Department of Geography. On a suggestion from my first honors advisor, I took a few geography courses during my freshman year and was a Geography and Film double major since.

What do Geography and Film have to do with one another? My fellow students have spared no creativity in rearticulating this question. "So, do you wanna, um, make documentaries for National Geographic…or create chloropleth maps of celebrity sightings?"

Geography is not, despite what we may have garnered from our high school educations, simply state maps and capitals. It is the study of any phenomenon over space. In the Kantian sense, at least in terms of his *a priori* human categorizers of time and space, Geography is as essential as History—the study of any phenomenon over time. While most academic disciplines, including the cinema, thoroughly examine themselves in relation to time, they miss an opportunity to do so with space. For me then, Geography enables the intellectual development of one's capabilities to render and analyze space. After all, when a director blocks characters and camera, what is he or she doing but creating spatial relationships that reinforce the emotive content of a scene? Furthermore, the concept of *place* is intimately bound within multiform relations of power (conceived here in Foucaultian terms) that "direct" such *geographical* choices as where films are made, where films do or supposedly do take place (setting), and where the people come from who make the films (actors, writers, directors, producers, etc.).

Columbia University

My choosing Columbia University is not because I want to be a New York filmmaker or make films about New York City. How could I make a more meaningful film about New York than that person, Woody Allen, who allowed me to fall in love with the cinema in the first place? At the moment, I doubt that I will even want to stay in the city beyond graduate school. My interest is elsewhere in a more rural aesthetic—not the imaginary/metaphorical rural of the western, but an authentic rural as told by such filmmakers as Terrence Malick and more recently David Gordon Green.

What I want from New York and Columbia is an opportunity to let my talents and personal vision marinate with those of other filmmakers and artists who are working at the highest level. I want to influence and be influenced, experiment and fail, and develop as a visual storyteller under the guidance and support of a faculty and program renowned for their narrative work—which is, despite my fondness for both my professors and friends, not Mythic University. Most importantly, I do not want to need each short film to make or break me like so many independent filmmakers I meet at festivals—most of whom do not get anything but a new audience at each festival to their disappointment, although this is really the most wonderful thing, to my lights. At Columbia, I want to work with the same zeal and spirit as when I was a high school senior making VHS movies after seeing *Annie Hall*. I want to create more of my own cinematic children, and, in doing so, continue to discover my own voice, my own poetry.

EXTENSIVE SCHOLARSHIP ESSAY: BIOLOGICAL SCIENCE
(This material is critiqued on page 87.)

Motivation and Background

Since C.S. Elton's observations first began the field of invasion biology in 1958[1], the problem of invasive species management has continued to be a prominent issue, despite advances in science and technology. Biological invasions of pest species pose a threat to the stability of ecosystems, both natural and managed.[2] A tremendous amount of effort is put into the detection and eradication of invasives, but not necessarily in the most economically or biologically efficient manner. In my research, I am using optimization with Stochastic Dynamic Programming (SDP) as a tool to examine the best spatial strategy of attack on a particular invasive species—the gypsy moth (*Lymantria dispar*).

The ongoing gypsy moth invasion in North America makes an exemplary case study because of the extensive life history data available describing its spread, and because of prior research to examine various methods to slow that spread. The gypsy moth has been moving across the U.S. since its accidental release in Boston in 1869.[3] The spread rates of the gypsy moth were estimated to be fairly high (9.45 km/yr) from 1900 to 1915, low (2.82 km/yr) from 1916 to 1965, and finally very high (20.78 km/yr) from 1966 to 1990.[4] Gypsy moth caterpillars are responsible for changing entire ecosystems because of their wide-ranging diet consisting of trees, shrubs, and plants. Their feeding weakens trees through defoliation, leaving forests vulnerable to disease and other attacks.[3] Nearly 311 million acres of forest land and urban and rural treed areas in the U.S. are at risk for gypsy moth invasion.[3] To manage such a pest, it is important to know the order in which events happen throughout the course of a year. The transition cycle that I am using to optimize management decisions is explained in Figure 1.

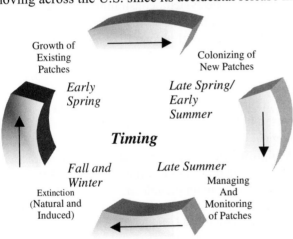

Figure 1: Gypsy moth population transition cycle.

Master's Thesis Research

The gypsy moth population is growing in two distinct ways—both as a wavelike front from the main population and as several dispersing "island" populations that may eventually merge with the slow-moving main population.[4] This type of movement is called "stratified-diffusion."[5] In my research, I assume that the gypsy moth population behaves like a mainland-island metapopulation, i.e., "a population of populations"[6] consisting of a mainland population and several smaller dispersed island populations. The best management solution may be a mixed strategy involving intervention on both the small dispersed island populations and the main population front.[7] By examining the gypsy moth population as a metapopulation, we can focus mainly on the dynamics of the small patches but also assume that the source of dispersal is from the main wavelike large population front. My research is aimed at developing a useful mathematical tool to optimize the plan of attack for the control of this invasive species.

Stochastic Dynamic Programming as a Management Tool

Stochastic Dynamic Programming (SDP) is an ideal management tool in the case of invasive species control because it can be used to generate solutions to problems of optimal decision-making. SDP requires the assumption that the state of the system is dynamic and therefore can change, but in order to use it we must define a discrete state space. To further limit the changes in the state of the system, constraints must be imposed on the system and finally the optimization criterion must be outlined. Because the dimensions of the state space can become overwhelmingly large, SDP models are typically solved numerically.[8,9]

After receiving widespread attention in behavioral ecology,[8] SDP has emerged as a valuable problem-solving tool in studies of biological control, agroecology, and conservation.[10] For example, SDP was used to find the strategy that maximizes the number of successful releases of a biological control agent.[11] In problems of fire management, SDP helped determine the optimal fire management strategy where threatened species were concerned.[12] SDP was also used to examine the optimal management of Saiga antelope, with climate as the main parameter.[13] For weed control, SDP helped researchers examine herbicide recommendations for wheat crops[14] and also to examine optimal economic crop rotation for wheat.[15] Methods of invasive species management are extremely costly and time-intensive. Mathematical models such as SDP in conjunction with research could contribute to a more cost-efficient and practical method of investigating and recommending management decisions for invasive species.

Model Outline

In my research, I have begun to outline and define the necessary assumptions and parameters to successfully construct an appropriate SDP for gypsy moth management. I plan to build the initial model based on the outline here, then continue my research by 1) adding to the initial model to create a more general model of invasive species management, and 2) exploring other mathematical tools to answer similar questions.

The SDP algorithm will be the set of strategies that will result in the "least invasive" state of the system within a defined time frame.[10] In order to reach the least invasive state, the probability of transition between states (based on the state of the system at the previous time step) will be determined for each point in time.

The state space of the system can be defined by five transitions with patches moving between three states: empty, medium, and large (Figure 2). The model assumes 1) a finite number of patches, 2) identical patches, 3) each patch as being in one of three states depending on how much of the patch is populated by the invasive species, and 4) no "small" patches. The final assumption of no small patches was made for two reasons. First, detecting small patches of isolated populations is very difficult and expensive, so most populations are not detected until they are slightly larger. Secondly, Allee effects contribute to the natural death of small populations.[16]

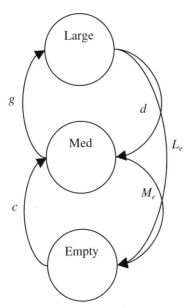

Figure 2: State space model of gypsy moth dynamics.

The five parameters can be broken down into three processes—growth, colonization, and extinction—that will shape the population transition matrix of the final model. Growth includes the probability of growth, g, from a medium patch to a large patch. Colonization includes the probability, c, of individuals from the large main population front colonizing an empty patch. Here, the assumption is made that only the main front generates new patches.

Finally, extinction includes the probability of a large patch going extinct, L_e; the probability of a medium patch going extinct, M_e; and the probability of a large patch declining to a medium patch, d. The large, main wavelike front, or "mainland," is considered only in terms of colonizing new, empty patches.

Five strategies will be applied to optimize management based on how many large, medium, and empty patches are present (see Table 1). With the exception of the "do nothing" strategy, which incurs no cost, each management strategy has an equal cost. Costs were made equivalent by varying the number of patches affected by each strategy. Strategies are all based on pesticide application, since it is the most common management practice for gypsy moth infestations.[3] In that sense, "containing" would mean applying pesticide to the edge of a population or spraying with a lower pesticide application rate so that extinction might not be likely, but the population would be unable to grow and might actually decrease in size and impact. "Spraying" would encompass applying pesticide with the motivation of complete patch extinction. "Do nothing" would allow the system to continue without intervention.

Table 1: Five management strategies to be considered for model optimization.

Management Strategy	Impact on Dynamics
Contain main population front	Decrease c
Contain 4 large sites	Increase d
Spray 2 large sites	Increase L_e
Spray 4 medium sites	Increase M_e, and indirectly decrease g
Do nothing	No impact

Each of the parameters will be tested for sensitivity. Values for colonization, growth, and extinction probabilities will be based on up-to-date knowledge of biological tendencies, and determined in consultation with USDA gypsy moth researcher Dr. Andrew Liebhold.

At any time, we assign a value or reward to a particular state. The reward value is defined by the function:

$$f(l, m) = \frac{1 + \frac{m}{4}}{P} \qquad where: l + m \le P$$

where l is the number of large patches, m is the number of medium patches, and P is a constant value describing the total number of patches in the system. Thus, in order to determine the optimal decision at any given point, we select the strategy that yields the minimum reward value. Assuming that a large patch is less desirable than a medium patch, the worst possible state of the system is when there are P large and 0 medium or empty patches, yielding the maximum value of 1. On the other hand, the best possible state occurs when there are 0 large and 0 medium patches, yielding the minimum value of 0.

The reward function will be revisited in order to examine the effects of altering the weight placed on large versus medium patches. The assumption that large patches are less desirable than medium patches will be relaxed in order to determine how the management strategy changes according to the perception of large and medium patches.

Future Research Considerations

The initial mathematical model of management will yield answers to fundamental questions of management based on strategies of pesticide application to control gypsy moths. Other areas I plan to further explore as part of my master's research are i) the effect of monitoring on the management strategy, ii) the possibility for biological control, and iii) the impact of a different strain of gypsy moth on management decisions.

i) Monitoring gypsy moth population levels through the use of pheromone traps is common practice across the U.S.[3] Incorporating monitoring into the management strategies described above and altering the costs of those strategies would add another element of reality and may change the optimal decision. Increased monitoring incurs a cost, but may allow for future savings through the detection of smaller patches that are less costly to eliminate, making it worthwhile to explore the interplay of management and monitoring strategies.

ii) Using the fungal pathogen *Entomophaga maimaiga*—an effective natural enemy of the gypsy moth capable of preventing outbreaks—as a biological control agent may be a viable management strategy in the near future. Current research is being conducted to further explore the dynamics of the fungus and its role in controlling gypsy moth populations.[17] SDP would be useful in determining optimal release strategies of the fungus.[11]

iii) Finally, to anticipate the invasion of the Asian strain of the gypsy moth (AGM), it may be important to consider how we would manage this strain should it become established in the United States. A few cases of the AGM have been found but not established in North America, first in 1991 and a second time in 1993. Eradication efforts were successful in both cases, but incredibly costly.[3] In one year, $25 million was spent in the northwestern U.S. to eradicate the AGM; $9 million was spent in the Carolinas for the same purpose.[18,19]
The AGM is characterized by female flight and an even broader range of hosts. Compared to the current North American strain with little population variability and flightless females, the AGM, once established, would spread much faster and leave a more devastating path through forests and other treed areas of the U.S. and Canada. Females of the AGM can travel more than 18 miles to deposit eggs, whereas females of the North American strain rarely move far from their birthplace to lay eggs.[3] Because of the flight capabilities of females of the AGM, the transition cycle would need to be altered to account for the timing of events in the model. Different dispersal abilities may affect the optimal management strategy.

Ultimately I plan to expand upon the gypsy moth system to make the model applicable to other invasive species. Species-specific modifications will have to be made, but the general SDP will help in the process of developing a framework for applied problems of invasive species management.

Academic Career and Future Outlook

Vital questions such as those involving invasive species management are often too costly or difficult to conduct experimentally but can be tackled mathematically. My undergraduate background in mathematics and applied analysis along with my interest in biology provides me with a unique foundation as an ecologist. By pursuing graduate work at Mythic University, I will be able to expand my biological and ecological background and integrate that with my mathematical abilities, laying the foundation for a successful career in mathematical ecology. Following the completion of my master's degree in Ecology in the spring of 20xx, I plan to pursue a research career in the field of ecology through a Ph.D. degree, focusing on experimental and mathematical work in the areas of biological invasion and conservation biology.

References

1. Elton, C.S. 1958. *The Ecology of Invasions by Animals and Plants.* Methuen, London.
2. Liebhold, A.M., et al. 1995. Invasion by Exotic Forest Pests - a Threat to Forest Ecosystems. *Forest Science*, 41(2): 1-49.
3. U.S. Department of Agriculture. 1995. Gypsy moth management in the United States: a cooperative approach. *Final Environmental Impact Statement*, 2.
4. Sharov, A.A. and A.M. Liebhold. 1998. Model of slowing the spread of gypsy moth (Lepidoptera : Lymantriidae) with a barrier zone. *Ecological Applications*, 8(4): 1170-1179.
5. Shigesada, N. and K. Kawasaki. 1997. *Biological Invasions: Theory and Practice.* Oxford University Press, Oxford.
6. Levins, R. 1970. Extinction. In M. Gerstenhaber (Ed.) *Some Mathematical Problems in Biology:* 77-107. Providence, R.I.: American Mathematical Society.
7. Shea, K., *et al.* 2002. Active adaptive management in insect pest and weed control: Intervention with a plan for learning. *Ecological Applications*, 12(3): 927-936.
8. Mangel, M. and C.W. Clark. 1988. *Dynamic Modeling in Behavioral Ecology.* Princeton University Press, USA.
9. Freckleton, R.P. 2000. Biological control as a learning process. *Trends in Ecology and Evolution*, 15(7): 263-264.
10. Clark, C.W. and M. Mangel. 2000. *Dynamic State Variable Models in Ecology.* Oxford University Press, Oxford.

11. Shea, K. and H.P. Possingham. 2000. Optimal release strategies for biological control agents: an application of stochastic dynamic programming to population management. *Journal of Applied Ecology*. 37: 77-86.

12. Possingham, H.P. and G. Tuck. 1997. Application of stochastic dynamic programming to optimal fire management of a spatially structured threatened species. in *Proceedings of Modsim*: Hobart, Tasmania.

13. Milner-Gulland, E.J. 1997. A stochastic dynamic programming model for the management of the saiga antelope. *Ecological Applications*, 7(1): 130-142.

14. Pandey, S. and R.W. Medd. 1991. A stochastic dynamic programming framework for weed control decision making: an application to Avena fatua L. *Agricultural Economics*, 6: 115-128.

15. Fisher, B.S. and R.R. Lee. 1981. A dynamic programming approach to the economic control of weed and disease infestations in wheat. *Review of Marketing and Agricultural Economics*, 49(3): 175-187.

16. Liebhold, A.M. and J. Bascompte. 2003. The Allee effect, stochastic dynamics and the eradication of alien species. *Ecology Letters*, 6: 133-140.

17. Weseloh, R.M. 2004. *Biological Control*. 29: 138-144.

18. Tveten, J. and G. Tveten. 1 July 1995. Another moth threatens U.S. forests, in *The Houston Chronicle*. Houston, TX. E8.

19. Brody, J. 30 May 1995. Invader from Asia increases gypsy moth threat, in *The New York Times*. New York. C1.

APPLICATION ESSAY FOR ONLINE EDUCATION: MILTARY

(This material is critiqued on page 88.)

In my work as an Air Force pilot during the seven years since graduating college, I've continually found ways to show how the tools of a professional geographer can be used to help my organization do its job better. My experiences in combat since the fall of 20xx have only reinforced this assertion.

A revolution, driven by information, is underway in war fighting. The ability to collect and analyze information is as important to today's soldier as mass and maneuver was to Clauswitz. Battlespace situational awareness and the subsequent ability to shape the battlespace is an intrinsically geographic problem. During WW I, observers in hot air balloons and biplanes hand-sketched the location of enemy emplacements. That 'eye-in-the-sky' evolved into modern satellite imagery and signals intelligence. Historically, the wealth of collected data has been diminished by the time and expertise necessary to analyze it and the organizational stovepipes through which it was disseminated.

In contrast, Operation Enduring Freedom saw the first use of real-time sensor-to-shooter links over the mountains of Afghanistan. Unmanned USAF Predator aircraft, hosting a suite of multi-spectral sensors, were deployed to loiter over and survey areas of enemy activity. Decision-makers and front-line operators used those dynamic images to swiftly identify and attack the enemy. During Operation Iraqi Freedom, the National Geospatial-Intelligence Agency (NGA), for the first time, deployed personnel to front-line units. NGA teams' know-how and communication suites allowed combat commanders to reach back and exploit all of the agency's spatial data and technical expertise. Commenting on this theme in NGA's *Pathfinder* magazine, Major General Roger Over states, "That's exactly what I wanted, but I didn't know that until you showed me."

As a geographer, I understand that our community views problem-solving through a unique lens. GIS gives the professional geographer powerful tools to collect, analyze, and exploit spatial information. Unfortunately, many leaders and decision-makers are unaware of the speed and flexibility the geographer can bring to problem solving.

I've served as an Air Force pilot for the past six years and have logged several hundred combat hours during operations in Southwest Asia. I've experienced first-hand the power of well-applied spatial data in battle. During mission planning for a flight to a hostile dirt landing zone in southern Afghanistan, I used NIMA's computerized fly-by products to familiarize my crew with the area. Squadron tacticians merged our planned route and altitudes with images based on DTED and satellite data. These images gave me the invaluable experience of, virtually, having been there before. Later in the same mission, adverse weather blocked our planned route of flight. Using his onboard laptop, my navigator overlaid the day's air coordination plan depicting air refueling tracks and combat 'kill-boxes' with a tactical chart of the area. We safely avoided those danger zones and successfully completed the mission.

My expertise in flying, particularly airlift operations, puts me in a position to appreciate both the support our mission receives from geographers today and to envision the possibilities that exist through technical advances and more flexible organizational collaboration. I think that the most significant roadblocks to realizing these possibilities are fiscal constraints and ignorance within my own professional community about what the professional geographer brings to the fight. Personally, I can do little to affect Congressional funding. However, my military experience, wedded with a more advanced background in GIS, would help me to bridge the military and geo-spatial communities.

GIS and the geographers' approach to problem solving promises decision makers, at all levels, unprecedented situational awareness across any layer of the battlespace. I don't expect the military to begin training squadrons of GIS wizards. However, it's become increasingly important that a broader cross-section of people within our force understands how individual pieces of the puzzle can benefit from the geographer's tools.

That message can be delivered through cooperation among agencies like the Air Force's Air University, the Air Mobility Warfare Center, the NGA, and Mythic University's e-Education Institute. I imagine a 'geoinfo-awareness' course for officers attending Army Command and General Staff college or the Air Force Weapons Instructor school, proctored by a capabilities expert from NGA, and hosted on-line by our own geography department. The on-line format would allow an infinitely customizable curriculum outlaying the power of filtering information and solving problems within a spatial context. Moreover, the on-line forum, unconstrained by classroom space or time zones, would both enable and encourage professional collaboration across the military's often rigid organizational and functional lines. That kind of collaboration, linked with an awareness of capabilities, yields success when the ever-changing demands of conflict require innovative solutions.

I've articulated my professional motivation and logic for pursuing an on-line MGIS degree through Mythic University's innovative program. More personally, I'm excited to find this opportunity to become a more expert geographer while continuing my active duty military service. My experience as an Air Force pilot has been both enriching and adventurous, but I miss the intellectual challenges I faced as an undergrad. I see unlimited opportunities to put my professional experience and academic interest to good use, and the MGIS program promises a means to do so.

EXTENSIVE APPLICATION FOR
GRADUATE TRANSFER: TOXICOLOGY

(This material is critiqued on page 89.)

Statement of Purpose
Janet Lerner

To most laypeople and even scientists outside the fold of biology, *mechanistic* toxicologists are often mistaken for their forensic distant cousins. A more humorous, yet sinister role assigned to toxicologists is one more befitting a protagonist of a murder mystery than a research scientist. These popular notions about toxicologists neglect the contribution they make to biomedical research. To the mechanistic toxicologist, toxicants are powerful tools that inform our understanding of basic physiology or elucidate a disease process. This understanding of mechanistic toxicology reflects the way I have been trained to view toxicological research. It is what originally piqued my interest in toxicology, what motivated my decision to pursue graduate work in this field, and what drives me now to continue my training by transferring to Mythic University.

My graduate training in toxicology began unofficially in a single toxicology class during my first year as a master's student at Lesser University. That class, taught by a public health professor who peppered lectures on metabolism and carcinogenesis with connections to the basic sciences, convinced me to continue my graduate studies in a toxicology program. Three years later, I completed the course requirements for a master's and sufficient research for a thesis, but remained uncertain of my career goals and the options that existed for a PhD in the field of toxicology. I delayed the writing of my master's thesis for two years to work in the clinical pharmacology department of a pharmaceutical company and as a science and writing instructor at two local colleges. In this two-year period, I discovered that I was less enthusiastic about industry, but had a passion for teaching. Moreover, I missed the intellectual rigor of research. As I completed the writing of my master's thesis, how I would apply a PhD to my work life became clear: Doctoral training would prepare me to direct undergraduate research, design research-based science curricula, and teach in an undergraduate setting.

I returned to graduate school full-time to finish core requirements in the PhD program and electives in the biochemical toxicology concentration so that my studies could focus on the molecular mechanisms of toxicity. That year I also defended my master's thesis work which, under the direction of Dr. Janet Mentor, characterized a novel biomarker for nerve terminal degeneration in mice treated with methamphetamine. These studies and collaborations with others in Dr. Mentor's lab contributed to numerous abstracts and three publications that appeared in the *Journal of Neurochemistry* and the *Journal of Experimental Pharmacology and Therapeutics.*

After earning a master's degree in neurotoxicology, I joined the laboratory of Dr. John Mentor, who has a strong interest in molecular approaches to toxicology. In addition, Dr. Mentor is Lesser University's authority on alternative animal models of toxicity. This presented an opportunity to ask genetic-level questions in whole organisms and understand the benefits and limitations of non-traditional animal models. Using one of Dr. Mentor's species of small laboratory fish, I proposed to explore a mechanism for dioxin-induced suppression of ovulation, which has been documented in several mammalian species. My model was the female Japanese medaka, which ovulates daily under controlled environmental conditions. Unlike with mammals, the ovulatory cycle of the medaka would require no pharmacological manipulation. My hypothesis focused on the effect of dioxin on the expression of matrix metalloproteinases (MMPs), which are critical components of remodeling in all stages of folliculogenesis. I speculated that decreased expression of MMPs in mature follicles may account for "trapped" oocytes observed in dioxin-treated mammals. This project intrigued me, especially in light of the emerging role for the aryl hydrocarbon receptor (AhR) in normal ovarian development. The fish model, however, proved to be problematic. The rapid ovulatory cycle, seasonal variability in the cycle, and a shortage of species-specific reagents made this project difficult to execute. After discussing my preliminary data with my qualifying exam committee, it was suggested that this question, in fact, was better suited for a mammalian model.

Shortly after I passed the PhD candidacy exam at Lesser University, my advisor Dr. Mentor assumed the position of Acting Dean of Research at Lesser University. This position essentially took him out of the lab and away from opportunities to interact regularly with students. In Dr. Mentor's absence I began working closely with one of his colleagues, Dr. Janet Mentor2, a recently hired assistant professor in the Department of Biochemistry with an affiliation to my graduate program. Dr. Mentor2, whose expertise lies in the areas of molecular biology, matrix remodeling, dioxin, and carcinogenesis, served as a member of my orals committee. I was given access to her lab where I learned cell culture and basic molecular biology techniques, and where I enjoyed opportunities to interact daily with her and her technicians. I was entrusted with projects in the lab, which allowed me to develop my skills while working out the logistics of my dissertation research. Because of my interest in molecular toxicology and my active involvement in her studies, I joined Dr. Mentor2's lab as her first graduate student in toxicology.

Over the next year, my time in the lab was spent exploring several projects conceived by Dr. Mentor2. We believed that these projects, in addition to what I had proposed, would become the specific aims of my thesis. One project explored the role of dioxin in matrix remodeling during breast tubule morphogenesis. Our hypothesis was that the delay in tubule morphogenesis, which has been reported in mice treated with a dioxin-like compound, could be a consequence of altered expression of MMPs. My work showed that cancerous and normal murine mammary cell lines were responsive to dioxin, but did not demonstrate increased expression of MMP mRNA or protein. Before I could explore this question in coculture with fibroblasts or in three-dimensional culture, a funding shortage forced the lab to refocus its energies toward Dr. Mentor2's primary research interest, which explores the role of AhR in the progression of malignant melanoma. Having little positive preliminary data on which to base my own grant proposal, but a strong interest in carcinogenesis, I agreed to abandon projects that did not directly pertain to Dr. Mentor2's primary research and instead make melanoma progression the focus of my dissertation work.

Recently, the lab's struggle to procure funding for the melanoma project has brought much of our work in melanoma to a halt. While Dr. Mentor2 re-envisions the direction of her research program, I have been involved in a pilot project using wounded fish pretreated with dioxin to explore the toxicant's effects on matrix remodeling. This collaboration between Drs. Mentor2 and Mentor, still in its nascent stage experimentally and conceptually, utilizes real-time RT-PCR to measure alterations in MMP expression in wound tissue. The first phase of this project focused on isolating total RNA from the wounded caudal fins of fish. This proved not to be a trivial task, but with the help of an undergraduate whom I supervise, I developed a simple and relatively inexpensive technique for isolating an adequate amount of total RNA from caudal fin tissue. Our preliminary data revealed temporal and dose-dependent changes in expression of MMPs in the wound tissue of fish pretreated with environmentally relevant doses of dioxin. These studies are the first to show an effect of dioxin on MMP expression in an alternative animal model. With a collaborator's guidance, I am presently directing the efforts of two undergraduates who are helping us characterize this system as a model of dioxin's effects on the proliferative phase of wound repair in fish. Although interesting from the standpoint of comparative physiology and identifying novel biomarkers of exposure, the project may not be suitable for a dissertation that needs to be both molecular in scope and mechanistically based. In view of this and the shortage of work in Dr. Mentor2's lab, Dr. Mentor2, at my insistence, has agreed to allow me to spend the remainder of the academic year in the more established molecular endocrinology lab of her colleague Dr. Janet Mentor3. This seven-month laboratory rotation, which will culminate my studies at Lesser University this summer, will permit me to resume training in molecular-level research and further prepare me for a transition to a molecular lab within the toxicology program at Mythic University.

My reasons for considering a transfer to the Integrative Biosciences program in Molecular Toxicology at Mythic University have as much to do with my progress in graduate school as they do with my personal life. The ambiguous direction of my research, limited funding, and the prospect of a significant change of direction for our lab, coupled with strong personal ties to the Mythic University area, are factors that equally motivate my decision. My goal in graduate school is to be involved in research that relies upon the tools of molecular biology to ask genetic-level questions. Furthermore, what I see as my greatest need as a graduate student is the opportunity to develop a better grasp of the decision-making process that is critical to successful research. While editing Dr. Mentor2's grant proposals, I have gained a sense of the importance of making sound choices about lines of inquiry to pursue, models to use, and experimental approaches to take. I also appreciate the importance of communicating these choices effectively. As a student, I hope to have ample exposure to the decision-making that underlies good science and an opportunity to take a greater role in articulating these decisions through the grant writing process. The research that interests me, in particular, is how alterations in signaling pathways alter gene expression during carcinogenesis and other disease processes. I have identified several investigators in the Program in Molecular Toxicology whose labs and research programs would allow me to build on the strong foundation that has been laid at Lesser University.

As a transfer student, I would bring to the program a mastery of the didactic work I have completed at Lesser University and an openness toward learning in a new setting. To a new lab, I would bring proficiency in basic biochemical and molecular techniques, a desire to improve and expand my skills, and a drive to produce and communicate results. To the classroom, I would bring a wide range of teaching experiences and a willingness to teach well. More importantly, I bring to the field an enthusiasm for toxicology, which has been shaped by exceptional professors and advisors at Lesser University and numerous interactions with the toxicological community through meetings, presentations, and memberships in professional societies.

I hope to have the opportunity to continue my graduate education in toxicology at Mythic University where I can build upon my previous training and prepare to enter a field that relies increasingly on the tools of molecular biology to elucidate the mechanisms of toxicity and disease.

CHAPTER 5

PERSONAL STATEMENTS AND APPLICATION ESSAYS FOR NATIONAL SCHOLARSHIPS

> *A good essay must have this permanent quality about it; it must draw its curtain round us, but it must be a curtain that shuts us in not out.*
> —*Virginia Woolf*

Nowhere does a student's ability to communicate well about personal attitudes and accomplishments become more important than in applications for national scholarships. With a mostly even playing field among scholars when it comes to GPA, personal statements and answers to application questions truly do help selectors winnow out the best choices, seeking a tidy match between individual candidates and available opportunities. A Marshall Scholar might not be right for a Truman Scholarship, and vice versa; a returning adult student might be ineligible for many scholarships but perfect for the Jack Kent Cooke Scholarship.

This chapter summarizes ten of the nation's most coveted scholarships, with samples of personal statements and essays following each two-page scholarship description. All of the samples here are strong, and about half of them come from scholarship winners and finalists, culled from about 100 students representing about 20 states. Using the material in this chapter, educate yourself on your target scholarship and study its samples thoroughly, recognizing the rhetorical strategies used as well as how carefully writers match their backgrounds to the scholarship criteria. Visit the scholarship websites and read the profiles of past winners when available, envisioning yourself as a featured student on the website in the following year. Most importantly, be prepared to spend 50+ hours studying, reflecting, and writing as part of the scholarship application process, as winners typically report they do. Whether you win or not, the time will be well spent.

The Udall Scholarship

The Udall Scholarship honors Morris K. Udall, an Arizona Congressman who authored legislation to protect wilderness areas and demonstrated commitment to the Native American and Alaska Native populations. Sophomores and juniors are eligible for the scholarship, which covers educational expenses for one year up to a maximum of $5,000. Udall Scholars come from various fields, ranging from environmental science to engineering to political science, and share in common a commitment to preserving or improving the environment. Udall Scholarships also include special categories for nominees who are Native American or Alaska Native with a commitment to the areas of tribal policy and health care.

The Udall Scholarship Selection Criteria

Udall Scholarship applications are reviewed by at least two readers, ranging from professors of environmental science to scholarship directors to representatives from the EPA. Four principal categories are used to rank each applicant:
- commitment to the environment, health care, or tribal public policy;
- academic achievements;
- nominee's personal essay;
- personal characteristics as revealed by such evidence as volunteerism and testimonials in letters of reference.

For a helpful window into the Udall selection process from the point of view of a former selection committee member, refer to "What You Need to Know About the Udall Scholarship" (http://www.udall.gov/pdf/janeudalltips.pdf).

Answering the Udall Application Essay Questions

The Udall application is extensive, including short essays written in response to a series of questions. These questions invite detail in such areas as your professional aspirations, career goals, research experience, leadership, personal motivation, and service, and there's even an open-ended question asking what additional information you wish to share. In answering these questions, former Udall applicants have described active membership in professional service organizations, a spring break Habitat for Humanity project, a life-changing semester of study in Ecuador, and a project using bird counts as a marker to assess the biological integrity of a local landscape. To answer the open-ended question, which the selection committee uses to sometimes award discretionary points, former applicants have emphasized an interest in environmental education outreach, discussed their role as the first member of their family to attend college, or noted their struggles as a single parent on financial aid.

Most important in answering these application questions is that you read the questions carefully to discern the desired criteria, that you use specifics and avoid unnecessary redundancy with other parts of the application, and that you avoid leaving any of the questions blank or providing answers that are out of proportion to your other answers in length or intent. Seek a balanced, efficient presentation.

Evaluation of Two Sample Sets of Udall Application Materials

The two sample sets of Udall application materials that follow are richly detailed, with both writers thoroughly discussing research and field experiences. In discussing his environmental commitment, the first writer, an environmental engineering student, focuses on a field trip to a Superfund site where he witnessed remediation in action, while the second writer, studying mathematics and ecology, discusses a course she is taking on environmental issues in South Africa and a sailing adventure in the Florida Keys. Of note in the first writer's essay is his creative answer to question #4, about leadership in his campus community, where he discusses his participation in an outreach service project. The first writer was put forth as a finalist but did not receive a Udall. The second writer did receive a scholarship, after winning honorable mention in the previous year.

The final application question is especially challenging, requiring you to compose an 800-word essay discussing Udall's ideas and connect them to your own interests. Through the detail of the two samples, we sense that these writers are genuine rather than simply parroting back answers they anticipate the committee wants to hear, and that they studied Udall's work carefully to inform their essays. The first writer focuses on Udall's contributions to "the philosophical evolution of the environmental movement," while the second writer takes the gutsy approach of discussing legislation that Udall fought hard for but later came to regret because of some of its impacts. This writer also draws an interesting case for simpatico views she has with Udall regarding her current environmental project.

Information on applying for a Udall Scholarship is at
http://www.udall.gov/p_scholarship.asp

SAMPLE RESPONSES TO SELECT QUESTIONS
ON THE UDALL SCHOLARSHIP APPLICATION

B. Your Aspirations

Question# 2. What are your professional aspirations? Indicate in which area(s) of the environment, Native American health care, or tribal public policy you are considering making your career and specify how your academic program and your overall educational plans will assist you in achieving this goal.

Though industry has historically been responsible for much of the environmental degradation in the United States, I strongly believe that the private sector will be an important catalyst in the revitalization of our environment. Notwithstanding the short-term, profit-driven negligence of a few corporations, the majority of American companies are coming to realize that it is simply better business to conduct themselves in an environmentally sound manner rather than face costly litigation and inflated remediation costs. I hope to be part of the emerging generation of ecologically conscious men and women who will lead the development of a new business model that regards proper stewardship of the environment as standard practice. Whether I confront environmental problems as an engineer, businessman, or lawyer, the focus of my career will be to ameliorate past abuses while proactively managing future pollution sources. I feel that by working within industry to promote positive change, I can achieve tangible progress in improving the way our business community interacts with the environment.

My current studies in Environmental Engineering (EnvE) and my planned minor in Global Business Strategies (GBS) will be valuable two-fold preparation for such a role in the growing environmental profession. My EnvE degree will train me to address the changing environmental needs of modern industry by providing a unique engineering education that integrates traditional process design with a strong background in the environmental sciences. Through the completion of my coursework in contaminant hydrology, microbiology, fuel science, mineral processing, hydrogeology, and engineering design, I will be qualified both to help reclaim contaminated environments and minimize the impact of future air, soil, and water pollution. The GBS minor complements my technical education by providing the basic finance, management, and entrepreneurial skills necessary to succeed in the business world. This practical balance of my undergraduate education creates multiple options after my graduation. Though I plan to work for several years to achieve my Professional Engineer (PE) credential before returning to complete an advanced degree, I will be well-prepared to reenter higher education to pursue a master's in environmental engineering, a company-financed MBA, or an environmental law degree. Any of these educational paths will help me accomplish my ultimate goal: to pursue a lifelong career protecting and restoring the natural environment through a pragmatic, market-oriented approach.

D. Your Programs and Activities

Question# 3. Describe non-course-related research experience, if applicable. Indicate which areas of the environment, tribal public policy or health care your research affects, and the ways in which the experience will assist you in achieving your goals as stated in section B, #2.

This past semester I began independent research into the in-situ bioremediation of hexavalent chromium, a major industrial pollutant in the United States. On my own initiative and working outside of my academic department, I contacted a number of professors over the summer in search of interesting undergraduate research opportunities to supplement my coursework. After receiving several offers, I chose to work with Dr. Janet Teacher and Dr. John Teacher of the Department of Civil and Environmental Engineering, since their expertise in bioremediation complements my major's emphasis on physical remediation techniques. I developed a simple 36-hour experiment examining the biological reduction of carcinogenic hexavalent chromium to innocuous trivalent chromium using *Shewanella putrefaciens* CN32 bacterium. This initial "learning experiment" will likely be the foundation of more original work for my senior honors thesis. I also enrolled in a graduate literature review course that discussed the biological reduction of metals, a topic that greatly aided my understanding of the underlying science supporting the burgeoning bioremediation field.

Question# 4. Describe a leadership experience in which you made a difference on campus or in your community.

My two most recent leadership activities did not involve my campus community, but could make a difference in a number of developing communities. I am an active member of Engineers Working for a Sustainable World (EWSW). Though unable to participate directly in any of the organization's development projects in El Salvador, Jamaica, or Nigeria because of coursework and time commitments, I have contributed to the organization in other ways, namely by completing two non-technical writing projects over the past year as fundraising and recruiting tools. Last spring, I worked closely with the club's faculty advisor drafting a grant proposal for multiple service projects in the rural village of Nueva Ezperanza, El Salvador. This document will be given to a number of development foundations to solicit the necessary financing for continued bridge construction and house retrofitting. More recently, I led a team of EWSW volunteers in creating a brochure for the organization. I arranged meetings, delegated responsibilities, and edited the final product. The brochure will be professionally published and used to promote EWSW throughout the university. By advertising the organization, I am helping to attract more dedicated people to EWSW. In the future, I hope to lead a technical project of my own, possibly the design and implementation of an arsenic removal system for the drinking water of an Argentine village.

Question #5. Describe a specific activity or experience that has been important in clarifying or strengthening your commitment to the environment, Native American health care, or tribal public policy.

During my first semester at Mythic University, I was able to attend a field trip to a local Superfund site with my advisor and about a dozen of my peers through the Society of Environmental Engineers (SEE). The field trip was a valuable learning experience that reaffirmed my career goals by allowing me to see firsthand the interesting, worthwhile work that environmental engineers do involving site characterization and remediation.

The Mythic Organics facility that we visited was both a registered Superfund site and a working chemical processing plant. In the early 1960s, herbicide precursors had been dumped at the property in open, unlined pits. Testing in later years showed that the hazardous chemicals were migrating to nearby groundwater sources and damaging the aquatic ecosystems. With the enactment of the Comprehensive Environmental Response, Compensation, and Liability Act (CERCLA) in 1980, the company became legally responsible for the mitigation of its poor pre-regulatory disposal practices and was required to implement an appropriate reclamation strategy. Our SEE group was given a full tour of the facility and learned about the specific remediation techniques the company was utilizing to remove the chemicals from the environment. Recognizing that the herbicide precursors are volatile organic compounds (VOCs), the Mythic Organics engineers determined that a soil vapor extraction system was the best approach. By mechanically pumping ambient air into the contaminated soil, the VOCs are volatilized into gases and then extracted by pumps and passed through a series of special filters that remove the compounds from the air. With the proper regulatory nudge, Mythic Organics has assumed responsibility for its past actions and is actively addressing them.

I was impressed by the simple efficiency of the remediation strategy and how it represented the real-world integration of a broad spectrum of knowledge including basic organic chemistry and engineering design. Observing a successful reclamation plan for the first time, I realized that our Superfund process was working and that my undergraduate education was preparing me for a meaningful career. I was excited to be in my engineering program and look forward to completing my degree because of the engaging, constructive work I can do with the skills I acquire.

Question# 6. Describe briefly any public service or community activities associated with your interests in the environment, Native American health care, or tribal public policy in which you regularly participate. Explain the duration, degree, and significance of your involvement.

My interest in the environment has always been practical rather than romantic, focused on improving the way people interact with their world over championing natural aesthetics. This guiding emphasis has especially influenced how I view the complex environmental dilemmas of the developing world and its constant struggle in an increasingly competitive global society. I sympathize with the desire to achieve a more comfortable modern lifestyle by exploiting one's abundant natural resources, but recognize that the Western-inspired path many underdeveloped countries are currently following could be self-destructive. The uncontrolled, haphazard industrialization of 19th century Europe and North America cannot be repeated in Asia, South America, and Africa or the environmental consequences and resulting human suffering will be grave. The international community must assist the developing world in establishing balanced, equitable growth that does not sacrifice environmental quality and social welfare in the name of economic expediency. Sustainable development programs that promote self-reliance, respect local customs, utilize appropriate technology, and re-establish traditional cultural stewardship are the only way that these countries can improve the daily lives of their average citizens without misusing their resources.

This firm commitment to sustainable development led me to join Engineers Working for a Sustainable World. Over the past three years, I have attended monthly meetings, contributed my time to several fundraising activities, and have worked closely with our faculty advisor on two writing projects. In the future, I hope to lead a technical project that will allow me to travel to and directly assist a developing community.

Question# 7. What additional information (not already addressed in the application) do you wish to share with the Udall Scholarship review committee?

Environmental advocacy demands the extensive knowledge and communication of complex, interrelated subject matter. It is not enough to just argue that our remaining redwood forests should be preserved for the sake of their aesthetics; an activist must be able to explain in convincing detail to sometimes hostile audiences just how ecologically damaging their loss would be. It is not enough to allege that pollution disproportionately affects the poor; hard evidence must be presented that integrates human geography, medical studies, and environmental sampling. To advance the evolving environmental agenda, the next generation of activists must overcome the stridency of vocal critics and reach out to the public with clarity and well-reasoned arguments. My environmental engineering education will provide the essential framework for a productive career of environmental advocacy from within the business community, a significant component of American culture traditionally resistant to regulation. By understanding the technical side of environmental issues, I will be well-prepared to play my part in promoting the transformation of industry into a responsible, accountable steward of the environment.

SAMPLE UDALL SCHOLARSHIP ESSAY

E. Essay

In 800 words or less, discuss a significant public speech, legislative act, or public policy statement by Congressman Udall and its impact on your field of study, interests, and career goals.

Congressman Udall and the Foundations of Modern Environmentalism

The 1970s represent a historic period of evolution in the American environmental movement, a critical time of transition that fundamentally changed the way concerned citizens and policymakers understand and confront pervasive environmental problems. It was a decade that celebrated the rich heritage of Muir and Thoreau while recognizing that traditional preservation alone could not adequately address the complex, interrelated social, economic, and environmental dilemmas of a growing nation and a globalizing world. It was a defining era of maturation when the environmental movement progressed beyond romantic idealism to practical action. Among the leaders of this dramatic refashioning was Congressman Morris K. Udall, a remarkable civil servant whose pragmatic vision embodies the philosophical foundation of modern environmentalism.

While reading a number of Congressman Udall's public speeches, I was immediately captivated by the basic agreement of his ideas and principles with my developing views on the same issues. Though nearly three decades have passed, I was particularly impressed by a speech he made to the Izaak Walton League of America in July of 1975 entitled "Environment vs. Economy: Exploding a Phony Issue." His arguments are well-reasoned, well-written, and well-defended, and most significantly, they portend the emerging sentiments of an entire generation of likeminded environmental advocates, myself included. Focusing on his three Es—energy, environment, and economics—Congressman Udall succinctly defined the central themes of my educational program and eloquently articulated many of my personal beliefs about the essential interconnectedness of our national responsibilities to the environment and each other.

One of the most admirable qualities of Congressman Udall's speech is his progressive, yet balanced position on a number of contentious issues. It would have been very easy for him to slip into hyperbole and rail across-the-board against the evils of industrialization as certain "barefoot elitist" environmentalists of his time did. But he resisted the rhetorical temptation and instead concentrated on presenting useful criticisms in accordance with the pressing realities of the day. Nowhere is this measured commentary more effective than in his careful critique of our country's flawed energy policy. Congressman Udall's reservations about nuclear power and the expansion of domestic oil and gas drilling, his criticism of inefficient automobiles and our unfortunate tradition of profligate resource consumption, his belief that dramatic improvements could and should be made to the mining industry, and his insistence on judicious conservation are all concepts that I learn about daily in my coursework in the Department of

Environmental Engineering at Mythic University. It is a testament to Congressman Udall's foresight and understanding of the issues that these same ideas are integral to my curriculum today.

A second component of Congressman Udall's speech that highlights his contribution to the philosophical evolution of the environmental movement is the historic connection he makes between environmental quality and social welfare. While previous generations of naturalists had disregarded the human costs of haphazard industrialization, Congressman Udall was one of the first politicians to recognize the underlying link between poverty and environmental degradation. Reasoning that overcrowded, dilapidated urban slums are as much a failure of environmental management as denuded landscapes, Congressman Udall was an early voice for the environmental concerns of minorities and other underrepresented groups. With sensitivity and poise, he helped bring this worthy cause into the mainstream movement of the 1970s. The fact that the concept of environmental justice is a guiding tenet of progressive politics today is further tribute to his enduring legacy.

The pronounced economic focus of Congressman Udall's speech is indicative of another innovation in environmentalism: While regressive-minded businessmen and reactionary politicians had attacked the environmental movement as inherently detrimental to the economy, Congressman Udall was one of the first to counter this overly simplistic assertion. Arguing that proper stewardship over the long term would strengthen the economy rather than detract from it by precluding future reclamation costs and health-related damages, he showed that environmental regulation is not some radical erosion of free enterprise that will take jobs away from people. It is a catalyst for better business practices that will ultimately improve the American economy. This perspective that Congressman Udall helped develop has been critical in shaping the way environmentalists combat the scare tactics of antagonistic elements in industry and government.

"Don't let anyone tell you that being for the environment means you have to be against progress," Congressman Udall boldly declared midway through his public address. This single, poignant statement captures the underlying theme of my education and the foundation of my pragmatic ideals—i.e., the careful advancement of an environmental agenda will bolster, not impede, our country's development. Congressman Udall's support of sensible resource conservation, his concern with environmental justice, his defense of active government regulation, and his demand for industry accountability are all central components of modern environmentalism. The current generation of environmentalists owes the philosophical basis of our education, our beliefs, and our career goals to the trailblazing work of people like Congressman Udall. I truly believe that his lifetime of civic service is a model for all of us to follow.

SAMPLE RESPONSES TO SELECT QUESTIONS ON THE UDALL SCHOLARSHIP APPLICATION

B. Your Aspirations

Question# 2. What are your professional aspirations? Indicate in which area(s) of the environment, Native American health care, or tribal public policy you are considering making your career and specify how your academic program and your overall educational plans will assist you in achieving this goal.

When working toward the management of invasive species, the protection of natural resources, the conservation of endangered species, and the improvement of environmental health, important decisions must be made, often with limited knowledge. As T.J. Case (2000) commented in *An Illustrated Guide to Theoretical Ecology*, "…an understanding of these problems and how precisely to achieve our goals is inevitably a quantitative and inferential subject." Finding solutions to these problems in a purely experimental fashion is often financially or physically impossible. However, applying mathematical modeling to problems of biological concern can provide managers with solutions to real problems, especially in conjunction with experimental work.

In my current research at Mythic University, I am using a mathematical model to consider optimal management and monitoring strategies for a particular invasive species, the North American gypsy moth (*Lymantria dispar)*, and I am learning firsthand how to create and use mathematical models to answer ecological questions. Ultimately I plan to expand upon the gypsy moth system and apply the model to other invasive species. Species-specific modifications will have to be made, but a general model will help to develop a framework for applied problems of invasive species management.

As an undergraduate in the Mythic University Honors College, I have the unique opportunity to stay at Mythic University for an additional year in order to complete a graduate program of study through the Integrated Undergraduate/Graduate Program. Continuing at Mythic University for an M.S. in Ecology, in addition to receiving my B.S. in Mathematics, will enable me to bring my ecological and biological understanding up to the level of my mathematical understanding, giving me an equally strong background in both mathematics and ecology. After the completion of my work at Mythic University, I plan to pursue a Ph.D. in Ecology and conduct research in the area of invasion biology and natural resource conservation, using both mathematical models and field experimentation. Beyond my educational goals I plan to teach and conduct research in the area of quantitative ecology at the university level. I will continue to use my mathematical and ecological knowledge to look at applied problems. My work as a quantitative ecologist will be important in finding solutions, especially when large-scale experimental work is too costly or difficult to conduct.

D. Your Programs and Activities

Question# 3. Describe non-course-related research experience, if applicable. Indicate which areas of the environment, tribal public policy or health care your research affects, and the ways in which the experience will assist you in achieving your goals as stated in section B, #2.

Conducting independent graduate-level research on the use of mathematical modeling to answer questions of the management of a particular invasive species, the gypsy moth, has strengthened both my ecological and mathematical backgrounds. The gypsy moth is a widespread forest pest of great economic concern to the United States. In order to better understand the invasion of this pest and obtain life history data, I am working with Dr. Andrew Liebhold of the United States Department of Agriculture (USDA) Northeast Forest Research Station. Working with Dr. Liebhold allows me to have a direct application of research to policy and management decisions, while my work at Mythic University with Dr. Janet Teacher allows me to gain experience in ecological research and modeling applications. The research I am doing, therefore, not only involves pure mathematical modeling and biological experimentation in a laboratory setting, but also incorporates the practical aspects of applying research to management decisions.

Question# 4. Describe a leadership experience in which you made a difference on campus or in your community.

In March of 20xx, Mythic University will host the Northeast Ecology and Evolution Conference (NEEC), an annual event for post-docs, graduate students, and advanced undergraduate students. The 20xx conference will include two days of talks, a poster session, and evening receptions and lectures. I am not only presenting a poster for NEEC, but also, since the conference is entirely student-run, I have taken on membership in multiple committees and assisted in the overall development of the upcoming conference as a part of the Ecology Graduate Student Organization. Working on the events for the first night of the conference through the Registration and Opening Events Committee, I secured guest speakers and panelists to speak about the future of ecology and evolution and the different career opportunities for up-and-coming ecologists and biologists. Additionally, I am working with the Facilities and Logistics Committee to reserve room space for speaker sessions and recruit volunteers to monitor and run the six different sessions throughout the weekend. Finally, I have helped in the promotion of the event by sharing information with other undergraduate students across the university who are involved in the sciences.

Not only participating in, but working toward the overall development of NEEC has given me leadership and teamwork experience while also affording me the opportunity to meet with graduate students and professionals in my field, helping to build a network for my future work as an ecologist.

Question #5. Describe a specific activity or experience that has been important in clarifying or strengthening your commitment to the environment, Native American health care, or tribal public policy.

Environmental Justice in South Africa, Mythic University, Jan. 20xx-July 20xx
This spring and summer I am taking a course entitled "Environmental Justice in South Africa." The course culminates in a three-week trip to South Africa devoted to researching and implementing projects in South Africa that seek to improve environmental and living conditions in a post-apartheid nation. Through coursework and communications with students and professors in Cape Town, South Africa, I am learning about the environmental outcomes of war and land division, while considering the societal and economic repercussions. The course allows me to not only conduct scientific research but also to make recommendations and assist with the implementation of environmental management decisions. Even thus far, my limited understanding of environmental justice in South Africa has given me a more global perspective on environmental issues and has strengthened my commitment to the environment.

Florida Keys Sailing, Hurricane Island Outward Bound School, March 20xx
Sailing on an open sprit-rigged ketch through the pristine environment of the Florida Keys solidified my desire to commit to and preserve the environment. In an ordinary week, five days and four nights seem trivial, but when spent living, learning, and playing on an open sailing ship in the Gulf of Mexico, five days turned into 120 life-changing hours. The passion and fascination that I developed from working in outdoor environmental education and summer camping turned into a desire to create change and commit to working for the environment. While I lived in rather close quarters with my 11 other fellow students and instructors on the boat, we were able to discuss important issues of environmental concern while witnessing firsthand the problems that we were discussing, including water pollution from commercial and recreational traffic and coral reef damage. Even the back country of the Florida Keys is touched by human influences and it was made evident to me that the environment needs to be a higher priority in the United States and internationally. Living simply, without setting foot on land or access to any of the typical comforts—that suddenly seemed like luxuries—gave me a deeper appreciation and respect for the environment along with a desire to create change.

Question# 6. Describe briefly any public service or community activities associated with your interests in the environment, Native American health care, or tribal public policy in which you regularly participate. Explain the duration, degree, and significance of your involvement.

Science and Mathematics Tutoring at Mythic University: Through the mathematics department I tutored a group of first- and second-year undergraduate students in the bottom 10% of their calculus classes. Through an NCAA grant I also tutored student athletes in introductory mathematics courses. The students that I taught were all students studying science—mainly biology majors—who needed extra assistance to get through their mathematics requirements. Tutoring these students helped me play a part in reducing attrition from the sciences by these students.

Educational Programming at the National Aviary in Pittsburgh: I spent 5-10 hours a week during high school volunteering my time as an intern and educational programmer. Throughout the internship I handled birds, gave tours of the Aviary, and facilitated educational outreach programs for local schools in addition to the visitors at the Aviary.

Environmental Education in the Classroom: Throughout my senior year of high school, I wrote lesson plans and was invited to be a guest teacher for first grade classrooms in one of the local elementary schools. One of the lessons I designed taught the first graders about the different layers of the rainforest, and using the Dr. Seuss book, *The Lorax*, conveyed the importance of preserving natural resources. At the conclusion of the school year, I trained ten high school freshmen to teach a group lesson on birds, and they ran several small workshops with the first graders.

Environmental Education in the Out-of-Doors: Summer camping—although a paid job— is certainly all-consuming. I spent six weeks leading young children as a cabin counselor and sailing director for a camp in the Adirondack Mountains. Being able to share my knowledge of ecology and impart a "Leave No Trace" style of life on young children in such a pristine wilderness setting is a small but important step in the fight for the preservation of and commitment to the environment.

Question# 7. What additional information (not already addressed in the application) do you wish to share with the Udall Scholarship review committee?

I was raised by two strong women—my mother and my grandmother. Three generations of women living under one roof provided me with a unique experience while growing up. My mother was the first woman in my family to pursue higher education and continued her pursuit even after having a child. As I was growing up I watched her finish her nursing degree at Oakland University and begin a career in Neonatal Nursing. My interest in the sciences and the environment most definitely stemmed initially from my mother's interest and passion for the subject. While my mother was attending classes and studying, my grandmother was my primary caregiver and she too encouraged my exploration and growth. Throughout my life, my mother and grandmother have continued to be my source of inspiration and encouragement.

SAMPLE UDALL SCHOLARSHIP ESSAY

E. Essay

In 800 words or less, discuss a significant public speech, legislative act, or public policy statement by Congressman Udall and its impact on your field of study, interests, and career goals.

Benjamin Franklin aptly stated, "When the well is dry, we know the worth of water." Morris K. Udall spent a significant part of his early career fighting for the passage of The Central Arizona Project (CAP) legislation, aimed at diverting water from the Colorado River Basin to the deserts of Arizona. The CAP included an aqueduct from the Colorado River to Phoenix and elsewhere in Arizona, in addition to plans to augment the river to prevent predicted water shortages. Although Udall steadfastly defended the CAP, he later regretted the project and the environmental and societal damage it caused.

Since 1910, Arizona had recognized its need for more water, yet at the time of the CAP it was nearly 1968, and Udall picked up his state's long struggle. He knew that Arizona needed water, and in the interest of his constituents, he saw the CAP as the solution. In his 1967 speech, "Countdown on the Colorado," given at the Town Hall in Los Angeles, CA, Udall spoke to many California residents who were against the CAP because it diverted water from their state. He likened the fight for water to a Judgment Day not only for Arizona, but for the other states of the Colorado River Basin, including California.

Given the history of Arizona and its struggle to gain access to new water sources, Udall put all of his energy behind the CAP and the construction of dams in the Colorado River Basin. Udall and other members of Congress noticed that the legislation, as it progressed through Congress, contributed to the unification of environmentalists, resulting in one of the largest letter writing campaigns in history (Carson and Johnson 2001). However, once the CAP legislation made it through Congress and was passed, it was delayed multiple times due to funding and environmental controversies. Amidst these difficulties, Udall persisted and the project was completed in 1993. However, water users were left to pay off federal loans in the amount of $4.4 billion. Udall soon realized that water from the CAP was serving urban centers instead of the outlying farming areas where it was needed most. Doubting the worth of the project, Udall said:

> By the time we finally got it passed, the environmental movement had arrived. Now what I thought would be the centerpiece of my career looks very dubious— to me and a lot of other people (Carson and Johnson 2001).

Looking back on his dedication to the CAP, Udall did what he thought was best for his constituents, but was also able to reflect intelligently on the final outcome of the project.

Like Udall, policy makers and managers are faced with situations in which decisions must be made in the face of uncertainty. My work in mathematical modeling is aimed at helping to improve our ability to make decisions when limited by uncertainty, time, and money. Specifically, I will be working this summer to examine the Lesotho Highlands Water Project (LHWP) and the issue of water distribution in South Africa, posing questions fundamentally similar to those faced by Udall in Arizona. The LHWP began in 1986 with the signing of the Lesotho Highlands Water Project Treaty and was meant to divert rainwater to urban areas of South Africa through a series of dams. So far, the LHWP has cost $8 billion, and is described as a "costly, corrupt, poorly designed, badly implemented, economically damaging, ecologically disastrous, and distributionally regressive mega-project" (Bond 2002).

With the understanding that there will nearly always be some level of uncertainty in decision making, I plan to examine management options using mathematical modeling and field work during my trip to South Africa to weigh viable options to the problem of water distribution. Considerations must be made not only from an environmental standpoint, but also from a societal point-of-view, as Udall very-well knew. As was the case for Arizona farming areas, water is still widely unavailable to the poor, urban households of South Africa because of increasing costs and excessive 'luxury' consumption by much of the middle- and upper-class households (Bond 2002).

The problem of water limitation in Arizona needed to be solved, and Udall worked for the most viable option available—the CAP. Eventually, Udall recognized that the CAP was not effective and worked toward repairing environmental and societal damages caused by the project. In South Africa, the problem is again water distribution and the implemented solution has proven, to an extent, unsuccessful. My goal, as an ecologist and mathematician, is to investigate solutions to the question of water distribution in South Africa and to apply what I learn to other questions of environmental management.

References:

Bond, P. 2002. "A Political Economy of Dam Building and Household Water Supply in Lesotho and South Africa." 223-269. In *Environmental Justice in South Africa.* ed McDonald, D.A. Ohio University Press: Athens, OH. 341.

Carson, D.W. and J.W. Johnson. 2001. *Mo: The Life & Times of Morris K. Udall.* University of Arizona Press: Tucson, AZ. 331.

Udall, M.K. "Countdown on the Colorado." 19 Dec 1967. Town Hall: Los Angeles, CA. Reprint of speech in Congressman's Report, 15 Jan 1968. Vol. VII, No.1. http://dizzy.library.arizona.edu/branches/spc/udall/countdown.pdf.

The National Science Foundation Graduate Research Fellowship

The National Science Foundation (NSF) awards fellowships for graduate study in science, mathematics, and engineering to candidates who are expected to contribute significantly to research, teaching, and industrial applications. Fellowships support students for one year or several, and the stipend is generous (in 2004 each fellow received $30,000 for a 12-month tenure), with an additional cost-of-education allowance granted to the fellowship institution ($10,500 in 2004). Obviously these awards are highly competitive, and selection panels choose students who will have a great impact on their fields and bring further reputation to their institutions. The NSF program also includes special awards for women in engineering and computer and information science. Individuals can apply during their senior year of college as well as during graduate school.

The NSF Fellowship Selection Criteria

NSF applications are reviewed by discipline-specific panels of mathematicians, scientists, professors, and engineers. Reviewers attend specifically to two criteria:

- *intellectual merit*, including the strength of the candidate's academic record, the research plan and previous research, and ability to communicate and interpret research findings;
- *broader impacts*, reflecting the review panel's desire to encourage diversity and benefit society through NSF awards.

Once the review panel makes its selections, NSF staff further review the fellowship recommendations, considering additional criteria such as geographic region, discipline, and other policy-specific selection factors.

Answering the NSF Application Essay Questions

The NSF application includes almost 20 questions, four of which must be answered in the form of extensive essays. Essays must be uploaded online through a process called FastLane, with all essays typed in no smaller than a 10-point font size and strict adherence to the dictated page limits.

For the essay questions requiring full narrative responses, applicants must carefully determine the substance of the question and frame responses so that the answers complement each other rather than result in needless redundancy. In this regard, it is useful to think of these questions in the context of just one or two words (e.g., personal motivation, scientific commitment, previous research, proposed research), and frame your answers accordingly. Extrapolate from the lengthy wording of the questions to generate ideas for examples, keeping in mind the fundamental context of the question and sticking to that context.

Evaluation of Two Sample Sets of NSF Application Essays

The two sample responses to NSF application questions provided in the following pages make for an excellent study in contrast. Also noteworthy: despite the great differences in these two approaches, both students did indeed receive an NSF.

The first sample essays are grounded completely in narrative and do not include any figures, tables, or references. The style is sometimes highly informal, to the point of what some might call a slightly hubristic tone, the use of an exclamation point (!), and even an admittance by the candidate that he has not yet decided on a particular graduate program. Nevertheless, if you read closely you realize that the informality is mostly placed within context of the personal motivation and scientific commitment discussions, while the discussions of previous research and proposed research are scientific and concerned with solving relevant problems related to microelectricalmechanical systems (MEMS). The research hypothesis and applications are also spelled out directly. Thus, we obtain a strong sense of the person (and personality) of this candidate, and we gain confidence in his abilities as a researcher.

In the second sample essays, discussions of previous and proposed research resemble formal literature reviews, each one citing numerous references from refereed journals and presenting figures generated by the author. The applications of the research, which has implications for rebuilding cartilage tissue and relieving musculoskeletal pain, are straightforward and beneficial to society. Meanwhile, we also get a sense of this writer's personal character, as she cites examples of tutoring other students and her role as captain of a women's soccer team sponsored by the Biomedical Engineering Society. In short, we meet both the scientist and the humanist—equal concerns for the NSF selectors.

> To apply for the NSF Graduate Research Fellowship program, begin the process at
> https://www.fastlane.nsf.gov/fastlane.jsp

SAMPLE RESPONSES TO SELECT QUESTIONS ON THE NSF GRADUATE RESEARCH FELLOWSHIP APPLICATION

Question Summary: Describe any personal, professional, or educational experiences or situations that have contributed to your desire to pursue advanced study in science, mathematics, or engineering.

Simply put, learning for the sake of understanding the world better is what drives my intellectual pursuits. This desire to know pervades my daily life—too much so according to some. However, by this point in my life, I have come to realize and accept that many people find my outlook on learning and life somewhat odd. Still, learning is my passion, and through this "odd" view of the world I have come to recognize an important pattern in the educational process. By fervently studying one subject area you begin to appreciate its enormity. Once reaching this appreciation, you become capable of selecting an appealing subset of that area to further study. Yet this subset expands beyond any hope of total understanding, forcing you to choose an even more specific area and thus continuing the cycle. Paramount to understanding how this cycle relates to my educational goals is to realize that my passion for learning increases (exponentially so) as I choose more and more specific fields to study. But perhaps I have gotten ahead of myself and should start from the beginning: high school.

In high school I took all of the advanced science and math courses available. With this expansive background, I realized that I enjoyed science and wanted to study it further but appreciated the need to find a specific focus. Hence, when I stumbled upon materials science, I recognized it as an amalgamation of the scientific areas I most enjoyed studying. Without my broad scientific background, though, I would not have been able to make this decision as definitively. This appreciation for having a well-rounded knowledge of a field has remained with me during my undergraduate studies. For example, although I have already chosen to focus on electronic/photonic materials, I have opted to take additional courses, which explore polymers, glasses, and refractories. These classes benefit me in two ways. First, they expand my knowledge base. Second, by exposing me to such topics as conducting polymers and glass-ceramic electronic packages, these classes diversify my appreciation for electronic/photonic materials. Moreover, in contrast to my general fondness for high school science classes, studying materials science generates a fervor for learning in me that I never thought possible.

As my passion for materials science grows, I realize that it is time once more to refine and focus my learning objectives. To some extent, this change will be a difficult one because I honestly love the entire field of materials science. However, through my various work experiences, I have come to realize that there exists yet another level of learning in which you act as both student and teacher. At this level you can become so engrossed in learning that you feel a sense of ownership for the work. Such learning has shown me education's ultimate satisfaction. Such learning is called research.

Unfortunately, my previous exposures to research have only provided me partial fulfillment. With just a single summer to complete a research project, the feeling of ownership only begins to coalesce near the end of the appointment. In fact, I often feel a void within myself when I am forced to leave the project incomplete. To that end, I have been known to work extra hours, even weekends, just to satisfy my own needs of completeness in my research. This is why I have chosen to pursue graduate school. In graduate school I will be able to continue my passion for learning in a research-oriented environment. Hence, it will become possible to expand that feeling of ownership for a project beyond any of my previous experiences. Simultaneously, I will be creating my own learning—learning that I genuinely hope will benefit the rest of society.

Question Summary: Describe your experiences in the following or describe how you would address the following in your professional career: integrating research and education, advancing diversity in science, enhancing scientific and technical understanding, and otherwise benefiting society.

As an undergraduate I have been very involved with student organizations in both my college and department. I have been a member of the Mythic University Student Council and the student branch of the American Ceramics Society (ACerS). Furthermore, I have held various positions in these organizations ranging from vice president to social chair. Thus, I consider myself quite active in the professional, educational, and social proceedings that affect me most, and I plan to continue my involvement after graduation. More relevant, though, is my motivation for becoming involved in these specific groups.

Six years ago, when I witnessed a demonstration of shape-memory alloys at an engineering convention, I became enticed to enter the field of materials science. Since that time, I have wanted to educate others about the field in the hopes of also captivating their interests. Discussing materials science with others is one of my favorite hobbies, and I have been pursuing this mission since that fateful day six years ago. Even from conversations with friends during my meagerly informed high school days, I was able to influence one peer to pursue a degree in materials science and another to pick up a minor in polymers. (I guess pure excitement alone can be sufficiently persuasive at times.) However, in college I wanted to extend this personal campaign even further, and therefore chose to join groups that allowed me the opportunity to communicate with prospective students and undecided undergraduates.

During my undergraduate career, I have been involved with every recruiting opportunity made available to me. At these events, my goal has never been to simply coax these students to come to Mythic University, but instead to inform them of what a fantastic career choice materials science and engineering can be. In the early spring, I am awake several hours before dawn to prepare decorations and displays for the Mythic University's annual open house, which is organized by the student council. Although this deprives me of several hours of sleep (on a Saturday even!), I still manage to exude excitement when I explain to prospective students all the wonderful "stuff" that materials scientists get to explore. Similarly, as a part of ACerS, I participated in a materials science departmental tour for high schoolers visiting Mythic University for the annual Junior Science and Humanities Symposium. This activity involved leading discussions on materials-related exhibits set up throughout the department. A third activity that I continually participate in is the Mythic University's annual phone-a-thon. This involves calling all prospective students accepted to the college for the upcoming year. I found this experience so rewarding that last year I took over as chair of the event. Additionally, I have also participated in various other engineering open houses and outreach programs, acting as a representative of the materials science department.

Recently I met up with a student who thanked me for persistently leading her and her parents to the materials science exhibits at the spring open house. That experience made her select materials science as her field of study. Like many others, she had never heard of materials science until that day but was immediately drawn to all of the opportunities it offered. This unexplainable magnetism that materials science can induce drives me to further educate others and compels me to extend my outreach efforts.
In the future, I would like to develop a short interactive lecture that could be presented in high school chemistry or physics classrooms and would relate concepts these students already know to the field of materials science. This would expose the students to the field, show them its similarities and applications to subjects they are already familiar with, and hopefully inspire a few to pursue a degree in materials science. It is my hope that student branches of materials-related professional organizations (like ACerS) could act as the distributors for such classes. Whether such a project would then lead to even more involved endeavors like websites or textbooks is unclear, but no matter where my career takes me, I will continue informing others about the wonders of materials science.

Question Summary: In a clear, concise, and original statement, describe research topics you may pursue while on fellowship tenure, and include how you became interested in these topics. Your statement should reflect your own thinking and work, demonstrate your understanding of research principles necessary to pursue these interests, and explain the relationship to your previous research, if any. Present your plan with a clear hypothesis or questions to be asked by the research. If you have not yet formulated a plan of research, your statement should include a description of one question that interests you and an analysis of how you think the question may best be answered.

As early as grade school, I was intrigued by the fact that energy can transform between multiple forms. This notion that heat, light, motion, and electricity are all forms of the same abstract quantity known as energy continues to fascinate me even today. Therefore, it should be of little surprise that as a materials scientist, I am most intrigued by the properties of materials that convert energy from one form to another. These materials are valuable because certain forms of energy are often more useful than others. Hence, numerous practical devices rely on these principles, including thermocouples, solar cells, and light-emitting diodes. However, of greatest interest to me are ferroelectric/piezoelectric materials that are capable of transforming electrical energy into mechanical motion.

One of the most innovative uses of piezoelectrics in recent years is as a component of microelectromechanical systems (MEMS). Piezoelectric materials truly represent a means for coupling electronics with mechanical motion and so seem destined for integration into MEMS technology. The material of most interest for these applications is the solid solution, ferroelectric lead zirconate titanate (PZT).

At room temperature, PZT is equilibrated as a tetragonal or rhombohedral perovksite phase depending on the composition. The piezoelectric response of this phase can be divided into two components: the intrinsic and extrinsic contributions. The intrinsic contribution is simply the result of the B-site cation shifted along the c-axis with respect to the oxygen sub-lattice. Although slightly more complex, the extrinsic contribution is typically attributed to domain wall movement between adjacent domains with non-$180°$ orientations. Each of these factors contribute about 50% to the piezoelectric response of bulk PZT.

However, PZT thin films show a significant decline in piezoelectric response. In the literature, this unfortunate outcome is often attributed to mechanical constraints placed on the film, which hinder the extrinsic contribution. To appreciate the mechanisms for this constraint, consider the Si-PZT system. Silicon has a considerably lower thermal expansion coefficient than PZT. Hence, upon cooling a crystallized PZT film, tensile stresses will arise in the PZT layer. Because crystallization is performed well above the Curie temperature, PZT will be in the non-ferroelectric cubic phase. However, as the film is cooled below the Curie temperature, the tensile stresses present will energetically favor tetragonal phases with the c-axis parallel to the plane of the film. Therefore, very few non-$180°$ domain walls will develop, and the extrinsic contribution will be vastly diminished. Thus, silicon-based MEMS must work around this limitation when incorporating PZT into the device.

However, during my recent senior thesis work, I have become fascinated with the possibilities of ceramic microsystems. Similar to how MEMS evolved from silicon processing technology, ceramic microsystems are spawning from multilayer ceramic technology, which was originally developed for electronic packaging and multilayer capacitors. Today, this technology is becoming a viable way for constructing three-dimensional systems on the micro-scale for applications such as microfluidics and micro-combustion. These ceramic microsystems offer many advantages over silicon MEMS such as parallel processing, ease in packaging, and lower equipment costs. More relevant, though, is the closer match in thermal expansions between these ceramic substrates and PZT in comparison to the match between silicon and PZT. Thus, I propose a project that would focus on determining the piezoelectric capabilities of thin film PZT on multilayer ceramic substrates.

The first step in such a process would be to fabricate these PZT films on electroded ceramic substrates. I am intimately familiar with this topic since it is the crux of my current undergraduate thesis. Therefore, I confidently anticipate that these films will be fabricated using sol-gel techniques. Once this process is reasonably optimized, uniform test samples will need to be prepared. A set of control samples with silicon substrates should also be prepared. Next, electrical tests will need to be performed to determine the extent of intrinsic and extrinsic contributions to the piezoelectric effect and dielectric constant. Typically, this information is extracted from one of two methods. The first involves making measurements as a function of increasing frequency. At high frequencies, the extrinsic contribution is eliminated and the pure intrinsic contribution can be determined. However, this technique is only applicable for dielectric measurements. To determine the contributions to the piezoelectric response, measurements must be made as a function of temperature. At temperatures near absolute zero, the thermally activated extrinsic component is effectively nullified and again the intrinsic component can be determined. However, both of these techniques have their shortcomings, and I will need to take these issues into consideration while developing these experiments.

Furthermore, piezoelectric measurements on thin films are complicated at best. The same mechanical constraints imposed by the substrate that limit the extrinsic response are also responsible for limiting the indirect piezoelectric response. Often a more appropriate approach is to derive the piezoelectric coefficient from the direct response. This measurement involves applying stress to the film and monitoring the charge build-up. The ferroelectric group at Mythic University has been a world leader in developing techniques to make such measurements, and this fact has contributed to my serious consideration of continuing at this institution for my advanced degree.

In summary, the basic hypothesis for this work is that PZT thin films with thermal expansion matched ceramic substrates will have a higher extrinsic contribution to piezoelectric and dielectric properties than films on substrates with lesser thermal expansion matches, such as silicon. If this hypothesis is found to be valid, then PZT films on ceramic substrates should show stronger piezoelectric responses, assuming all other film properties (such as structure, thickness, and composition) are equal. Consequently, such films would be extremely useful in advancing ceramic MEMS technology.

Apparatuses such as pumps for microfluidics and valves for microcombustion chambers could all be possible consequences of such technology. In addition, this research would lead to a better scientific understanding of the intrinsic and extrinsic contributions to ferroelectric properties.

As a final note, let me briefly comment on my selection for possible graduate school institutions. Clearly, Mythic University is a leader in ferroelectric materials science, and a transition into its graduate program would be nearly seamless for me. Thus, I could promptly begin my research and have the opportunity to work with faculty at the top of their field. On the other hand, I realize the professional advantages of changing environments, and as a result, I am also seriously considering other institutions. My two major criteria for evaluating institutions are my own interests in the research opportunities available and the facilities that these institutions offer.

Question Summary: Describe any scientific research activities in which you have participated, such as experience in undergraduate research programs, or research experience gained through summer or part-time employment or in work-study programs, or other research activities, either academic or job-related. Explain the purpose of the research and your specific role in the research, including the extent to which you worked independently and/or as part of a team, and what you learned from your research. In your statement, distinguish between undergraduate and graduate research experience. If you have no direct research experience, describe any activities that you believe have prepared you to undertake research.

During my short scientific career, I have conscientiously strived to gain as much research experience as possible. In fact, I began my first research project in materials science while still in high school. During the summer of 20xx, I worked at a local failure analysis company, MATCO Incorporated. For my project, I performed some basic studies on the oxidation of titanium and examined how different processing parameters affected the resulting color change. With the close of the summer, I submitted a report based on my findings and outside research. Admittedly, the project was rather mundane, and in fact, at the time I failed to grasp all of the underlying science involved. Yet, my work at MATCO gave me valuable experience in a laboratory environment, as well as exposed me to the daily routine of a materials science engineer. Most importantly, though, this experience solidified my desire to study materials science and seeded the notion to follow a research-oriented career path.

During my undergraduate career, I quickly developed an exact yet flexible plan on how I intended to spend my summers. My goal was to acquire three internships, one for each summer, and have these internships cover the three major working environments in which I could possibly find myself once I graduated: industry, academia, and government. I can happily say that I have accomplished this goal.

I spent my first summer in a research experience for undergraduates (REU) program at Mythic University. In this program I worked in a biomaterials laboratory learning how to manipulate the surface wettability of glass substrates. My objective was to create radially symmetric gradients of wettability. To accomplish this task I diffused hydrocarbon molecules with silane functional groups through a gel that was in contact with the glass surface. These molecules would then "silanate" the surface creating a region of lower wettability. Since the silane was diffused from a central location, the amount of "silanation" decreased radially from this point, hence forming a wettability gradient. To analyze my gradients, I used a Wilhelmy balance. I also developed a fairly basic, although useful, mathematical model (based on wetting forces) that helped to explain the data I collected from the Wilhelmy balance. Perhaps my most ingenious accomplishment, though, was analyzing the silanated glass substrates with optical microscopy while cooling them on a piece of ice. Cooling the glass samples forced water to condense on the surface. These condensed water droplets would bead in different shapes and sizes depending on the surface characteristics, hence allowing me to "see" my wettability gradients. This tool, which I discovered on my own, proved invaluable in providing me with both qualitative and semi-quantitative data. Overall, this research experience was outstanding because although the initial idea was my mentor's, I was left to independently carry out the research. By the end of the summer, I had a much better grasp on the scientific process and the importance of creating a research plan and modifying it when necessary.

I spent my second summer working at Carpenter Technologies, a specialty steel manufacturer. This was my introduction to working in industry. Although the work I did at Carpenter did not necessarily follow a purist's view of the scientific process, it did allow me to hone my skills in sample preparation, optical microscopy, and hardness testing. However, more importantly, this internship exposed me to working in a team environment and interfacing with multiple people to solve problems. In fact, at one point I traveled with my mentor to a hot rolling conversion facility outside the company to discuss problems occurring with Carpenter billets that they had been hot rolling. Also on that trip, we visited with a slitting facility to discuss possible methods of reducing the amount of scrap. These experiences and many others became invaluable lessons in how to communicate ideas and network with technical and non-technical personnel in order to achieve a desired goal. Hence, the communication tools that I gained from my work at Carpenter will better allow me to interface with professors, technicians, and other graduate students once I enter graduate school. Additionally, I have learned that working in a group can often be the wisest path for solving a problem.

However, my internship this previous summer at Oak Ridge National Laboratory (ORNL) proved to be the most rewarding and enjoyable of the three. This extremely positive experience was certainly the result of being able to synthesize my past experiences and use these lessons to perform research that was both efficient and valuable. Essentially, my project entailed coating metallic and ceramic components using pack cementation and then evaluating the effects microwave heating had on the process. My laboratory duties included preparing the samples and powder pack, operating the furnaces, mounting and polishing samples, and performing the necessary characterization. The important characterization tools I used were optical microscopy, scanning electron microscopy, energy-dispersive x-ray analysis, x-ray diffraction, and hardness testing. Furthermore, I performed nearly all of the data analysis on my own and reported my conclusions in both a poster and a technical paper. During the three months I spent at ORNL, I was the sole researcher on this project and was allowed to direct my own course of research.

Of course, initially I did receive training on the equipment, but even during these sessions I was treated as an intellectual equal who already understood the underlying scientific concepts of each technique. In fact, this was the treatment I received during my entire stay at ORNL. Because of this, I gained more confidence in my "textbook education" and in my ability to apply this knowledge. For the first time, I felt like a capable and valuable researcher. Still, I did acquire many knew skills that will benefit my future research endeavors. The two most vital skills were maintaining a lab notebook and analyzing collected data. My ability to keep a complete and well-organized lab notebook improved over the summer and was aided by suggestions from my mentors. Now, I feel much more comfortable with maintaining a scientific record of my work.

Currently, I am performing research at Mythic University's Materials Research Laboratory as part of my senior thesis project. In this project, I collaborate with one of the faculty members and present my results in a thesis that will be archived in the library. My specific project involves depositing lead zirconate titanate films with liquid source misted chemical deposition on ceramic substrates similar to those used in electronic packaging. In the process, I will also be learning how to operate sputtering equipment and how to measure dielectric and piezoelectric properties of thin films. This work will certainly serve to further my research experience as well as teach me how to organize a literature review and prepare a thesis. I look forward to the challenges that this project presents as well as the opportunities for further maturation as a practicing scientist.

SAMPLE RESPONSES TO SELECT QUESTIONS ON THE NSF GRADUATE RESEARCH FELLOWSHIP APPLICATION

Question Summary: Describe any personal, professional, or educational experiences or situations that have contributed to your desire to pursue advanced study in science, mathematics, or engineering.

Although math and science have been my favorite subjects since elementary school, with math games such as "Around the World" and "24" piquing my interest, it was not until high school that I decided upon engineering as my future career. In tenth grade, I began to study C++ and computer programming and learned to love the feeling of accomplishment that came with the solution of a difficult problem. In eleventh and twelfth grades, I participated in the American Computer Science League competitions with a team of two other students. Both years, our team earned a trip to the National All-Star competition where we placed in the top ten, and I was awarded for my individual performance. Success in this contest and in other traditionally male-dominated classes such as calculus, chemistry, and physics led me to believe that I could succeed in the field of engineering.

Another long-standing desire of mine has been to help others. From a young age, I have volunteered with different organizations in a range of capacities. In particular, since elementary school, I have enjoyed tutoring fellow students; helping a peer to understand a difficult concept is an extremely rewarding experience. Because of this, I searched for a way to integrate mentoring, math, and science into a career. I explored becoming a doctor or a teacher, but I found neither satisfactorily combined my academic and personal interests.

An event in my junior year of high school solved this enigma. That year, I toured the Bioengineering Department at the Mythic Medical Center. While there, I realized what I wanted to do with my life: become a bioengineering professor at a major research university, concentrating in the area of tissue engineering. This career path appears to be the perfect combination: I can apply my research to improve health care, while at the same time, mentoring and instructing future scientists and engineers.

Since then, I have pursued my career choice by becoming actively involved in biomedical research, beginning in my sophomore year. I find research challenging, and I enjoy the sense of accomplishment when a difficult problem is solved, yielding new knowledge that contributes to the betterment of society. Finally, I greatly enjoy working in the academic atmosphere that embraces the sharing of this new knowledge.

My academic success in college and my involvement with science-related extracurricular activities have encouraged me to persist in my goal of earning a Ph.D. in bioengineering. I am in the top 0.5% of my class and, in the last year, have been awarded the Barry M. Goldwater and the Astronaut Scholarship Foundation Scholarships. I have also helped to found an undergraduate chapter of the Biomedical Engineering Society (BMES) at Mythic University and have served as webmaster for the club. Through this club, I have had the opportunity to participate in outreach to high school students. Finally, I have confirmed my desire to become a professor by serving as a mentor to incoming freshmen in the Mythic University Honors College.

All of these factors have led me to believe that a career in academic research will best match my passions.

Question Summary: Describe your experiences in the following or describe how you would address the following in your professional career: integrating research and education, advancing diversity in science, enhancing scientific and technical understanding, and otherwise benefiting society.

"A hundred years from now it will not matter what my bank account was, the sort of house I lived in, or the kind of car I drove. But the world may be different because I was important in the life of a [child]."
—Forest Witcraft, Boy Scouts of America

My belief in the veracity of the statement by Witcraft is one of the reasons I have decided to become a research professor. I believe that this career will allow me to share my fervor for science and discovery with future generations, especially young women. From a young age, and continuing throughout my college career, I have tried to embody this principle and to volunteer in other capacities in order to improve the community around me.

One of the ways in which I have been able to share my field of bioengineering with others has been through the Biomedical Engineering Society (BMES). Last year, I worked with Prof. John Teacher and a few of my peers to co-found an undergraduate chapter of BMES at Mythic University. The purpose of this club, according to the BMES, is to "promote the increase of biomedical engineering knowledge and its utilization." Our chapter seeks to fulfill this mission by bringing together undergraduate and graduate students and supporting activities such as mentoring, career information sessions, and outside speakers. As part of our outreach, I had the opportunity to return to my high school over spring break to speak to science classes about biomedical engineering and to share some of my experiences of college life. I have also assisted the BMES at the annual Engineering Open House, which is an event geared to helping high school seniors learn more about the different engineering disciplines, hopefully encouraging them to consider engineering as a career. In addition, I have served as the captain of a BMES-sponsored intramural women's soccer team. Team sports depend upon each player cooperating and putting forth 100% effort toward a common goal, which directly translates to the demands of a research environment. This team not only encouraged bioengineers to interact outside of classes, but it also gave me the opportunity to promote communication between science and non-science majors, since I actively invited non-bioengineers to join the team.

Since beginning my honors thesis research as a sophomore, I have had many opportunities to share the knowledge I have gained by presenting my results in various settings. These have included a publication ("Procoagulant Stimulus Processing by the Intrinsic Pathway of Blood Plasma Coagulation," in *Biomaterials*) and several poster presentations among members of my field. I also participated in a poster presentation that included entries from all undergraduate majors. This presentation gave me the chance to explain my work to people from non-science backgrounds, challenging me to present technical details in a way that is meaningful to a wide variety of viewers.

I have also positively impacted the lives of incoming freshmen by serving as a mentor for the Mythic University Honors College students. I have helped these freshmen to make a smooth transition from high school to college by offering advice on ways to succeed in and out of the classroom and also by lending an ear to whatever troubles they may be experiencing. One of my former mentees recently informed me that I inspired her to succeed in her engineering studies despite it being a traditionally male-dominated field. She also gained interest in working towards the Goldwater Scholarship as a result of my award last year.

Finally, I seek to serve the rest of the surrounding community through my participation in Habitat for Humanity. Our chapter helps to raise money to build houses for people who would not ordinarily be able to afford them by performing odd jobs for people in the community, asking for donations from local people and businesses, and by holding an annual "House Walk," in which each walker is sponsored by family, friends, and members of Mythic University community.

Throughout my career, I hope to continue my commitment to public service by serving as a mentor to young women, volunteering for summer science enrichment programs, and performing other acts of community service such as participating in the Adopt-a-Highway program. In this way, I can share with others the blessings that have been given to me throughout my life.

Introduction and Relevance: Musculoskeletal pain was the most cited reason for visiting a physician in the year 2000.[1] Current orthopedic repairs utilize artificial materials such as ceramics, metals, and polymers, which cannot replicate the function of natural tissue and do not fully integrate with the body. Tissue engineering seeks to cultivate tissues that are physiologically similar to native tissue to solve these problems. Impeding the realization of these complex structures is the failure to successfully integrate cells, scaffolds, and signaling. My goal is to create a scaffold that will facilitate incorporation of implanted cells, growth factors, and extracellular matrix proteins in order to rebuild and repair cartilage tissue in joints.

Molecular self-assembly, or building from the "bottom-up," is increasingly being recognized as the next step in the development of novel biomaterials. In particular, researchers have begun investigating the utility of self-assembling polymers and peptides in the field of tissue engineering. In the development of tissue-engineered scaffolds, peptides have several advantages over polymers, including versatility in composition, chemical properties, and morphology. For example, polymer scaffolds typically only include one or two different biological ligands on their surfaces because it is difficult to control the concentration and arrangement of these ligands. Peptides offer the ability to easily synthesize different sequences with different properties that can then be combined to form self-assembled scaffolds. Peptides can also be designed to form gel structures under physiologic conditions.

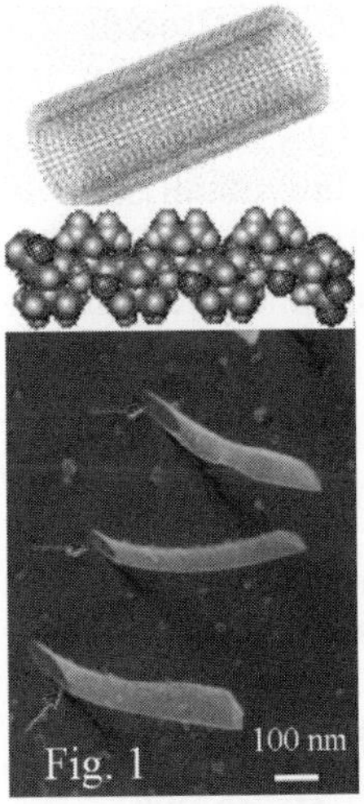

Fig. 1   100 nm

Ground-breaking studies by Zhang et al.[2] demonstrated that chondrocyte proliferation can be supported by self-assembling peptides made of alternating hydrophobic and hydrophilic residues that do not elicit an immune response. However, these peptides have been shown to only assemble into the beta-sheet type nanofibril, the kind typically seen in the amyloid fibrils of Alzheimer's disease. This group has also recently developed surfactant peptides that self-assemble to form nanotube structures as seen in Fig. 1.[3] These surfactant peptides have the advantage of forming well-defined hydrogel structures while remaining relatively easy to modify, which may lead to the ability to incorporate cell-binding sequences and other biomolecular sites on their surfaces. Stupp et al.[4] have recently reported on the construction of scaffolds made of self-assembling amphiphile peptides that contain a sequence promoting neurite growth. These scaffolds were seeded with neural progenitor cells and successfully induced neuron differentiation *in vitro*. Stupp et al. have also shown that the scaffold can self-assemble when a peptide solution is injected into tissue.

Background and Research Objective: I have focused my undergraduate degree of Bioengineering on biomaterials by choosing a concentration in materials science and by performing my honors thesis research in a biomaterials laboratory. I intend to build upon this foundation by pursuing my Ph.D. in Biomedical Engineering under the guidance of Dr. Phillip Messersmith at Northwestern University. Northwestern University is a leader in the nanotechnology field and recently expanded its facilities with the addition of the Robert H. Lurie Medical Research Building. This building is the new home of the Institute for BioNanotechnology in Medicine (IBNAM), which performs research in fields such as self-assembly, tissue engineering, genomics, and smart drug delivery. Dr. Messersmith's research is based upon utilizing biological strategies to develop new biomaterials and tissue engineering approaches for the repair, replacement, or augmentation of human tissue. His group has investigated the use of the natural tissue enzyme, transglutaminase (TG), in combination with stimuli-responsive lipid vesicles containing calcium (Ca) to induce the rapid *in situ* formation and cross-linking of peptide, protein, and polymeric hydrogels.[5,6]

My research will build on this background, with the goal of developing a self-assembling scaffold made of surfactant peptides, which employs Ca-dependent TG cross-linking. This peptide will include the cell-adhesion sequence RGD, intended to attach chondrocytes to the scaffold. Cross-linking will be triggered *in situ* by the release of Ca from lipid vesicles upon exposure to light, as demonstrated by Messersmith.[5] Growth factors—transforming growth factor beta (TGFb) and basic fibroblast growth factor (bFGF)—will also be included in the vesicles in order to encourage cell growth and differentiation. While each of these components has been investigated individually, the proposed combination of them is novel and will advance the goal of producing injectable scaffolds for the repair and regeneration of tissue. In order to prepare for this research, I will take courses at Northwestern University in biochemistry, biophysics, nanotechnology, tissue engineering, and self-assembled materials.

Research Design: The surfactant peptides described by Zhang et al.[3] include hydrophilic head groups and hydrophobic tails of the form n'-AAAAAAD-c'. My molecule will use this backbone, but sites for TG (Q, K) and cell binding (RGD) will be added. As a starting point, I propose the amino acid sequence: n'-AAAAQARGDK-c'. A peptide solution will be formed by mixing the cell-binding peptide with peptides that do not contain the cell-binding sequence of the structure: n'-AAAAAAQAAK-c'. Self-assembly will be confirmed by analyzing the peptides with transmission electron microscopy (TEM), circular dichroism, and other methods. If these molecules do not self-assemble quickly enough for clinical applications (within three minutes), the Q may be disrupting the hydrophobicity of the tail, in which case the A sequence of the tail will be changed to the more hydrophobic V or L. Additionally, the position of the TG sites could be varied: more Q and/or K sites may be added, or the current sites may be moved.

I have included TG sites in my peptide because this family of enzymes is found in fluids and extracellular matrix (ECM) throughout the body, and components of cartilage ECM cross-link with TG, enabling the scaffolds to integrate with native tissue. Sperinde and Griffith[7] have shown that poly(ethylene glycol) can be cross-linked with a lysine-containing polypeptide by the use of TG, thereby improving mechanical properties. This combination can form a hydrogel network that can be injected into the body.

Since TG is dependent upon Ca, the eventual goal will be to deliver Ca to the body by the use of vesicles that release their contents upon exposure to a light source of a certain wavelength and intensity. But first, I will test the ability of my peptides to cross-link by adding different concentrations of $CaCl_2$ and animal-derived TG to a solution of peptides *in vitro*. Once cross-linking has been optimized, I will then advance to testing my system with Ca-containing vesicles *in vitro*. Finally, the possibility of adding the growth factors TGFb and bFGF to phototriggerable vesicles will be explored. These growth factors are important for stimulating chondrocyte activity and also for decreasing cartilage degradation.

Next, I will test the cell-binding capabilities of the RGD sequence by incubating assembled scaffolds with chondrocytes harvested from calves at the cell density of 15×10^6 cells/mL. After 3, 6, and 9 weeks, sections of scaffold will undergo histological examination in order to determine the amounts and kinds of collagen being produced by the embedded chondrocytes. Based on the results of these tests, the ratio of peptides with and without the cell-binding sequence in the peptide solution will be varied.

Finally, the *in vivo* properties of the scaffold and vesicles will be tested by injecting a solution into an animal model and triggering gelation with a light source. The scaffold's mechanical, immunological, and histological properties will be analyzed.

Long-term Goals: In the future, the incorporation of peptides with a variety of cell-signaling sequences will be investigated with the ultimate goal of injecting the scaffold into human subjects to repair damaged cartilage. This will potentially have a great impact on the treatment of osteoarthritis, a debilitating joint condition that affects millions of Americans each year. My career goal is to become a Professor of Bioengineering at a major research university concentrating in the area of tissue engineering and regenerative medicine. I look forward to sharing my research with the next generation of scientists and engineers in the classroom and in the surrounding community.

References:
1. National Center for Health Statistics, Advance Data: National Ambulatory Medical Care Survey, 2000 Summary: http://www.cdc.gov/nchs/data/ad/ad328.pdf
2. Zhang S. Fabrication of novel biomaterials through molecular self-assembly. *Nature Biotechnology.* 2003. 21:1171-1178.
3. Zhang S. and X. Zhao. Design of molecular biological materials using peptide motifs. *J. Mater. Chem.* 2004. 14:2082-2086.
4. Silva G., Czeisler C., Niece K., Beniash E., Harrington D., Kessler J., and S. Stupp. Selective Differentiation of Neural Progenitor Cells by High-Epitope Density Nanofibers. *Science.* 2004. 303:1352-1355.
5. Zhang Z., Shum P., Yates M., Messersmith P., and D. Thompson. Formation of Fibrinogen-Based Hydrogels Using Phototriggerable Diplasmalogen Liposomes. *Bioconjugate Chem.* 2002. 13:640-646.
6. Collier J., and P. Messersmith. Enzymatic Modification of Self-Assembled Peptide Structures with Tissue Transglutaminase. *Bioconjugate Chem.* 2003. 14:748-755.
7. Sperinde J. and L. Griffith. Synthesis and characterization of enzymatically-cross-linked poly(ethylene glycol) hydrogels. *Macromolecules.* 1997. 30:5255-5264.

Question Summary: Describe any scientific research activities in which you have participated, such as experience in undergraduate research programs, or research experience gained through summer or part-time employment or in work-study programs, or other research activities, either academic or job-related. Explain the purpose of the research and your specific role in the research, including the extent to which you worked independently and/or as part of a team, and what you learned from your research. In your statement, distinguish between undergraduate and graduate research experience. If you have no direct research experience, describe any activities that you believe have prepared you to undertake research.

Biomedical devices, ranging from catheters to ventricular assist devices, are used by the millions annually. Many novel coatings and materials have been developed for these applications, yet the ideal materials for these varied uses remain to be discovered.[1] In particular, for blood-contacting applications, the body's reaction to biomaterials continues to be plagued by two major problems: bleeding and thrombosis.[2,3] Thrombosis is usually the result of adverse interactions between the artificial material and the body. Bleeding becomes a problem when attempting to prevent thrombosis by administering excessive anti-coagulants. Therefore, without a better understanding of the process by which the body responds to foreign materials, promising technologies such as self-assembled nanomaterials cannot reach their full potential as hemocompatible materials.[4,5] I have been performing research towards my honors thesis since my sophomore year, under the guidance of Prof. John Teacher at Mythic University. This research has focused on understanding how the body reacts to the introduction of foreign materials. In particular, I have concentrated on blood-surface interactions and the engineering of novel hemocompatible surfaces.

Blood coagulation occurs through a cascade of enzymatic reactions involving many plasma proteins, lipids, and ions resulting in the production of a fibrin clot. This cascade can be divided into the intrinsic, extrinsic, and common pathways. The intrinsic and extrinsic pathways are initiated by distinct events and converge into the common pathway. The intrinsic pathway is activated when blood interacts with an artificial surface, while a tissue injury activates the extrinsic pathway.[6] The intrinsic to common pathway can be conceptualized as occurring through linked sets of enzyme reactions, termed compartments. In this work, the intrinsic cascade has been modeled in terms of three such compartments: activation, transfer, and coagulation.

My research on blood-surface interactions seeks to quantify dose-response relationships, connecting surface properties of a biomaterial with the tendency to activate the intrinsic pathway of the blood coagulation cascade. In the various experimental assays used in my work, the "dose" results from applying a surface to human plasma or from adding an activating enzyme to human plasma. The "response" is the formation of a plasma clot as measured by coagulation time. Two primary questions raised by these experiments ask: How does dose propagate through the cascade to yield a response? What is the relationship between intensity of the dose and response?

Another aspect of my research, mathematical modeling, seeks to answer these questions. The model uses the compartmentalized cascade to treat the intrinsic pathway as a "black box" leading to the output of thrombin in the common pathway. This model allows me to apply derived equations to the experimental data to obtain rate parameters that will give quantitative information about the entire coagulation process. This information is expected to lead to a better understanding of how changing material properties affects hemocompatibility.

The effect of adding an amount of surface area to plasma is one example of a dose-response relationship explored in my research. I performed experiments in human plasma with beads made of two different materials: glass and silanized octadecyltrichlorosilane (OTS). Glass is a high-energy, hydrophilic surface, while OTS is a low-energy, hydrophobic surface. These experiments have shown that glass activates the coagulation cascade significantly more than OTS based on coagulation times. Mathematical modeling quantified this observation, showing that the activating potential of the surface scales exponentially with surface energy. Another interesting result is that both materials begin to saturate at the same amount of surface area. This observation has led to the hypothesis that thrombin is produced as a bolus in proportion to the amount of surface area added, instead of being slowly produced the entire time until coagulation. This work is currently in press in *Biomaterials*, a leading peer-reviewed journal in the field.[7]

During the past two summers, I began work on engineering surfaces that have regions of one chemical functionality on the nanometer scale within a continuous matrix of a second functionality. The goal of this research is to test the hypothesis that nanoscopic organization of chemistry can influence the activation of blood coagulation. In order to create these nano-surfaces, I chose to use the method of forming self-assembled monolayers of organosilanes on glass substrates. Self-assembled monolayers (SAMs) are ordered assemblies that form spontaneously by the adsorption of a surfactant with a specific affinity of its headgroup to a substrate.[8]

In this work, I have used two organosilanes: 3-aminopropyltriethoxysilane (APTES) and n-butyltrichlorosilane (BTS). A monolayer of APTES has an intermediate surface energy, while a monolayer of BTS has a low surface energy similar to that of OTS. APTES and BTS molecules have nearly the same chain length. Therefore, the combination of these two silanes on the same substrate results in a smooth surface. First, I created partial monolayers, or "islands," of APTES on a clean glass surface. Next, I back-filled the surface with BTS. I then examined the surfaces using atomic force

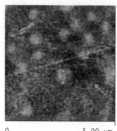

0   5.00 μm
Data type   Friction
Z range   0.07500 V

Fig. 1

microscopy (AFM) in contact mode. Because the surfaces were smooth, with an average roughness of only 0.15 nm, I relied on friction images to determine the make-up of these surfaces. Through this analysis, I determined that the islands of APTES had an average diameter of 500 nm and appeared in a regular arrangement across the substrate (Fig. 1). The next step was to create glass beads with APTES islands and back-fill with BTS in order to perform surface area titrations as described earlier. This allowed me to compare these new surfaces with previously characterized surfaces. The result of a surface area titration of the APTES/BTS beads showed that these beads activate the coagulation cascade less than beads made of purely APTES or purely BTS. To better understand these potentially positive results and to finalize them for publication, I am completing surface characterization by techniques such as atomic force microscopy, contact angle tensiometry, and x-ray photoelectron spectrometry.

Solving the problem of how dose is propagated through the plasma coagulation cascade will contribute to the understanding of how a surface activates the blood coagulation process. Ultimately, this understanding will aid in the design of a hemocompatible material that results in the lowest activation of the cascade. This improved interaction with the body will enable patients to take less anti-coagulant medicine, producing better results following the use of biomedical devices.

References

1. Beiko D., Knudsen B., Watterson J., and J. Denstedt. Biomaterials in Urology. *Current Urology Reports*. 2003. Feb 4(1):51-55.

2. Rose E., Gelijns A., Moskowitz A., Heitjan D., Stevenson L., Dembitsky W., et al. Long-term Use of a Left Ventricular Assist Device for End-Stage Heart Failure. *New England Journal of Medicine*. 2001. 345:1435-1443.

3. Lavine M., Roberts M., and O. Smith. Bodybuilding: The Bionic Human. *Science*. 2002. 295:995-1032.

4. Ratner B. The Blood Compatibility Catastrophe. *Journal of Biomedical Materials Research*. 1993. 27: 283-287.

5. Ratner B. Blood Compatibility – A Perspective. *Journal of Biomaterials Science, Polymer Edition*. 2000. 11:1107-1119.

6. Nemerson Y. The Tissue Factor Pathway of Blood Coagulation. *Hemostasis and Thrombosis: Basic Principles and Clinical Practice*. J.B. Lippincott Company: Philadelphia, 81-93. 1994.

7. Zhuo R, Miller R, Bussard K, Siedlecki C, and E Vogler. Procoagulant Stimulus Processing by the Intrinsic Pathway of Blood Plasma Coagulation. In Press: *Biomaterials*. 2004.

8. Schreiber, F. Structure and growth of self-assembling monolayers. *Progress in Surface Science*. 2000. 65:151-256.

The Fulbright Scholarship

The Fulbright Scholarship provides funds sufficient to complete a proposed research or study abroad project for one year. Applicants submit written outlines of their research or study plans, which may include a year of graduate study, original dissertation research, a creative or performing arts project, or a teaching assistantship. Because the study is undertaken abroad, applicants must have sufficient maturity, character, and literacy to work within the host country.

The Fulbright Scholarship Selection Criteria

Criteria that selectors use to award Fulbright Scholarships include:

- likelihood of the candidate and project to help advance the program and promote mutual understanding among nations;
- sufficient written and spoken literacy in the host country's language;
- feasibility and specificity of the proposed plan.

A final criterion is the ratio between the number of awards offered in the target country and the number of applications received—i.e., students applying to countries that receive fewer applications have a greater statistical chance of acceptance. Applicants can assess competition statistics and other details for a particular country by consulting the Fulbright website noted on the next page.

Composing a Curriculum Vitae and Statement of Proposed Study

The primary written portions of the Fulbright application are the curriculum vitae (CV) and statement of proposed study. Though most students are used to thinking of a CV as a resume (the terms are often used interchangeably), the Fulbright application defines a CV as a "personal/intellectual biography in narrative form." The CV is your opportunity to discuss personal motivations, your experience and activities, and future goals. Though your examples should still be concrete, you have the room to reveal your personality—indeed many applicants view this as their chance to let the selectors know them as individually as possible, and they use lightly entertaining anecdotes to set themselves apart from other candidates. In plain terms, the goal is to write a CV that no other person could have written.

In writing the statement of proposed study or research, begin by making sure not to repeat material from other parts of the application unnecessarily, and present detail tailored as much as possible to the host country. If you can show that you have performed research on (or, better yet, *in*) the host country already and have made contacts with potential supervisors, you increase your odds of success dramatically. The Fulbright website cautions writers against the use of discipline-specific jargon, and a good rule of thumb is to define any jargon that you do use in context, keeping the focus of your proposal on addressing problems that will provide valuable contributions to society and within your field. Also, practicality and feasibility are principal concerns, so the best applicants provide a timeline, discuss their methodology and goals, and analyze such variables as the host country's cultural and political climate and resources. Finally, of course, you must demonstrate as necessary your linguistic ability as it applies to the country and your proposed plan, especially if your primary goal is a teaching assistantship.

Evaluation of Written Materials from Two Sample Fulbright Applications

The first sample CV and proposal, covering the following five pages, do an excellent job of making the case for the writer's personal and intellectual readiness for the proposed project. The CV focuses on the student's experiences as inspired by his service-oriented grandparents—members of the Mennonite Church. These role models inspired the student to travel to Peru and contact the Mennonite Economic Development Associates (MEDA). As we learn in the student's proposal, he wishes to work on a grassroots project in Peru related to rice farming, and he shows that he has earned the support of the MEDA Consulting Group, underscoring the feasibility of his plan.

The second CV and proposal are also neatly intertwined, and the writer opens the CV with a delightful anecdote about her family puzzling over why a woman would be interested in geological research. The student uses the CV to detail her science background and educational travel, including a month in Thailand, where she plans to do her proposed seismic research. To underscore the urgency of such research, she opens her proposal with a poignant narrative and statistics about the devastating effects of a 1999 earthquake in Central Taiwan. Some readers might have valid concerns over whether the proposal is too technical at times, and whether its sources should be cited internally, yet these essays remain impressive overall. Indeed, the writer was named as a scholarship alternate.

Information on the Fulbright Scholarship program is available at
http://www.iie.org/FulbrightTemplate.cfm?Section=U_S_Student_Program

SAMPLE CURRICULUM VITAE FOR THE FULBRIGHT SCHOLARSHIP

Curriculum Vitae for John Lerner

My grandparents have touched many lives: former drug addicts, refugees, neighbors, and my own. They have an uncommon ability to build relationships; they are a paradigm of service—where service is more than what you do and is also defined by who you are.

In my own life, I have aspired to affect people in the manner of my grandparents and others in the Mennonite Church. I still have that aspiration, but my vision has expanded. Prior to attending Mythic College, I pictured myself living in Mythic County near my family and my roots. I grew up attached to the local way of life, working at my family's snack food business, raising crops to earn money, and leading the local Future Farmers of America. During high school, I read the international section of the paper but the people and events seemed a world away. At Mythic College, professors challenged me with realities such as the fate of 500 million people who are chronically malnourished. I began to ask myself, "Why will I have thirty food options at breakfast tomorrow while whole populations around the world will wake up with almost nothing to eat?"

In the summer of 20xx, I traveled to Ecuador, equipped with rudimentary Spanish, a background in international politics and economics, and a desire to meet people, hear their stories, and learn from them. In Ecuador, the effects of a devastating financial crisis in 2000 still lingered. Many people had watched helplessly as banks froze savings accounts while the national currency plummeted, melting the life savings of many Ecuadorians.

Like helplessness, dependency often stems from a lack of opportunities. The children who begged on the streets of Quito depended upon strangers for money. If they were going to eat they had to beg. Reflecting on such matters, as part of my studies I had asked myself, "What is the goal of development?" Through the plight I witnessed among Ecuadorians, I came to define development as building the productive and institutional capacities that give people opportunities to lead lives that they value.

After my travels, I returned to Mythic County in December of 20xx and ate Christmas dinner at my grandparents' farmhouse. I knew that this area was my home, and that my family was the source of my inspiration. I also knew that my passion for studying international development would take me away from Mythic County. But my grandparents had taught me to empathize and act. While aware of problems within

Mythic County, I had seen much greater need in Latin America. Driven by the values instilled in me, I contacted Mennonite Economic Development Associates (MEDA) to work on a development project.

In June of 20xx, I traveled to Peru to assist with an innovative approach to agriculture lending pioneered by MEDA. While working for MEDA, I assessed a microcredit project involving rice farmers. The experience impressed upon me the value of a grassroots understanding as well as the importance of sound macro-level policies. Tariff rates, financial regulations, and public infrastructure plans could mean the difference between the project's success or failure. I left Peru convinced that sound trade and development policies could profoundly affect people's lives. Shaping macro-level policies became my goal.

With this goal in mind, I hope to pursue a law degree and a Master of Public Policy with an emphasis in international development. These degrees will give me the tools to craft and analyze development policy. I will use my experiences and education to hope to shape such policies in Latin America. Later, I plan to teach development studies at the university level.

SAMPLE STATEMENT OF PROPOSED STUDY FOR THE FULBRIGHT SCHOLARSHIP

John Lerner
Study Proposal—Peru
Economic Development

Through my Fulbright independent research project I hope to better understand the production decisions made by Peruvian rice farmers in northern Peru. On what factors do farmers base their decisions to enter, to continue, or to exit rice farming? On what factors do farmers base their specific production decisions, i.e. how much rice to plant? Can accepted microeconomic theory explain these decisions or is another explanation needed? How do cultural or socioeconomic factors influence the decision-making process of these farmers? Finally, how should the answers to these questions affect agriculture development policy in Peru? Should the Peruvian government use the new state-run Agro Banco to subsidize rice farmers whom the formal capital markets ignore?

Understanding production decisions of small-scale farmers requires an understanding of the context in which they operate. Therefore, I will focus the first part of my project on understanding this context. One critical consideration is assessing the current trade, investment, and agriculture policies, such as the Agriculture Financial Rescue bill (RFA), that affect small-scale producers. Other important context issues include the production and price trends in the Peruvian rice market and the major international and domestic players in that market.

Developing a grassroots understanding of small-scale rice farming is both timely and necessary. It is timely because it complements current development organization trends. The Bagua Grande microcredit project, which I was involved with this year, is part of a larger shift in focus of development organizations that has occurred in the last ten years. Popularized by the success of the Grameen Bank, microcredit lending has boomed. The latest trend within microcredit lending is small-scale agriculture. This trend is popular among small development organizations as well as large agencies such as the U.S. Agency for International Development (USAID). In fact, USAID funded the Bagua Grande project as part of its multi-million dollar poverty alleviation project in Peru known as Project PRA.

Understanding small-scale agriculture is crucial in addressing poverty in Peru. According to the Peruvian Institute of Statistics and Information (INEI), the rural poverty rate was 35% higher than urban poverty rate in 2002. Child malnutrition and under five mortality are twice as high in rural areas compared to urban areas. Furthermore, INEI data show that among rural populations, small-scale farmers are the most vulnerable to rapid changes in income.

The policy context in which small-scale rice farmers operate has changed dramatically in the last fifteen years. In the early 1990s, Peruvian officials adopted a more market-oriented agriculture policy, reducing import restrictions on agriculture goods and dissolving the state-run agriculture commercialization companies. In 1992, Banco Agrario, which subsidized the agriculture sector, was eliminated. As the Peruvian Ministry of Agriculture Strategic Plan states, these policy changes should cause a reorientation in the agriculture sector that reflects the new market conditions. The Strategic Plan confirms, however, that such reorientation has been slow, if not imperceptible. A 1994 Peruvian census found that the majority of Peruvian farmers did not consider prices as the most important signal in deciding what crop to plant. If farmers are not following price signals, what signals are they following?

My supporting institution, Mennonite Economic Development Associates (MEDA) Consulting Group Peru, has a wealth of experience working in the Peruvian rice industry. MEDA Consulting Group Peru offers both invaluable contacts and industry-specific knowledge that will facilitate my investigation. I have personally met with Sonia Dominguez, the MEDA Consulting Group Peru country manager, and she has offered her organization's support to me. Further, my previous study abroad experiences in Chile and Ecuador and my ten-week internship in Peru have allowed me to develop my Spanish speaking and writing skills, making this project feasible from a language and cultural awareness standpoint.

I will conduct most of my research in the coastal city of Chiclayo, the center of the rice industry in northern Peru. Much of the rice from northern Peru is taken to Chiclayo where it is milled and distributed to regional or national markets. Farmers from a wide region accompany their crop to the mill where they oversee its sale. Two of these mills, Molino Las Delicias and Molino Tropical, have worked directly with my supporting institution in a rice microcredit project in the region. As a result, Chiclayo offers the most promising opportunities for me to both research the rice industry and to conduct surveys.

Surveys obtained at mills in Chiclayo will be supported by surveys obtained at local input suppliers in towns with a large rice industry such as Bagua Grande, Bagua Chica, Jaen, Moyobamaba, and Picota. MEDA has worked directly with input suppliers in Bagua Grande and Picota and can offer contacts in those towns. Traveling to smaller towns will permit me to access more small-scale farmers who sell their rice to intermediaries instead of directly to a mill, and help me understand how they make these decisions.

Through this Fulbright project I can further develop my ability to engage in cultural exchange. As I learned while working for MEDA, surveying farmers is difficult. The surveyor must learn how to earn the cooperation of strangers by starting the conversation appropriately and by putting the person being surveyed at ease. When someone feels comfortable in a conversation they will more fully express their opinions, and they will probably also diverge into other issues as if they were talking to an acquaintance.

Surveying rice farmers in Peru will also give me an invaluable grassroots perspective on development issues. This understanding of how individuals respond to macro-level policies is vital to my career goal of working in international development policy. Upon returning from this Fulbright project, I plan to enroll in a Juris Doctorate and Master in Public Policy joint degree program. In both the J.D. and M.P.P programs I will focus on trade and development issues.

This project will also benefit development organizations that operate agriculture projects in the region. MEDA Consulting Group Peru has expressed interest in my findings. I will also offer my study to the many development organizations working in the region, including those that operate the Economic Services Centers as part of USAID's Project PRA. USAID has plans to continue funding development organizations in the region as part of its Economic Growth, Alternative Development, and Peru-Ecuador Border Region Development programs.

I plan on leaving for Chiclayo in early August of 20xx. I will spend the first month researching the rice industry of the region by gathering data from the regional agriculture offices, mill contacts, and contacts in rural credit institutions. In the following three months, I will survey farmers at mills in Chiclayo. To supplement those surveys, I will use months 5 and 6 to conduct surveys of farmers who visit agriculture input supply stores in towns such as Bagua, Jaen, Picota, and Piura in Northern Peru. Finally, I will use months 7 and 8 to analyze the data obtained from the surveys, finish a formal paper on the entire research project, and disseminate my findings to interested development organizations.

SAMPLE CURRICULUM VITAE FOR THE FULBRIGHT SCHOLARSHIP

Curriculum Vitae for Janet Lerner

I decided that I wanted to be a scientist while I was still in elementary school, but even in high school where I was praised for my academic successes, my relatives were still against the whole idea. My grandma still asks me every Christmas what my major is and once I start telling her about earthquakes and mountain formation, she quickly changes the subject. Coming from a small town in Mythic County and being only the second person on either side of my family to attend college, it has been an ongoing issue to convince my family that a person, let alone a woman, can make a living doing geologic research.

As a freshman at Mythic University, I was accepted for a research assistantship designed for incoming freshman women. Through this program I worked with a Mythic University geochemistry professor on the sequestration of pollutants in aquifers. Going into the program, I expected merely to be washing lab equipment and capping bottles, but instead I got to make solutions, run pH experiments and learn how to use spectroscopy instruments. By my sophomore year, I was running samples and interpreting data. It was through this experience that I learned a valuable lesson: opportunities are endless if one is prepared for them.

The spring of my sophomore year I applied for a research course that required me to learn to scuba dive. Through this course I was certified as a PADI open water diver and was able to go to the island of San Salvador in the Bahamas. In San Salvador I was part of a team that conducted research on the island's coral reefs, which involved surveying them for disease and damage, through a program called Reef Check. That summer I also received a scholarship through Mythic University's Biogeochemical Research Initiative for Education to continue the geochemistry research I started as a freshman. Later that summer I left for a semester abroad at the University of Western Australia in Perth, Australia. Before returning home, I visited Thailand for over a month to satisfy my curiosity about Asian cultures and to obtain my advanced and rescue diver certifications.

To say the least, my study abroad experience dramatically changed my life. I had never really been away from home for very long at one time other than college, but even there I was only an hour away from home and had close friends who also attend Mythic University. Being in Australia taught me the true meaning of independence and gave me a new sense of confidence. In addition, I gained an international perspective on many issues that I had never considered before. My experience in Thailand opened my eyes to many misconceptions I had about Asian people, and it gave me a new appreciation for the term "culture."

The spring semester of my junior year I was accepted into a collaborative research class in which we began to prepare an online geology course for Mythic University's world campus classroom. In the summer we spent three weeks in many of the southwestern US national parks producing short educational films to be used in the class. This fall we are editing the films and giving presentations about our experiences with the class. As I write this I am in the first semester of my senior year and I have just started my thesis research with a grant from the National Science Foundation. My work investigates uplift in the Himalayan Plateau.

Since studying abroad, I have gained a more compassionate outlook on life, which has caused me to re-evaluate my career choices. For a short time I considered changing fields to a major that would be more beneficial to humanity and thus more self-fulfilling. But after contemplating the issue for some time, I decided that I can make a difference in the world with any career choice. Now, I am devoted to using my geologic knowledge for the betterment of humanity. This is the main reason why I have chosen a project dealing with earthquakes in Taiwan. The research is not just about geology but about advances that will help to save people's lives.

In addition, I am very excited to learn more about the Asian culture, which I have taken a special interest in since my short visit to Thailand. I believe I am highly qualified to conduct my proposed research. Although my research interactions will be done in English, I have started Chinese lessons this fall at Mythic University to make my experience in Taiwan even more meaningful. I will have completed Chinese II by the time I graduate and I hope to take personal language lessons over the summer before traveling to Taiwan. After this experience I plan to obtain by PhD at a geology school in California, integrating the knowledge I obtained in Taiwan to studies on fault zones in the United States.

SAMPLE STATEMENT OF PROPOSED STUDY
FOR THE FULBRIGHT SCHOLARSHIP

Janet Lerner
Study Proposal—Taiwan
Earthquake Dynamics

At 1:47 in the morning, September 21, 1999, the town of Chi Chi in Nantou County, Central Taiwan began to shake violently. A release of built-up stress deep in the Earth caused the eastern side of the Chelongpu Fault to rise, rupturing the surface for an approximate extent of 86 km and creating a lasting offset upon the surface of the Earth.

The earthquake caused buildings to tumble and triggered landslides in some areas. A report from the Central Weather Bureau in Taipei reported a death toll of 2,333 and 10,002 injured. Over 46,700 buildings totally collapsed with 100,000 people left homeless. The initial tremor was followed by over 10,000 aftershocks, five of which were termed moderate earthquakes which caused minor death and damage. Direct and indirect losses associated with the Chi Chi earthquake totals 30 billion dollars. The Chi Chi earthquake was a catastrophe for the Taiwanese people and the largest recorded earthquake ever to hit the island.

I am interested in studying earthquake dynamics, and Taiwan is an excellent place in which to do so. Taiwan is an area of active mountain building and it lies along the boundary between the Luzon arc of the Philippine Sea Plate and the Chinese continental margin, where plate collision is occurring. The Chelongpu Fault in particular offers a special opportunity to study faults. Not only is it a major event that is geologically recent but the fault is well-mapped and relatively well-known. The Chi Chi earthquake is unique in that it provided a multitude of modern digital data for seismologist and earthquake engineers. These data can be attributed to an extensive seismic instrumentation program that had been successfully implemented in Taiwan three years prior to the Chi Chi Earthquake. In addition, recent drilling along the fault is allowing access to fault rocks at depths where rupturing initiates.

By studying the physical characteristics of the rocks, one can gain a better understanding of fault development and ultimately come one step closer to the earthquake mechanism. As motion on a fault commences, the rocks can either experience velocity strengthening, where an increase in slip rate makes further slip less probable, or velocity weakening, where an increase in slip rate makes the rocks weaker. Velocity strengthening and weakening are primarily a function of material properties of the rock bodies surrounding the fault. These properties of the fault zone can mean the difference between a steady creep in which fault blocks move without seismic slip, or a major earthshaking event like that of the Chi Chi earthquake. The faulted rocks of the Chelongpu Fault are especially valuable to geologists in that they record the history and evolution of deformation caused by the Chi Chi Earthquake.

Previous studies have determined the architectural pattern of major thrusting fault zones as asymmetric, meaning the damaged zone is thicker above the fault core than below. In addition, the fracture density tends to increase with depth, reaching a maximum at the fault core and abruptly decreasing thereafter. Observations such as these have been made on previous fault zones, but solid research on fault dynamics and how it relates to this architecture is lacking. Consequently, my research will focus on the asymmetric development of fault zone evolution.

With the help of Mythic University structural geologist Dr. John Teacher, I have been in contact with Dr. Yue-Gau Chen, Professor of Geosciences at the National Taiwan University, who organizes Sino-American collaborations in Taiwan, and Dr. En-Chao Yeh from the Deep Sea Research Department at the Japan Agency for Marine-Earth Science and Technology (JAMSTEC). JAMSTEC will be receiving drill cores from the Taiwan Continental Drilling Project (TCDP), an international effort dedicated to drilling the Chelongpu Fault zone. Dr. En-Chao Yeh is responsible for evaluation of drill cores at JAMSTEC and will be participating in a series of micro-scale and meso-scale analyses that will be done on the cores. These analyses include structural, physical property, rock mechanic, and geochemical examinations of the fault zone rocks. Each of these examinations is assigned to a separate group of researchers, and I have been given an invitation from Dr. En-Chao Yeh to work with him on the structural examinations and an invitation from Dr. Yue-Gau Chen to be associated with the National Taiwan University in Taipei, which would culminate in a master's degree in geology.

There are five tests that I would be performing on the drill cores, as follows:

1). Core observations will be done to characterize the meso-scale structures and textures on the cores and on scanned images. These structures can be associated with individual earthquake events to give an idea of how and to what extent the fault moved during each event and to decide a development direction: upwards, stationary or downwards.

2). Thin sections will be taken to look at micro-scale structures and textures under an optical microscope. Micro-structures can be used to develop cross-cutting relationships and allow for a better understanding of development sequence of the fault zone.

3). The Scanning Electron Microscope (SEM) will allow for examination of even smaller features including mineral phases and micro-textures.

4). Transmission Electron Microscopy (TEM) will be used to identify the detailed atomic structures and the presence of glass which is only produced under high pressure conditions.

5). Microscopic X-ray Computed Tomography (Micro-XCT) will be used to determine the porosity, permeability and fluid dynamics across the fault zone.

These analyses would be conducted for a half year of study and would be followed up by a half year of interpretation of results, comparison to other studies, and linking to the bigger picture through collaboration with other drill hole examiners. It is expected that this work will result in a comprehensive overview of the asymmetric architecture of the Chelongpu Fault. Through characterization of a single fault where earthquake dynamics are well-known, principles will be generated that can be applied to other areas of potential seismic hazard.

My proposed project (which would start in September 20xx and end in June 20xx) is an excellent opportunity for geology to serve as a medium whereby intellectual exchange can be the basis for cultural connection. Earthquakes are an ever-present danger in Taiwan and the United States (particularly the San Andreas Fault area); a collaboration on research is not only about technology but about uniting powers to save lives and resources. Although both countries already have extensive programs that focus on earthquake research, it is only through combined efforts that the most rapid advances can be made. Furthermore, this opportunity has the potential to greatly enhance my professional career as a geologist. Not only is this project at the forefront of structural geology studies, but it will give me an international perspective on geologic and cultural issues alike. Finally, the project is an especially unique opportunity for a woman in a male-dominated field.

Sources:
Personal Communication: Dr. John Teacher and Dr. Yue-Gau Chen.
Statistics taken from: California's Partnership 2000 Conference website at:
http://www.ciwmb.ca.gov/Part2000/Events/00Conf/Presentations/EarthQks.htm.

The Goldwater Scholarship

The Goldwater Scholarship (honoring Senator Barry M. Goldwater) awards sophomore and junior students up to a maximum of $7500 annually for tuition, books, fees, and room and board. Its aim is to provide a continuing source of highly qualified scholars to work as scientists, mathematicians, and engineers. Students are chosen based on their commitment and potential to make significant future contributions in their fields, and it is expected that Goldwater Scholars will pursue graduate degrees.

The Goldwater Scholarship Selection Criteria

Goldwater applications are reviewed by an independent committee appointed by the Goldwater Foundation, and the committee's selection criteria include:

- potential for a commitment to a career in the sciences, engineering, or mathematics, as demonstrated by the student's overall application;
- excellence in academic performance.

As with many other national scholarships, candidates for the Goldwater are nominated by their institutions, and final selection of Goldwater Scholars is made by the Goldwater Board of Trustees, which reviews the assessment made by both the nominating institution and the independent selection committee.

Answering the Goldwater Essay Questions and Writing the Nominee's Essay

The last few questions of the Goldwater application invite narrative responses, with approximate length dictated by the size of the space available to answer the questions. These three questions involve the applicant's professional aspirations, personal motivations, and diversity (broadly defined). Clearly, a lot of flexibility is built into answering such questions, and students tend to approach these questions accordingly, narrating personal anecdotes and information about their families to let the selectors know what kind of people they are. While still emphasizing science and research, past applicants have shared information about a childhood or other formative experience, the desire to become a professor or write a textbook, their ethnic background, and even information about hardships of their parents. In answering these questions—especially the question inviting comments on diversity—it is important to be genuine and sound natural in your examples. Readers tend to sniff out and suspect aspirations that reach too high, or motivations that are insincere, or diversity that is forced.

For the nominee's essay (limited to two pages), you must describe an issue or problem associated with your field and describe any related ongoing or intended research. Most writers document any sources cited in APA Style (see http://www.wisc.edu/writing/Handbook/DocAPA.html), and they are especially careful to credit sources of information and graphics as well as clarify their exact role in the research project. Your aim is to show how you can excel in a research environment, or work as part of a design team, or contribute to the understanding of a technical problem. Remember, too, that members of the selection panel will have the expertise to understand a complex problem in your field.

Evaluation of Two Sample Sets of Goldwater Application Essays

In the following pages, two sample Goldwater essay sets are provided, and both writers show a facility with presenting themselves as budding scientists.

In answering the narrative questions, the first writer stresses his aspiration to lead a team of researchers studying pollution control in industrial chemical processes, and cites specific problems he has encountered in his current research on bacteria growth. His tone is almost philosophical at times, discussing the rewards of both achievement and failure in the sciences, and he notes that he is the first in his family to pursue a technical degree. His nominee's essay stresses the long-term goal of his research in bacterial adhesion, and he carefully describes his team's use of video microscopy to record particles as they adhere to bacteria.

The second writer addresses the narrative questions by outlining her participation in programs related to women in science and her personal aspirations, ranging from serving as part of a NASA research team to working as a glass blower at a Renaissance Faire. Her diversity background is grounded in her hailing from a highly rural area (even her influential father is a "senior bank auditor but country man at heart"). Finally, her nominee's essay, addressing the goal to improve the durability of window glass, offers precisely detailed information even to the extent of giving exact nanometer depths that yielded different data points. Such an approach closely resembles a technical abstract that would appear in a journal. Significantly, this student did receive a Goldwater Scholarship.

Nomination materials for the Goldwater Scholarship are available at
http://www.act.org/goldwater/yysnm.html

SAMPLE RESPONSES TO SELECT QUESTIONS
ON THE GOLDWATER SCHOLARSHIP APPLICATION

Question D: What are your professional aspirations? Indicate in which area(s) of mathematics, science, or engineering you are considering making your career and specify how your current academic program and your overall educational plans will assist you in achieving this goal.

Few generations have had the amazing power to impact our environment on a worldwide scale. Even fewer generations have realized humankind could have such a large impact on the Earth. The past century has seen many advancements in technology and quality of life. These great achievements have also given humankind the power to permanently alter our Earth and its fragile ecosystems. It is important to improve our quality of life, but it is also important not to compromise that of future generations by sacrificing our natural environment. My professional aspirations are to lead a team conducting research on new methods to reduce and control pollution output from industrial chemical processes. My research will be performed either in an industrial setting or in combination with teaching as a college professor.

My current academic program in chemical engineering provides knowledge of industrial chemical processes along with a solid background in mathematics and chemistry. My current research project provides a jumpstart on the type of research I can expect to perform as a graduate student and as a professional investigator. Graduate school in chemical engineering provides the in-depth knowledge required to understand and improve pollution control in industrial chemical processes. A Ph.D. degree will provide me with the essential skills needed to develop my own research projects and lead a team of researchers.

Question E: Describe an activity or experience that has been important in clarifying or strengthening your motivation for a career in science, mathematics, or engineering.

My research experience this past summer has greatly solidified my interest in pursuing a career in scientific and engineering research. I have always had an interest in how the world operates and how humankind has obtained its vast wealth of knowledge, but I was not certain how I would pursue these interests in my career. In my first month of laboratory research, I encountered several unique challenges. Bacteria would not grow properly and the ionic strength of sample solutions and ratios of particles to bacteria had to be constantly altered and adjusted. I soon realized the tremendous degree of work, number of failed attempts, and good amount of luck that can go into even the smallest of advances. It gave me a newfound respect and admiration for the great minds of the past to which we owe our knowledge of the world. When I was ultimately able to perform a successful bacterial adhesion experiment, I had a great feeling of satisfaction. It reminded me that the most rewarding achievements are often those that require many failures before success is achieved.

Working with the graduate students in lab, each of whom had his or her own specialized research topic, was inspiring. I realized that there are plenty of opportunities available and there is plenty of room to make an impact. Most of all I realized that I would genuinely enjoy working to solve new problems and learning more about our world as a scientific researcher.

Question F: Goldwater Scholars will be representative of the diverse economic, ethnic, and occupational backgrounds of families in the United States. Describe any characteristics or other personal information about yourself or your family that you wish to share with the review committee.

I grew up in a highly rural area. My father works as a Union Ironworker traveling between jobsites throughout the seasons while my mother works as a bookkeeper. I will be the first member of my family to pursue a technical degree and a career in science. I was fortunate enough to be raised by a family that worked very hard to provide the opportunities available to me and instilled in me the importance of respecting people of diverse backgrounds and differing views on life.

To gain a more global perspective, I will study abroad in New Zealand next semester. I am excited about the opportunity to be immersed in a new culture. I hope that I can continue to expand my horizons by experiencing new cultures throughout my life.

SAMPLE NOMINEE'S ESSAY FOR THE GOLDWATER SCHOLARSHIP

Question Summary: Discuss a significant issue or problem in your field of study that is of particular interest to you.

Title: "Investigating the Role of Orientation in Bacterial Adhesion"

Bacterial adhesion can cause industrial equipment biofouling,[1] medical implant failure,[2] and is a problem for *in situ* bioremediation of polluted soils.[3] Despite extensive studies, mechanisms of bacterial adhesion remain inadequately understood. This makes it difficult to treat or control biofilm formation (a result of bacterial adhesion), which is the long-term goal of this research.

As a bacterium nears a surface, a balance between several forces will determine its course of action. Such forces include van der Waals, electrostatics, hydrophobic, solvation, depletion, and biospecific interactions. The importance of these forces can depend on a number of factors including the structure of the bacterial surface, solution ionic strength, and properties of the inert surface. The large variety in bacterial surfaces and the conditions under which adhesion can occur prove to complicate the bacterial adhesion process.[4]

There have been only a few studies examining the *orientation* of a bacterium as it adheres to a surface.[5,6] One such study performed by Jones et al. has observed that when the bacterium *Escherichia coli* adheres to colloidal particles, over 90% of the particles adhere to nanoscale regions at the ends of the rod-shaped bacterium.[7] These findings suggest that the ends of the bacterium may play a key role in the adhesion process. It is possible that the ends of the bacterium contain surface nonuniformities that facilitate the adhesion process. Surface nonuniformities may include lipopolysaccharide (LPS) chains and surface proteins in addition to the often-seen flagella.[5] If these surface nonuniformities can be isolated and identified, it may be possible to control the adhesion process through molecular biology.

In my undergraduate research project, the work of Jones et al. has been extended to two strains of the bacterium *Bulkholderia cepacia*. *B. cepacia* has been shown to degrade both trichloroethylene (TCE) and tetrachloroethylene, molecules representative of many halogenated pollutants.[7,8] Injection of this bacterium into polluted soils is a promising method of bioremediation, but bacterial adhesion to soil prevents movement through porous media.[9,10] As the particles adhere to the bacteria, the bacteria are less likely to be transported through small micro-pores in the soil. It would be advantageous to decrease adhesion in order to enable the bacteria to better disperse through polluted soils during *in situ* bioremediation.

In order to examine bacterial adhesion, we used video microscopy to observe and record the orientation of various sized particles as they adhered to bacteria. Images of rod-shaped bacteria adhering to various-sized spheroid particles are shown below.

B.cepacia G4 1.54 µm silica particle   *B. cepacia* G4 0.9 µm silica particle

The rate of end-on adhesion for the *B. cepacia* was observed to be near 75% with the same-sized particles used by Jones et al. in studying *E. coli* bacteria. This indicates that there may be different surface nonuniformities on *B. cepacia* or perhaps a different mechanism of adhesion. It was also observed that the size of the particles plays an important role in determining where the particle will adhere to the bacterium. Larger particles tend to adhere on cell ends more often than smaller particles of the same silica or polystyrene material. The preference for bacteria to adhere to larger particles end-on can be partially explained by geometric coincidence. As a particle approaches a bacterium rotating under Brownian motion, depending on the particle size it may rarely be able to meet the middle of the bacterium without first encountering the ends.

Future work will include additional oriented adhesion experiments substituting spheroidal colloidal particles for bacteria. These experiments will provide a basis of comparison for the previous sets of data. We will examine whether the high end-on adhesion rates are observed when there are no biological factors in play. In addition, oriented bacterial adhesion experiments with varying particle sizes will be performed to see if a quantifiable relationship between particle size and rate of end-on adhesion can be obtained. This research will help identify molecular mechanisms of bacterial adhesion, which will enable strains of bacteria to be altered in order to improve bioremediation processes. This study will be submitted to a scientific journal for publication in the near future and will be included in my senior honors thesis in chemical engineering.

References:
[1] Flemming, H.C., and G. Schaule. 1996. Biofouling, p.39-54 *In* E. Heitz, H.C. Flemming, and W. Sand (ed.), Microbially influenced corrosion of materials. Springer-Verlag, Berlin, Germany.
[2] Costerton, J.W., P.S. Stewart, and E.P. Greenberg. 1999. Bacterial biofilms: a common cause of persistent infections. Science 284: 1318-1322.
[3] Steffan, R.J.; Sperry, K.L.; Walsh, M.T.; Vainberg, S.; Condee, C.W. *Environ. Sci. Technol.* 1999, 33, 2771.
[4] Fletcher, M. 1996. Bacterial Adhesion: Molecular and Ecological Diversity. Wiley Interscience, New York, N.Y.
[5] Marshall, K.C., R. Stout, and R. Michell. 1971. Mechanisms of the initial events in the sorption of marine bacteria to surfaces. *J. Gen. Microbiol.* 68: 337-348.
[6] Jones, J. F.; J. D. Feick; D. Imoudu; N. Chukwumah; M. Vigeant; D. Velegol, *Appl. Environ. Microbiol.* 2003, 69, 6515-6519
[7] Hanada, S.; T. Shigematsu; K. Shibuya; M. Eguchi; T. Hasegawa; F. Suda; Y. Kamagata; T. Kanagawa; R. Kurane, *J. of Fermentation and Bioengineering.* 1998, 86, 539-544.
[8] Tros, M.E., Schraa, G., Zehnder, A.J.B. *Appl. Environ. Microbiol.* 1996, 62, 437.
[9] Martin, R. E.; E. J. Bouwer; L. M. Hanna, *Environ. Sci. Technol.* 1992, 26, 1053-1058.
[10] Taylor, S.W., and P. R. Jaffe. 1990. Substrate and biomass transport in a porous medium. *Water Res.* 26:2181-2191.

SAMPLE RESPONSES TO SELECT QUESTIONS
ON THE GOLDWATER SCHOLARSHIP APPLICATION

Question D: What are your professional aspirations? Indicate in which area(s) of mathematics, science, or engineering you are considering making your career and specify how your current academic program and your overall educational plans will assist you in achieving this goal.

Currently, I am pursuing a combined B.S./M.S. through the Integrated Undergraduate Graduate program because it allows me to take upper-level classes in my major earlier than one would experience in the normal B.S. program. This accelerated coursework is preparing me for a technical internship this summer. My participation in the Women in Science and Engineering Research Program has given me the unusual opportunity to work in a research group of graduate students as an undergraduate sophomore. The research I have been doing on nanoindentation of glass and glass melting has provided a hands-on experience to complement my accelerated coursework. It is also a way to prepare for my honors thesis.

After I get my Ph.D., I plan to work in research and development for a national lab such as Sandia or a government institution such as NASA. I would like to have my own lab with a research team and eventually take a project into space as a mission specialist. To prepare for a future career in research, I am applying to Sandia National Labs for a summer internship.

I plan to continue to participate in the activity of glass blowing throughout my professional career. By occasionally working as a glass blower at a seasonal Renaissance Faire I would be able to raise the awareness of materials science through one of its more artistic forms.

Question E: Describe an activity or experience that has been important in clarifying or strengthening your motivation for a career in science, mathematics, or engineering.

I became aware of the field of Materials Science and Engineering (MatSE) during my junior year of high school when I attended the Society of Women Engineers High School Day at Carnegie Mellon University. Up until that point I had been considering Aerospace Engineering because of my acute interest in space. That day every student was sent to three workshops; one was for their preemptively chosen major and the other two were random. One of the workshops I attended was on Materials Engineering. I was instantly fascinated. The demonstration that I remember most vividly was the brittle fracture of metals after immersion in liquid nitrogen. I immediately decided to major in MatSE.

My next college visit was to Mythic University for an Engineering Open House. The glass blowing demonstration impacted me the most. The Materials Science and Engineering Department at Mythic University has a facility for off-hand glass blowing. I pursued that interest last semester by stopping by the glass lab for 3 or 4 hours every week to watch the graduate students blowing glass. My interest paid off because starting this semester I will be taking glass blowing lessons from the same graduate students I watched at the open house two years ago. I will also have the opportunity to help out with the glass blowing demonstration at this year's open house.

Question F: Goldwater Scholars will be representative of the diverse economic, ethnic, and occupational backgrounds of families in the United States. Describe any characteristics or other personal information about yourself or your family that you wish to share with the review committee.

My family lives in a very rural area, and as such there was sparse opportunity for distinction in high school. I did my best, graduated as valedictorian, and completed my graduation project my junior year. My graduation project was inspired by my long-standing interest in space and a search through a NASA website. With the help of my father, a senior bank auditor but country man at heart, I built a drop box with a special candle holder to successfully demonstrate the effect of microgravity on candle flames.

When I go home over breaks from school, I make a point to visit my former high school teachers and present MatSE information to their new students. Living in a rural area, while refreshing and without frills, often does not provide information about the wealth of opportunities available, including career opportunities such as engineering for women. I always look forward to these visits home to share my experiences with other upcoming students.

SAMPLE NOMINEE'S ESSAY FOR THE GOLDWATER SCHOLARSHIP

Question Summary: Discuss a significant issue or problem in your field of study that is of particular interest to you.

Title: "Nanoindentation Interrogation of Float Glass for Elastic Modulus and Hardness"

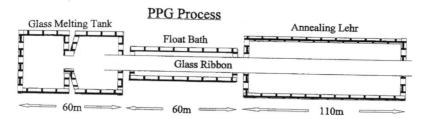

Contemporary window glass is made by the float bath process to ensure that both sides are perfectly parallel and smooth. The molten glass batch is poured from the melting tank onto a bath of molten tin. As the glass floats across the tin it cools. It then flows off the bath onto rollers that take it through an annealing lehr to remove thermal stress. As the glass rolls out of the lehr it is cut into pieces for further processing. Tin is chosen for the float because of its low reactivity with soda lime silica glass. However, it is not perfectly unreactive because contaminants enter the tin bath and change its chemistry. Some of the tin diffuses into the float side of the glass as $Sn2+$ and $Sn4+$. The diffusion of tin is governed by many factors including the composition of the glass and the time spent on the float bath. The thicker the glass is, the longer it spends on the bath. Consequently the tin has more time to diffuse. This difussion process typically produces a hump in tin content as shown.

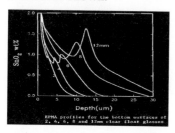

RPMA profiles for the bottom surfaces of 2, 4, 6, 8 and 12mm clear float glasses.

Traditionally, the bottom side of float glass is used as the external side of the glass when it is used in applications such as automobile windshields and commercial windows. This side was found to perform better during normal use. A better understanding of this phenomenon is desired in order to improve the mechanical and chemical durability of these glasses for future applications.

A hypothesis was formed by Dr. John Teacher that there should be a significant difference in the elastic modulus and hardness of the air and tin sides of float glass. This would be expected to alter the resilience of the float side of the glass relative to the unaltered surface. A nanoindentation technique was chosen to interrogate whether or not this is the case. Three different 4-mm-thick soda lime silica float glasses varying in iron content were chosen for examination. A Hysitron nanoindenter outfitted with a Berkocitch indenting tip was chosen for the analysis because it would be able to analyze the upper 400 nanometers of the chosen samples for hardness and elastic modulus. The loads used were 100, 300, 500, 1000, 2500, 5000, 10000, and 15000 micronewtons, yielding data points for depths of 20, 40, 60, 90, 150, 200, 300, and 380 nanometers, respectively. Nine indents were performed at each load per run and at least 3 runs were performed to ensure reproducibility.

The results obtained did not show the expected differences in elastic modulus or hardness. Instead they were almost identical at about 75 GPa for the elastic modulus. The elastic modulus of the fused silica with which the nanoindenter was calibrated was 72 Gpa.

These results suggest that the observed enhanced durability of the tin-side of float glass is due to more complex issures, possibly related to chemical interactivity between the glass and the atmosphere in service. The research group I work in is currently investigating these issues, through controlled atmospheric exposure and nanoindentation techniques. This research is expected to provide a fundamental insight into how to compositionally tailor float glass for improved chemical and mechanical durability in structural applications.

(*A statement identifying research team members appears in the original here.*)

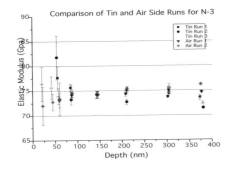 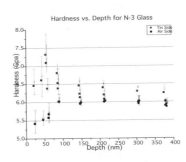

(*All figures in the original essay appeared in a larger size.*)

References:

M. Verita, F. Geotti-Bianchini, S. Hreglich, C. G. Pantano, and V. J. Bojan, "EPMA, RBS, and SIMS Analyses of Tin Profiles in Commercial Float Glasses," *Bol. Soc. Esp. Ceram. Vidrio*, **31c** [6] 415-420 (1992).
Paulson, Thomas Edward, "Thermodynamic and Kinetic Investigation of High-Temperature Interactions Between Float Glass and Tin," (1998).

The Rhodes Scholarship

Each year, 32 Rhodes Scholarships are awarded to US students, supporting two years of graduate study at Oxford University in any field. In addition to educational costs, Rhodes Scholars receive a maintenance allowance for term-time and vacation expenses. The scholarships are viewed as long-term investments in individuals with "excellence in qualities of mind and qualities of person," measured by their academic superiority and devotion to humankind. Selectors who compose Rhodes Scholarship committees come from fields including academia, law, government, medicine, and journalism.

The Rhodes Scholarship Selection Criteria

Standards by which Rhodes Scholars are judged include:

- exceptional literary and scholastic achievements;
- demonstrated devotion to service, moral character, and leadership.

An additional criterion that can weigh in a candidate's favor is success in athletics or another demonstration of physical vigor.

The Rhodes Personal Statement

Given the prestige of the Rhodes Scholarship and the staggering competition, many applicants struggle with the fact that they are limited to two fairly short writings in their applications. Candidates provide a list, not longer than two pages and in a font size no smaller than 10 points, of activities and honors in college, and a 1000-word essay setting forth personal aspirations and detailing a specific plan of study for their proposed academic work at Oxford. Needless to say, these documents are scrutinized with great care by selection committees.

The list of activities and honors should be selective and grouped logically into categories, as in a resume or curriculum vitae, and some very brief description could be used amidst this list to give context as necessary. Most important, though—in that the writer has the opportunity to interpret and persuade—is the writing of the personal statement. Excellent Rhodes personal statements are infused with concrete examples, a self-reflective tone, a showcasing of priorities and service, and an overall picture of yourself as a person of accomplishment and character. Some applicants make the mistake of seeing the essay as an academic mini-thesis or a narrative resume, while others treat it as an exercise in purple prose. Some even seem to make a demand for the scholarship or grovel at the feet of the selectors. Such poor visions of what a personal statement should be explain why the Rhodes application calls for the essay to be "written in as simple and direct a manner as possible." Meanwhile, remember the bottom line about the goal of the personal statement in the eyes of the readers: describing your specific area of proposed study and reasons for wishing to study at Oxford.

Evaluation of Two Sample Rhodes Personal Statements

The two sample Rhodes statements provided here are interesting to contrast with each other, in that the first student aims to study health, disease, and culture and the second to study British literature. Also, one writer links herself directly to Oxford only in the final paragraph, while the other links herself throughout.

One of the most striking features of the first sample is its introduction, in which the writer places herself soaked in sweat and deep in thought on a mound of rock in northern Kenya, contemplating the fate of a Homo erectus woman who died 1.7 million years ago. This narrative leads the writer to an extensive explanation, including service-based examples, of the marriage between her degrees in Women's Studies and Anthropology. Her second page is devoted to her research, including work at the Smithsonian Institute's National Museum of Natural History. We also find details evidencing physical rigor and athletic competition.

In the second sample, the writer opens with the simple phrase "I have found my mentor," then describes the very person she wishes to study with at Oxford, making further references to this professor in five of the essay's eight paragraphs. Amidst various literary references, we find examples of the student presenting a paper on Chaucer at a conference as a junior, and finally describing herself as one like Sir Gawain—an adventurer seeking a deeper understanding of self.

Though neither of these candidates received a Rhodes (which punctuates the keenness of competition), both were put forth as candidates by their schools and made it to the interview stage.

> Learn more about the Rhodes Scholarship and download the application at
> http://www.rhodesscholar.org/

SAMPLE RHODES SCHOLARSHIP PERSONAL STATEMENT

Soaked in sweat, I sat deep in thought on the small mound of sand and broken rocks in northern Kenya, where 1.7 million years ago a desperately ill Homo erectus woman had died. Her death had entranced me for years. KNM-ER 1808 had died of Hypervitaminosis A, wherein an overdose of Vitamin A causes extensive hemorrhaging throughout the skeleton and excruciating pain. Yet a thick rind of diseased bone all over her skeleton—ossified blood clots—tells that 1808 lived for weeks, even months, immobilized by pain and in the middle of the African bush. As noted in *The Wisdom of the Bones*, by Walker and Shipman, that means that someone had cared for her, brought her water, food, and kept away predators. At 1.7 million years of age, 1808's mere pile of bones is a breathtaking, poignant glimpse of how people have struggled with disease over the ages. Since that moment two summers ago, I've been fascinated by humans' relationship with disease. I want to research paleopathology, the study of ancient diseases, in relation to human culture, specifically sex and gender.

At first glance my education doesn't quite reflect my passion for paleopathology. I am often asked how bachelor's degrees in Women's Studies and Anthropology coadunate. Women's Studies and my related community service have honed my analytical skills, led me to the idea of studying sex and gender in relation to disease, and given my life and work a social conscience. I had participated in activism before college, yet my undergraduate experiences radically altered how I viewed the world and its potential for social change. Travel, conversation partnering, activism, and classes in Anthropology, African American, and Women's Studies taught me to think critically about human culture and behavior. Meanwhile, gender-equity organizing and assaults in the local community showed me the need for activism against sexual assault. I've focused on prevention, fueled by a strong personal need to make the world a less painful place. Most inspiring was organizing the "Outrage Rally against Sexual Assault," which attempted to raise awareness about and de-stigmatize assault in response to a series of assaults on the Mythic University campus. This rally had a positive impact in empowering survivors, evidenced by subsequent increased reporting of assault rates.

Organizing has also taught me successful leadership and teamwork skills, applicable to academic and social settings. I've learned the subtleties of integrating multiple perspectives into a shared vision and a success through networking with University administrators, Police Departments, nationally recognized activists, Congress persons, fellow students, and the general public. As head organizer for Mythic University's 20xx "Take Back the Night," attended by more than 500 people, I headed a seven-committee, twenty-person organizing team. In addition to recognition, as with the 20xx Service Award—Mythic University's highest undergraduate award for good citizenry and academics—organizing has honed my critical thinking skills and prepared me for performing innovative and multidisciplinary graduate research.

I want to study the relationship between human pathology and culture, looking specifically at disease in the context of sex and gender in non-modern European populations. My field of interest is new in paleopathology, so I will integrate paleoepidemiology and paleodemography—the studies of ancient disease processes and population dynamics—with gender and cultural studies and European history, contextualizing disease historically and culturally. My goal is to look at what health and disease can tell us macrocosmically and individually about social and sexual inequity, socioeconomic class, and gender-related quality of life.

Research experiences, such as working as a research assistant in a craniofacial morphometrics lab, studying skulls, and doing field work in Pennsylvania, Kenya, the Orkney Islands, West Virginia, and South Dakota, have prepared me well for graduate school. I've conducted ethnographic, paleontological, demographic, archaeological, cultural, and osteological research. I am currently co-authoring an article on the implications of Forager's mating and marriage practices for sociobiological theory, while working on a research paper on craniofacial morphology in Medieval Denmark. I also completed a senior thesis on Amerindian women's culturally influenced reproductive health issues. With confidence, I want to proceed with graduate work at Oxford to gain a higher degree and greater research opportunities in the midst of British culture.

My work this year at the Smithsonian Institute's National Museum of Natural History has galvanized and confirmed my devotion to paleopathology. An anthropological fantasy realized: I am surrounded by invaluable research opportunities and constant, stimulating dialogue with future colleagues, and vast and exotic collections including cave bear skulls, dinosaurs, and the renowned Terry skeletal Collection. Volunteer work cataloguing the Bab edh-Dra skeletal collection and independent research exploring metabolic diseases' effects on the skull using CT imaging technology have taught me the reality of professional research. Concurrently, this year has allowed me to further realize my personal interests. I practice fine arts, read extensively, love to travel, and have a whirlwind tour of Western Europe planned for December. I am hiking and backpacking on the Appalachian Trail, playing rugby, running, and I am training my four-year-old horse for jumping and cross-country riding and competitions.

I believe that my personal interests, experiences, and social conscience would contribute as much as my research skills to Oxford's social and intellectual culture. Oxford offers me an opportunity to pursue a Master's in European Archaeology while taking supplementary courses in pathology, anatomy, modern European History, and social and cultural anthropology. Equally, I could have research guidance from staff in Biological Anthropology and the Human Sciences program, where human culture, biology, and behavior in response to disease are being actively studied. At Oxford, I could nurture and share a unique set of social experiences, nurture and explore my research interests, and contribute an innovative, informative, and multidisciplinary new approach to my field. Ensconcing myself in British culture, intellectual environment, and vigorous research at Oxford is the chance of a lifetime. I hope to be able to seize it.

SAMPLE RHODES SCHOLARSHIP PERSONAL STATEMENT

Personal Statement by Janet Lerner for the Rhodes Scholarship

I have found my mentor, and I'd like to tell you who it is and how this has come about. I have not yet met him face-to-face, but he has already taught me how to begin this essay with his words. Professor Anthony D. Nuttall, writing in his book *Openings*, tells us, "…All good openings are somehow naturally rooted, more or less remote, of an original creative act: *in medias res*, as against 'In the beginning'." Nuttall describes the importance of an opening by demonstrating the difference between the actual opening lines and the first sense of action, which will become the plot.

The "original creative act" to which he refers applies as well to young scholars. I recognize now that I am in the process of becoming the scholar I will always be becoming. This process currently involves research that is the basis for my senior honors thesis: investigating two British poets' incorporation of classical Greek and Roman mythology into their poetry. I have begun studying Geoffrey Chaucer and Alfred Lord Tennyson, both of whom make active use of myth in their works. The philosophy of intertextuality, a specific interest of Professor Nuttall's, is apparent in his research on the influence of Roman and Greek classics on British poets, the very topic I have chosen for my honors thesis. While I am learning from reading Professor Nuttall's books, specifically his *A Common Sky: Philosophy and the Literary Imagination*, the opportunity to work with him would inspire me to pursue further research in this field and enrich my understanding of literature and its critical theories.

My interest in British poets and their use of classical literature evolves from a paper I presented at the 20xx *Novus Et Antiquus* Conference. I had the privilege of being selected as one of five undergraduates to attend this faculty conference, where I presented my work on classical mythology's influence on the medieval author Geoffrey Chaucer's poems *The Knight's Tale* and *The Parliament of Fowls*. There Chaucer uses the Roman gods and goddesses to orchestrate the fates of the two female characters. Through the intervention of these deities, Chaucer shows compassion for women and grants mercy to both females. My experience as a college junior presenting a paper at a faculty conference proved gratifying on another level as well: I was pleased to receive guidance from the professors, and also to be complimented on my pronunciation of Middle English quotations.

I came to Chaucer only after reading Chrétien de Troyes' *Lancelot*. In this Arthurian romance, Chrétien represents Lancelot as conflicted—the kind of chivalrous knight whom one expects to find only in myth, yet, in violation of the code of honor, desirous of his lord's queen. I began thinking of the tales of the Arthurian knights as more than legendary—as potentially credible historical accounts. I wrote a paper on Gawain's rhetoric as a means to elicit specific responses in *Sir Gawain and the Green Knight*. Gawain's rhetorical strategies and their manipulations ultimately led him to a deeper personal recognition and self-acceptance. This early exercise alerted me to strategies of language in the Middle Ages.

A post-graduate education at Oxford based on personal tutorials and independent research is precisely the type of program I now need to pursue. Through several independent study courses in my undergraduate curriculum, I have become even more self-motivated and have been gratified to discover that discussion between teacher and student has helped me develop my best work.

Professor Nuttall is a Fellow of Oxford's New College, the ideal place to continue my studies in medieval literature because it was built at the height of the medieval period, the era on which I plan to focus in my graduate study. I was pleased to discover that New College is also one of only four colleges that participate in the Oxford Access Scheme, a program that reaches out to inner-city students and encourages them to seek a higher education. This program provides all students with an equal opportunity to apply to a university as prestigious as Oxford. In participating in this program, New College seeks qualified students who may not have the socio-economic ability or confidence to apply to and attend Oxford. I would like to become involved in this program because I have worked with students in similar situations from the Boys and Girls Club near my hometown, and have found supporting these students to be very rewarding.

My reasons for applying for a Rhodes Scholarship to work with Professor Nuttall have roots in a study I undertook in 20xx. While reading Shakespeare's *The Tempest*, I found a single line in which the allegorical unicorn becomes a link between the medieval era and the Renaissance. I became interested in the villain Sebastian's professed disbelief in the unicorn, that imaginary animal symbolic of Jesus Christ in medieval bestiaries. My research on the historical symbolism of the unicorn in medieval literature led me to conclude that in rejecting the unicorn, Sebastian implies that he also rejects Christianity. An interesting aspect of *The Tempest* that I have not yet pursued is the masque, in which the Roman goddesses Iris, Ceres, and Juno descend upon the island in preparation for Miranda and Ferdinand's wedding. My earlier interest in Shakespeare's use of the allegorical unicorn will create a focus for study when combined with the masque of the Roman goddesses in *The Tempest*. Shakespeare's integration of Christianity and classical mythology is yet another area I would like to explore with Professor Nuttall, for not only has he published on philosophy; he has also written *Two Concepts of Allegory: A Study of Shakespeare's* The Tempest and the *Logic of Allegorical Expression*.

The adventure of Sir Gawain—which leads him to a deeper understanding of self—is not unlike the journey I have undertaken, a journey I hope will lead me to Oxford University, its Bodleian Library, and study with Anthony Nuttall and other mentors. Oxford will provide me the opportunity to learn directly from authorities in my field who will help guide me in my quest to become a scholar. Like Gawain, I am striving to realize my potential through my own adventure.

The Marshall Scholarship

The Marshall Scholarship is awarded for two years of study in any discipline, usually at the graduate level, and is tenable at any British university. Only the best students who apply make it beyond a school's internal selection committee to the regional review panel interviews, where about 130 students are interviewed out of 800 applicants, for about 40 awarded scholarships. Of these applicants, more than half typically have a perfect GPA. Marshall Scholars receive payment of tuition and travel as well as a personal allowance to cover living expenses.

The Marshall Scholarship Selection Criteria

Criteria used by Marshall selectors in awarding scholarships include:

- evidenced distinction of intellect and character;
- strong motivation and seriousness of purpose, as represented by the proposal of a specific, rigorous academic program.

Selectors also appreciate evidence that Marshall Scholars will view themselves as US cultural ambassadors to the United Kingdom, and vice versa.

The Marshall Scholarship Application Essays

Part of the Marshall application invites short written discussions about personal interests and non-academic activities, future career aims, and foreign travel and languages. Clearly, these discussions provide a great opportunity to present examples such as athletics, set some lofty goals, and demonstrate the maturity one needs to study abroad. Choose examples that don't require much explanation and that are not repeated in the lengthier application essays.

The most significant writings in the Marshall application are a personal statement of up to 1000 words and a one-page summary of the proposed academic programme. The personal statement typically discusses personal motivations, experience in research or teaching, academic activities, and career goals. Most writers keep this essay focused on motivations and ambitions, while some focus more on academic examples such as senior thesis work or research, and some writers introduce their target program in the final paragraph. In their personal statements, former applicants have expanded on such details as their parents' professions, an influential teacher or course, important texts they have read, theories and positions they uphold, applications of their research, and conference presentations and publications. Stressing academic achievements here is of little to no value, in that academic excellence in Marshall candidates is a given.

In the one-page proposed academic programme essay, tie your experience directly to the target school(s) and provide a clear study plan. Although students list two preferred universities elsewhere in their application, most use the one-page summary to discuss their first choice only. Clearly, the best writers evidence their suitability for the program while showcasing details to prove that they understand the program's offerings, especially if they have chosen specific individuals at the target program with whom they would like to study.

Evaluation of Two Sets of Sample Marshall Scholarship Application Essays

The first set of Marshall essays on the next three pages takes an interestingly creative approach, with the writer describing himself as a "biological anthropologist by day" and a "philosopher by night" in the personal statement. These two unlikely partnerships, wedded in one person, are exemplified by a paper the student wrote about a "consilience between Nietzsche and the theoretical work of Amotz Zahavi." We also find affecting narrative in the personal statement, with the writer depicting himself standing waist-deep in a Costa Rican swamp and working with human cadavers in a gross anatomy course. The accompanying academic programme essay is dominated by connections between the writer's background and his target program, the University of Leeds.

The second set of Marshall essays is generally more formal and research-based, but ultimately equally personal, with detail including the writer growing up as the son of two Presbyterian ministers and extensive descriptions about his physical activities, which he ties directly to the personal attribute of energy. As this student clarifies, his research concern is with fundamental principles of light and the philosophy of measurement, which he intends to study with a particular professor at Cambridge. Most importantly, the writer also notes in his academic programme essay that he aims to complete a third year of undergraduate studies followed by a one-year MPhil research program at the graduate level.

> More information on the Marshall Scholarship resides at
> http://www.marshallscholarship.org/

SAMPLE MARSHALL SCHOLARSHIP PERSONAL STATEMENT

In the sixth grade, I took a test to see if I was left- or right-brained. To my elementary eyes, the result of that quiz would be the truth from on high—a resolute word that would define the man to come as either analytic or artistic. Unfortunately, the oracle I sought gave me a perplexing answer. Much to my disbelief, my tallied score yielded a perfect split down the middle. Was I mentally ambidextrous or mentally challenged? I preferred to think the former; either way, I have never felt at home thinking in just one hemisphere.

When I tell people that I study biological anthropology *and* philosophy, they often curiously raise an eyebrow. "What an odd combination," they remark. Even though I have come to expect this, I understand their bewilderment. Though the sciences and the humanities were once braided into one holistic education, today, the two behave like estranged lovers settling a bitter divorce, resulting in separate academic quarters. One hundred years ago, every student at Mythic University—humanist, scientist, and farmer alike—was required to read Plato in the original Ancient Greek. Receiving a broad education was seen as part of becoming a true scholar. Despite their differences, when I look at the current interaction between the humanities and the exact sciences— specifically between philosophy and evolutionary biology—I see cause for hope, perchance even reconciliation, through philosophy of science. In this pursuit, I have tailored my undergraduate education to lay a foundation in both philosophy *and* science.

Biological anthropologist by day. Many of my days are spent at the Mythic University paleoanthropology lab, where I am fortunate to work as Dr. John Teacher's undergraduate research assistant, casting the semicircular canals of small mammals to study their morphology as it relates to movement. The semicircular canals house the organs of balance, and their morphology is inherently tied to locomotion. Through the analysis of these casts, we can analyze variation within readily available populations. High-resolution computed tomography (CT) scans allow for the non-invasive reconstruction of this tiny region of the inner ear in the minutest detail. This exciting approach is providing new insights into the locomotion of hominids and other ancient, extinct primates without damaging rare fossils. Studying the variation in canal morphology helps us assess the reliability of this technique.

The experience of this assistantship, along with two summers of standing in a waist-deep Costa Rican swamp, culminated in my honor's thesis, which investigates the agility of three species of New World monkeys through both observations of positional behavior and analysis of semicircular canal morphology. Agility is a rather nebulous concept. It is my hope that this comparative examination will yield an effective means of quantifying relative levels of agility among primates.

Understanding how primates move requires a functional understanding of mammalian anatomy—a passion of mine for the past three years. The opportunity to assistant-teach three undergraduate anatomy courses has been among the most fulfilling parts of my education. When I taught gross anatomy I had the opportunity to work with two cadavers. A person can learn a great deal about human anatomy from texts, but there is an eye-opening degree of realism that sinks in during cadaver study. Furthering my own knowledge of anatomy would be reward enough for teaching these classes. What really propels me to teach, though, is the possibility of helping my students germinate a genuine curiosity in a subject that I love.

Philosopher by night. While fascinated by my anthropological pursuits, I take tremendous pleasure from reading philosophy into the early morning hours, sitting in the back of the dimly lit Mythic University Diner, famously open 24 hours a day. Camaraderie is high at the Diner as a good number of philosophy graduate students study there every night, conversing over coffee. It was there where much of my interest in philosophy blossomed as I listened to many late-night debates about the virtues and failings of Aristotle and the nature of mind. For a while, I was seen as the token scientist, but after studying there for two years and taking a two graduate-level philosophy courses in ethics and the philosophy of mind, philosophy students are beginning to recognize me among their ranks. My experiences have led me to form a biweekly study group where undergraduate philosophy majors can interact and discuss their readings with the graduate students.

I became particularly interested in the interaction of philosophy and biology when I read Nietzsche's *On the Genealogy of Morals* for the first time. Seeing a unity of ideas between some of what Nietzsche wrote in *Genealogy* and aspects of contemporary evolutionary biology made me realize that a more fruitful exchange of ideas between biologists and philosophers could precipitate advances in both fields. When I read *Genealogy* again last year in my ethics seminar, I wrote a paper about a consilience between Nietzsche and the theoretical work of Amotz Zahavi—the ornithologist and author of *The Handicap Principle*—which I will submit for publication this fall.

This idea came as an epiphany—one shining moment of clarity that allowed me to unite seemingly disparate fields of knowledge for the first time. As I continue to investigate the relationship between philosophy and biology, I sense that more epiphanies are on the horizon. For me, continuing to bring the two fields together will not only require both sides of my mind, but also a mentor with the experience and breadth of knowledge to guide me in such an endeavor. Studying with Dr. Jonathan Hodge at the University of Leeds' History and Philosophy of Science program will put my mental ambidexterity to good use.

SAMPLE MARSHALL SCHOLARSHIP
PROPOSED ACADEMIC PROGRAMME ESSAY

At the University of Leeds I propose to pursue a research MPhil in the history and philosophy of science, with a focus on the philosophy of evolutionary biology under Dr. Jonathan Hodge. I also wish to seek out the mentorship of several members of the philosophy department in this endeavor.

My broad interest is in philosophy of biology. I am especially interested in the interaction between philosophy and evolutionary biology, insofar as I want to study the historical repetition and unity of ideas between philosophy and biology in an attempt precipitate advances in both fields. In other words, I study the consilience between specific philosophers' ideas and aspects of evolutionary theory (e.g., Nietzsche or Buddhism, and natural selection, or the relationship between the works of ethical philosophers and the ethical implications of evolutionary psychology). Such a program of study requires both a working knowledge of evolutionary theory and history in addition to discussion and understanding of relevant philosophers (Aristotle, Nietzsche, Darwin, and others).

Simply put, the History and Philosophy of Science program at The University of Leeds offers me opportunities not afforded by other universities. Its greatest asset is the presence of Dr. Hodge, who for the past several decades has been one of the world's foremost philosophers and historians of biology. Reading his article, "The notebook programmes and the projects of Darwin's London years" in *The Cambridge Companion to Darwin*, which he co-edited with Gregory Radick (also at Leeds), I immediately became aware of the remarkable breadth and depth of his knowledge about Darwin and the history of evolutionary theory. Dr. Hodge possesses the qualities I am looking for in an advisor—he has the capability to recognize and further my insightful hypotheses relating biology to philosophy and to help me fine-tune those that are too grandiose.

One of Leeds strongest attractions is the breadth of its departments. Not only will I be able to study philosophy of biology with professor Hodge, but I will also have the opportunity to study Nietzsche and Buddhist philosophy with Seiriol Morgan and Nik Jewell in the philosophy department, as well as Aristotle with Nafsika Athanassoulis. Thus, The University of Leeds can provide me with an opportunity to study philosophy outside of the biological realm, just as I desire.

Should the University of Leeds not be an option, I propose to pursue a MPhil in the History and Philosophy of Science Department at the University of Cambridge under the direction of Dr. Timothy Lewens. My project would remain the same; however, Cambridge lacks a philosopher of biology of equal merit to Dr. Jonathan Hodge, making The University of Leeds preferable.

SAMPLE MARSHALL SCHOLARSHIP PERSONAL STATEMENT

The driving influence in my life has always been to grasp the nature of the universe. Growing up as the son of two Presbyterian ministers, questions concerning the creation of the universe and the principles upon which it runs were staples in my home life. More than that, my parents always pushed me not to be content with merely understanding how the world works, but always to strive for the basic principles explaining why it works that way. I recall asking my father a simple question about a car and getting a three-hour lecture on the physics behind the internal combustion engine. This experience in and need to dig deeper into the workings of the world has brought me to the place that I am now, and I feel it guiding my future.

I have been doing physics research in varied fields since the summer after my freshman year, yet I have never been able to answer a question that has nagged me for years. How do we know that our systems of measurement are truly definitive? In my lab, I would be taking a temperature measurement with a thermocouple gauge and comparing it with a measurement by a standard thermometer, and the whole time I asked myself how I could know that I was really measuring the same thing—temperature—with both.

The basic problem is involved with the foundations of the scientific system of measurement. Traditionally, temperature would be measured by the height of a mercury column in a glass tube—a basic thermometer. Yet, the meter was defined as the length of a certain platinum rod at a specified temperature. Thus, there is circularity in our basic units of measurement. This is the basic problem in the philosophy of measurement to which I want to apply myself.

As is evident from the example of the thermometer used above, I see this question as a very historical one. But at the same time I feel that it is pertinent to modern physics. One of the underpinnings of quantum mechanics is that matter behaves like a wave until a measurement is taken, at which time the "particle" is made to choose a position, or velocity. This begs the question: What constitutes a measurement? Given that quantum theory is the essence of modern physics, this question cannot be ignored.

After my work in particle physics at the Deutsches Elektronen-Synchrotron (DESY) in Hamburg, Germany, I want to do research in theoretical particle physics. Yet, I feel that if I don't take time out now to carefully study the philosophy of measurement, I will not be able to address the issues facing modern physics theory as well as I could. My undergraduate studies have been interdisciplinary—I major in physics, math, and philosophy—and I feel that an interdisciplinary approach in my graduate studies will be the most fruitful. I say this because I have always felt that a well-rounded person is better able to tackle the complex problems of life. This is why I do not work only in academics, but also spend considerable time in athletics and community service.

Physically I am endlessly active. I have used college to explore a large variety of new activities. Freshman year, I was a member of the Mythic University Racquetball Club and competed in intercollegiate tournaments. As a sophomore, I joined the university's Crew Team and rowed in the first squad in men's novice lightweights. Last year, I joined the Shotokan Karate Club, earning a green belt in two semesters instead of the normal three. I also started long-distance running and am currently training for a marathon in the spring. If am not doing one of these things I am playing pick-up games of soccer, volleyball, or basketball with friends. I bike, sail, hike, and hang-glide.

The same energy that I have in sports I carry into my community service activities. I have helped with voter registration for the upcoming election, Adopt-A-Highway in my local area, and a local campaign to revive a dilapidated movie theater. My primary affiliation is with Habitat for Humanity. This year I am the fundraising director, in charge of raising enough money so that the Mythic University chapter of Habitat can build its second house for a deserving family. In Habitat, I have spent countless hours doing jobs such as drywalling, insulating, and painting. This past spring break I went to Winter Haven, Florida, to help paint a house with 15 other students.

It will also take great energy and versatility to be successful as a professor of physics. One must not only understand physics, but also be able to pass on one's knowledge of physics to others. A good background in the history of physics and the underpinnings of its principles will serve me well in passing on my physics knowledge in an exciting and helpful way. By working in examples from the history of physics, students will be more engaged with the impact of science on society and feel the human side of physics.

My undergraduate thesis at Mythic University will also help to prepare me for writing and research in my future career. The beginning of the historical work mentioned above will take the form of my honors undergraduate thesis. I will be examining four experiments in the history of optics, and showing how the experiments can be more effectively used in undergraduate classrooms to illustrate the principles of physics. I will study experiments of Newton, Fresnel, Faraday, and Einstein to address fundamental principles of light. We experience light every day; however, comprehending its nature has puzzled even the greatest of scientists. Einstein is quoted as saying: "Every physicist thinks that he knows what a photon is. I spent my life to find out what a photon is, and I still don't know it." I want to bring myself and my future students to try to tackle such issues.

This summer I visited Cambridge, and after much thought throughout my time in Europe, I have come to the conclusion that it would be the ideal place for my studies in the history and philosophy of science. Cambridge has a department that combines both historians and philosophers of science with an excellent museum carrying original pieces of scientific equipment. Moreover, Dr. Simon Schaffer is renowned for his work in the philosophy of measurement, and I would gain greatly by learning directly from him. For these reasons, I would like to complete the third year of undergraduate studies in the history and philosophy of science at Cambridge and then continue study in the MPhil one-year research course with funding from the Marshall Scholarship.

SAMPLE MARSHALL SCHOLARSHIP
PROPOSED ACADEMIC PROGRAMME ESSAY

If I receive the Marshall Scholarship I will study the history and philosophy of science at Cambridge University. Spending two years at Cambridge would improve the quality of the teaching and research that I plan on doing as a professor of physics. It would give me the knowledge and expertise to make my teaching interesting to students from a wide range of backgrounds by incorporating historical information. It would also gain me the background necessary to face the problems of modern theoretical physics.

While at Cambridge I would complete the third year of the undergraduate program and then the one-year research MPhil in the Department of History and Philosophy of Science and Medicine. The first year would broaden my knowledge and understanding of both the history and philosophy of physics. I already have a strong base in the subject. I have taken four classes in the philosophy of science and related topics at Mythic University and my undergraduate honors thesis is concerned with the history and philosophy of science at it applies to physics education. I have also done independent reading in the subject. My first year at Cambridge would be an extension of these studies, under some of the most prominent researchers in their respective fields.

My second year at Cambridge would serve to consider questions in the philosophy of measurement more deeply. I wish to focus primarily on the measurement of temperature in the nineteenth century, from both historical and philosophical perspectives. In considering history, I am concerned with the discussions within scientific circles during the nineteenth century about controversial principles of measurement. In addition, I would investigate the methods undertaken by instrument makers to ensure that temperatures measured with different types of devices could be reliably compared. I would focus on the transition during the century away from the traditional mercury thermometers to more modern thermocouple devices, and how these two devices were compared at the time. Philosophically, I am interested in our definitions of fundamental units, such as length and mass. I want to address questions of fundamental importance to quantum mechanics, which will have bearing on my future work in physics.

Given my aspirations described above, the program at Cambridge is an excellent fit for me. It is unique in allowing one year of intensive study followed by an independent research course. The department of interest to me is the largest of its kind in the UK, and combines both historians and philosophers together. In addition, the department is built around the Whipple Museum, which houses a fine collection of original scientific instruments for study, including thermometers from the nineteenth century. I have read and admire the work of Dr. Simon Schaffer and would love the opportunity to work with him. Spending two years at Cambridge would allow me to pursue a balance between history and philosophy that is difficult if not impossible elsewhere. Finally, I feel it is necessary for my development as a researcher and teacher.

The Truman Scholarship

The Truman Scholarship awards $30,000 towards graduate study, and undergraduates apply during their junior year. Applicants must have extensive records of community service, be committed to working in a government or public service position, and possess excellent communication skills. As of 2005, Truman Scholars are also required to fulfill a special public service requirement following completion of their graduate degree, as detailed on the Truman website.

The Truman Scholarship Selection Criteria

In culling about 200 finalists for Truman Scholarship interviews, the selection committee uses criteria including:

- quality and length of community or government service;
- leadership record, academic performance, and analytical skills.

Selectors give priority to candidates enrolling specifically in graduate programs related to service, ranging from public policy to environmental protection.

The Truman Scholarship Application Essays

The Truman Scholarship application requires extensive writing in the form of more than a dozen questions to answer with lists and short essays and a separate two-page policy proposal. The application questions include discussions of a specific example of your leadership, a recent service activity, a societal problem, influential courses you have taken, your target graduate program and future plans, and an open-ended question for "additional personal information." There are two important pieces of advice in answering these application questions. First, *don't leave any questions blank*—find creative ways to answer all of the questions based on your background, seeking advice from your school's Truman faculty representative. Secondly, *thoroughly scour the Truman website*, noted on the next page. Here you will find everything from suggestions by a past Truman participant to both satisfactory and unsatisfactory responses to application questions.

The website also details policy proposal tips and provides a sample proposal. In the policy proposal, your task is to choose a controversial, manageable, well-studied problem and write a recommendations-based proposal to a government official. Obviously, you are not expected to solve the problem—the committee is interested in how well you can analyze an issue and demonstrate both a passion and practicality for solving it. In writing this proposal, keep in mind the fundamental definition of a Truman Scholar: *an agent of social change.*

Evaluation of Two Sample Truman Scholarship Policy Proposals

In the two sample policy proposals that follow, you will find some noteworthy similarities: both use the same basic form and headings; both use statistical data to demonstrate the problem; both provide a specific solution (the first in the form of a bill, the second in the form of an education program) to address the problem; both cite a variety of references. These similarities are significant in that *every* Truman policy proposal needs to have these attributes in order to be successful.

Considering the proposals individually, the first focuses on the controversial topic of discrimination faced by the Lesbian, Gay, Bisexual, and Transgender (LGBT) community. This writer analyzes how members of this community experience problems ranging from employment to physician referrals, and correlates how such individuals might be protected in the same way that persons of color are protected under the Civil Rights Act of 1964. The writer shows particular savvy as she reminds her target senator that he recently supported the Employment Non-Discrimination Act, but that she proposes a bill whose net of protection would be even wider. As we read the final section of the proposal, purposely even-handed in tone, we recognize that the writer is politically active, aware, and potentially persuasive. Indeed, this candidate did receive a Truman Scholarship.

The second proposal focuses on Fetal Alcohol Syndrome (FAS), opening by noting the fate of the innocent victims, then branching into statistics about both binge drinking among women and low levels of FAS awareness. The writer's proposal is to deliver FAS awareness programs within colleges through increasingly popular first-year seminar classes, and the essay's end analyzes the considerable challenges involved in implementing this proposal. Some readers might find the proposal unpersuasive in that FAS problems themselves are not fleshed out and the relationship between cited data and proposed solution may be thin, but remember that the committee looks at this proposal in the context of the entire application, and intends to put a significant writing challenge.

An excellent website on the Truman Scholarship is available at
http://www.truman.gov/

SAMPLE TRUMAN SCHOLARSHIP POLICY PROPOSAL

<u>To</u>: John Office
<u>Office Held</u>: United States Senator (R, state name)
<u>Issue</u>: Lesbian, Gay, Bisexual, and Transgender Civil Rights

Problem Statement
One of the most urgent problems within the United States is the discrimination faced by the Lesbian, Gay, Bisexual, and Transgender (LGBT) community, who are routinely denied equal civil rights protections. Discrimination against LGBT people is legal in thirty-four states (NGLTF, 2004). According to the American Psychological Association, over one-third of LGB African-Americans and more than one-half of LGB White Americans have experienced discrimination based on their sexual orientation.

Discrimination occurs in many arenas including public accommodations, housing, school and employment. For example, within medical settings, about one-third of LGB physicians and medical students surveyed reported that, because of their sexual orientation, they had been denied employment, refused medical services or a loan, denied a promotion or referrals from other physicians, or were fired from their positions (Schatz and O'Hanlan, 1994). Discrimination affects the mental health of LGBT individuals, their access to equal opportunity, and their job performance (Waldo 1999). It hurts the children who cannot access medical benefits from their LGB parents and creates an American culture that is exclusive and divisive (HRC 2003).

Proposed Solution
According to political scientist Alan Yang, people are most accepting of LGBT people when they have a relationship with a member of the LGBT community (1997). It is only when LGBT people feel comfortable coming out to their friends, family and employers that our society will truly become supportive of this population. This means that a comprehensive federal anti-discrimination bill including protection for LGBT people in employment, public accommodations, housing and education must be passed.

It is absolutely necessary that LGBT have a legal remedy for the discrimination they are faced with in the same way that people of color are protected under the Civil Rights Act of 1964. Research indicates that places of employment with anti-discrimination policies shower higher job satisfaction and commitment among LGB people (Burton, 2001). This is further supported by research showing that LGB people are more likely to report discrimination in places of employment that do not have policies against discrimination based on sexual orientation ("Support for ENDA," 2003). According to these findings, LGB people are also more likely to be comfortable in their academic and living environments when non-discrimination policies exist.
Your recent support of the Employment Non-Discrimination Act is commendable, but this bill is not sufficient. It only protects LGBT people against employment discrimination. A bill must be drafted that prohibits discrimination in employment, public

accommodations, housing and education. LGBT people must be protected in all areas of society so that they are afforded equal access to all of the United States opportunities.

Major Obstacles/Implementation Challenges

Although a 2001 Gallup Poll indicates that eighty-five percent of respondents replied yes to the question, "In general, do you think homosexuals should or should not have equal rights in terms of opportunities?" there is a significant portion of Americans who believe that homosexuality is a sin ("Testimony," 2002), and members of this group actively fight legislation to promote their views. This group is well-organized and mobilizes its grassroots efforts efficiently and effectively. This group tends to misinterpret the idea that by seeking equal civil rights protections, LGBT people are asking for *special* rights.

There is also a strong possibility that employers may not support this bill because they will believe that it might require them to offer domestic partner benefits to their employees. This is an added cost that may challenge small businesses in particular.

Admittedly, this is not a policy that all of your constituents support, but it is one they can all benefit from. By working towards a society that is inclusive of all of its citizens, our community is strengthened and all people are afforded their constitutional right to equal opportunity.

References, Footnotes, and Exhibits

Burton, S. B. (2001). Organizational efforts to affirm sexual diversity: A cross-level examination. *Journal of Applied Psychology, 86*(1), 17-28.

National Gay and Lesbian Task Force. GLBT Civil Rights Laws in the U.S. 1 February 2004. http://www.ngltf.org/downloads/civilrightsmap.pdf.

Schatz, B., and O'Hanlan, K. (1994). Anti-gay discrimination in medicine: Results of a national survey of lesbian, gay, and bisexual physicians. *American Association of Physicians for Human Rights*. San Francisco.

"Support for ENDA." 2003. Human Rights Campaign. 29 Jan. 2004, <http://www.hrc.org/ContentManagement/ContentDisplay.cfm>.

"Testimony For the Hearing on ENDA." United States Senate, Washington D.C. 27 Feb. 2002. 28 Jan. 2004 <http://www.apa.org/ppo/issues/penda202.html>.

Waldo, C. (1999). Working in a majority context: A structural model of heterosexism as minority stress in the workplace. *Journal of Counseling Psychology, 46* (2), 218-232.

Yang, Alan S. Trends: Attitudes Toward Homosexuality. *Public Opinion Quarterly*, Vol. 61, No. 3. (Autumn, 1997), pp. 477-507.

SAMPLE TRUMAN SCHOLARSHIP POLICY PROPOSAL

<u>To</u>: Janet Office
<u>Office Held</u>: United States Secretary of Education
<u>Issue</u>: Fetal Alcohol Syndrome Awareness in Higher Education

Problem Statement

Every child born with Fetal Alcohol Syndrome (FAS) is unjustly handicapped by the alcohol consumption habits of his or her mother. The leading, preventable cause of birth defects in the US is alcohol, with FAS resulting in the most extreme cases (Floyd and Sidhu, 2004). Approximately half a million pregnant women report alcohol use each year, and 80,000 report binge drinking (Floyd and Sidhu, 2004).

Binge drinking among young women ages 18-44 is on the rise, increasing by 13 percent in a recent three-year period (Gardner, 2004). Binge drinking puts women at an increased risk for unintentional pregnancies and means they are more likely to drink while pregnant. These statistics are evidence of a major public health problem in the United States.

Low levels of FAS awareness in the nation ultimately contribute to the unwanted conception of FAS children. The 2002 National Health Interview Surveys found that 73% of women and only 55% of men have a measurable awareness of FAS (Nation et al., 2003), indicating that substantial numbers remain unaware of the dangers of alcohol consumption during pregnancy.

Proposed Solution

My proposed solution is to increase FAS awareness in higher education. Support would be sought from the US Department of Education's Policy and Program Studies Service, as its mission statement is in line with my project goals ("US Department of Education," 2004). Monies would be requested from the Fund for the Improvement of Post-Secondary Education (FIPSE), to be spent on prevention and intervention though education ("Office of Postsecondary Education," 2004). Prevention education would address both FAS and binge drinking in higher education and in future marital relations.

The awareness program would be delivered via First-Year Experience (FYE) classes, also known as First-Year Seminars (FYS). According to Bradley Cox of the National Resource Center for the First-Year Experience and Students and Transition, over 621 institutions of higher education host FYE/FYS programs (Cox, 2004) , making them a standardized setting for the delivery of the FAS program. FIPSE monies would be promoted to higher education institutions across the country to thereby increase FAS awareness and decrease the future conception of FAS children.

If successful, this program could be adapted for future intervention in public high schools and community colleges.

Major Obstacles/Implementation Challenges

There exist three significant challenges to the implementation of this FAS program. A realistic proposal would be needed to promote the curricular addition of FAS into FYE/FYS classes across the country. FYE courses are highly variable, both in conception and credit hours, and therefore the program will need to be comprehensive and concise enough as to be a reasonable addition.

The second challenge would include the delivery of the program by a professor. One major reason for the failure of prevention programs to date has been poorly trained presenters (Nation et al., 2003). An efficient, comprehensive training program would be needed to maximize program effectiveness. Coordination with established on-campus groups such as residence life and counseling programs would be ideal.

Thirdly, the FAS program must be established in a way pertinent to the college student's life and so that students take it seriously. College students do not engage in risky drinking habits with the intention of getting pregnant. Therefore the connection of risky drinking habits to the birth of FAS children can be difficult to establish.

References, Footnotes, and Exhibits

Cox, Bradley. Personal Communication. 2004.

Floyd, RL and Sidhu SS. Monitoring Prenatal Alcohol Exposure. *American Journal of Medical Genetics*, Vol 127C, 33-39, 2004.

Gardner, Amanda. "Report: Binge Drinking on Rise in Young Women." *Health Day.* 23 June 2004. <http://www3.komotv.com/Global/story.asp?S=1965365>

Golden, Janet. "An Argument That Goes Back to the Womb: The Demedicalization of Fetal Alcohol Syndrome, 1973-1992. *Journal of Social History*, Winter 1999. <http://www.findarticles.com/p/articles/mi_m2005/is_2_33/ai_58675447>

Nation et al. "What Works in Prevention: Principles of Effective Prevention Programs." *American Psychologist*, June/July 2003, Vol 58, No 6/7, 449-456.

"Office of Postsecondary Education – Programs Fund for the Improvement of Postsecondary Education (FIPSE)." 26 November 2004. <http://www.ed.gov/about/offices/list/ope/fipse/index.html>

"US Department of Education Principal Office Functional Statements: Office of the Secretary & Deputy Secretary." 26 November 2004. <http://www.ede.gov/about/offices/list/om/fs_po/osods/policy.html>

The Mitchell Scholarship

The Mitchell Scholarship is named to honor the former U.S. Senator George J. Mitchell, who served as Chairman of peace negotiations in Northern Ireland. The scholarship funds one year of graduate study at an Irish university and is awarded to approximately 12 students per year. The scholarship provides airfare, tuition, fees, housing, and a stipend for living expenses. The Mitchell Scholarship Selection Committee interviews 20 scholarship finalists in Washington, DC.

The Mitchell Scholarship Selection Criteria

The Mitchell website notes the criteria used to select Mitchell Scholars:

- achievement in academics, leadership, and community service;
- a concrete plan and commitment to study at an Irish university.

No minimum GPA is required and no GRE scores are used in the selection process, but high academic achievement is a necessity in a Mitchell Scholar. Also, a student's past experience in Ireland or previous acceptance into an Irish university program does *not* serve as an advantage, in that part of the scholarship's mission is to introduce new future leaders to Ireland.

Preparing the Mitchell Scholarship Application

The Mitchell application process takes place completely on-line, even for the applicant's recommenders. Thus, a good deal of time must be spent on familiarizing yourself with the on-line system. Meanwhile, a valuable way to prepare your application is to read the "Reflections on Ireland" online journal maintained by current Mitchell Scholars, as well as the profiles of past recipients. This practice will give you a good sense of both everyday life in Ireland and the kinds of students the selection committee has awarded in the past. Note that much of what you input in the application is the sort of material one lists in a curriculum vitae or resume, and this material will be balanced with your personal statement by the committee as part of the selection process. The application also invites you to list at least three preferences for schools, and the website notes that failure to do so can weaken an application slightly, in that institutional balance is a factor in placing students at universities.

In composing the personal statement, which is about two pages in length, the basic goal is to present a rationale for the proposed study program and provide concrete evidence of your readiness. Some students detail their achievements in academics, leadership, and service, while others focus heavily on the study program of their first school preference, trusting that their application as a whole will provide a balanced picture of their background. Still other students match themselves to Ireland or Northern Ireland as directly as they can, including travel abroad when relevant, and noting any Irish professors whom they have met or with whom they have had contact.

Evaluation of Two Sample Mitchell Scholarship Personal Statements

The two sample personal statements that follow on the next four pages are an interesting study in contrasts, in that the first focuses heavily on music performance and the second on political advocacy. While both are strong personal statements, it should be noted that neither student landed a Mitchell Scholarship, underscoring the competitiveness of the application pool.

The first sample statement opens with a narrative discussion of Irish dance performance, after which the writer fleshes out her background in dance and music performance extensively. Indeed, this student has already studied for a semester abroad at University College Dublin and received private lessons in performing Irish "trad" music. Thus, her goal of extended study in this area is well-grounded in experience, and after she discusses her three target programs, making it clear why the University of Limerick is her first choice, she forcefully notes: "I *must* study in Ireland if I plan to pursue my passion."

The second sample statement—written by a woman born of Peruvian parents and raised partly in Japan—opens with the writer defining her unique ethnic background and cultural diversity. As we learn throughout the essay, this background has informed her distinctive and deep involvement as an advocate for marginalized voices. She directly links this passion to her three academic programs of choice, and ends by artfully defining herself as a "world student and future political activist," making a brief reference to Senator Mitchell's work, and citing her commitment to ultimately helping US Latino citizens.

> For complete detail on the Mitchell Scholarship and to register to begin the on-line scholarship application process, go to
> http://www.us-irelandalliance.org/scholarships.html

SAMPLE MITCHELL SCHOLARSHIP PERSONAL STATEMENT

Feet like lightning. Arms pressed to the sides. Instruments sounding like nothing I had previously heard. The airing of *Riverdance* on PBS was my first introduction to anything that could be considered "traditional Irish." At that time, I had been dancing since I was five years old, so this newfound form of dance was naturally intriguing. My interest in dance and the arts continued to grow and at the age of nine, I began to play the flute. Almost immediately, music was my passion, and I knew someday I wanted to perform. For years, I focused solely on concert flute repertoire, assuming I would become a concert performer. During high school, though, I had the opportunity to collaborate with a hammered dulcimer player who gave me notated Irish music to read, and my interest skyrocketed. I began to listen to traditional Irish groups such as the Chieftains and "Celtic rock" groups such as Seven Nations. During my sophomore year as a flute performance major at Mythic University, I realized study in Ireland was the only way for me to properly learn traditional Irish music and culture.

Fall 20xx was my semester in the Junior Year Abroad (JYA) program at University College Dublin (UCD). Because the JYA program required two areas of emphasis, I chose Music and Celtic Civilization. Before arriving in Ireland, I knew the music department at UCD did not offer lessons with private instructors, so I contacted Mr. Bill Dowdall, professor at the Royal Irish Academy of Music and principal flautist of the National Concert Orchestra. Mr. Dowdall was willing to give me "classical flute" lessons, but he did not play traditional Irish music (often called "trad"). As my main reason for going to Ireland was to learn trad music, I had to find a teacher. With the help of Mr. Adrian Scahill, my "Irish Traditional Music" lecturer at UCD, and Mr. Dowdall, I found an Irish flute teacher, Mr. Seán Ò Broin.

At least once every week during my time in Ireland, I went to McNeill's Traditional Music Shop on Capel Street in Dublin to take a trad lesson with Mr. Ò Broin. Irish music is an aural tradition—meaning that in order to perform it authentically, one must learn tunes by ear. Being trained classically, I was used to reading notes on a page, but one cannot analyze Irish music from a classical viewpoint. Trad is a separate and unique art form with its own set of special rules. I learned that lesson firsthand and through an ethnomusicology course at UCD.

Since returning to the United States, I have observed that most people who play Irish music read from "fake books," which tend to approximate and simplify the complicated, time-honored tradition. Irish music must be learned aurally and personalized by each player with her own ornamentation, nuances, and interpretation of her teacher's style. I realize that when it comes to seriously studying traditional Irish music, I have only scratched the surface with one semester of lessons. I must return to Ireland if I am to continue the pursuit of knowledge that was begun.

During my graduate study in Ireland, I plan to attend the Irish World Music Centre (IWMC) at the University of Limerick to attain the MA in Irish Traditional Music Performance. The Centre is the only one of its kind in the world, and the degree is unique to this university. Although University College Cork offers a one-year MA in Music, and NUI Maynooth offers a one-year MA in Music (Performance and Musicology), the IWMC is the only school to offer Irish Traditional Music Performance. At my target University of Limerick program, advanced instrumental tuition is provided by world-renowned traditional performers and tutors, and the examinations of repertoire sources and styles of performance are supplemented by important modern non-performance skills such as music business and music technology. The IWMC offers other specialized courses besides my proposed MA, and elective modules in the program will allow me to pursue some of my other interests.

I believe other interests are an integral part of my education and plan to continue gaining more knowledge in each area while studying abroad again. Classes offered through the Irish Traditional Dance and Contemporary Dance Performance programs at the IWMC will allow me to further my dance knowledge outside my world of ballet. Mr. Niall Keegan, Course Director of my prospective MA program, tells me there will be opportunities to continue my concert studies in ensembles. Not only do I plan to continue with concert flute studies, I also intend to teach private classical lessons. My first ethnomusicology experience at UCD whetted my appetite for exposure to diverse musical cultures and inspired me to apply for the newly approved International Arts Minor at Mythic University. Classes through the Ethnomusicology program at the IWMC will teach me more about other cultures and their special musical traditions. Irish language studies will broaden my understanding of Irish music traditions, and I look forward to beginning these classes while in the country.

Eventually, my goal is to perform in ensembles that incorporate varying musical styles, especially Irish traditional music. Since returning from Dublin, I have led workshops, given recitals, performed a jury for the Mythic University woodwind faculty, and spoken with many people about my Irish learning experiences. My joy comes from educating people about trad music through performance and conversation. I am determined to follow my ambition to share this passion. When my JYA semester ended with my first experience studying in Ireland, I realized how much more I needed to learn about traditional Irish music and culture. I do not merely want to study in Ireland; I *must* study in Ireland if I plan to pursue my passion. Now, with the Mitchell Scholarship and its many benefits, mastery of Ireland's distinct musical art form and immersion in its culture are within my grasp. It is an honor to be considered for this perfect opportunity.

SAMPLE MITCHELL SCHOLARSHIP PERSONAL STATEMENT

I have always found comfort in my mother's words: *to find out where you're going, you need to know where home is.*

Home was never an easy concept to me—a girl born of Peruvian parents and raised in Japan. A family heritage and birthplace are common differentiators, a way to identify oneself in acceptable categories to the world. Instead, I was often treated like a wandering foreigner, without clear and defined categories. I have no simple answer when asked about my identity: I was born in Japan and lived there for seven years as a Peruvian. Now I am an American with ties all over the world. Even though I cannot embrace just one location, I established a home for myself in a metaphysical and emotional space: the space where my family, passions, and goals all intersect.

My perspective as an ethnic minority deeply influenced the way I engage my life. Just as with my own family, struggling upon entering Customs in the United States, I see the pattern of struggle among Latino families due to a disconnect between Latinos and the larger society. Latinos are not major players in the discourse on vital issues facing the United States. With an increasing curiosity on the conditions facing other minority groups, I continue to pursue my motivating drives: to stand up for minority groups and dedicate myself to service.

As part of my fight against barriers for equal access to the political system, my ongoing campaign for civic participation has called upon all students at Mythic University to raise their voices and demand accountability of politicians. As the President of the Student Political Science Association, I led efforts in "Get Out the Vote" campaigns and coordinated major speaking events to inform students of the pertinent political issues. Also dedicated to children's rights, I have collaborated with students to improve the conditions of street children in the Dominican Republic through fundraising and the construction of shelters in Santo Domingo. The group Rescue Childhood continually increases its educational efforts by informing the campus and community about children's rights issues. Last year, I was instrumental in gaining the support of Mythic University in hosting a children's rights activist, a survivor of Pol Pot's killing fields.

As part of my commitment to understanding challenges facing minorities, I participated in the service learning initiative in the summer of 20xx. As a volunteer for Habitat for Humanity and NET, a juvenile detention center, I began to internalize the space of poverty in my month-long stay in Mythic City: the run-down homes, drug dealings, and shootings at night. Through the classroom, I investigated the history of the city and learned of the negative economic and social trends facing many other urban areas, mostly populated by minority groups. I was appalled by the lack of opportunities for African-American and Latino residents. Inspired by the goals and the convictions of the community leaders, I worked to improve the conditions of my community.

My interest in marginalized and ethnic minority groups has evolved into an honors thesis: an analysis of the successes of Latino interest groups on influencing policymaking in Washington DC. I am undertaking a project tracking the successes of

Latino groups in specific policies over time. The results will show what factors play a significant role in increasing policymaking successes. My ultimate research goal is to investigate the ways in which Latinos can take part in the discussion of policies that will affect their daily lives. As the Latino minority grows larger, I fear rising tensions over immigration, education, and jobs will begin to polarize sectors of the population. These discussions must take place peacefully on the floor of Congress and not on the torn streets of places like Mythic City.

The Mitchell Scholarship is an incredible opportunity to study minority groups in a non-American institution. The focused, taught courses in Irish institutions offer the chance to develop a great expertise in an area. The Queen's University in Belfast offers an M.A. in Identity, Theory and Culture and Comparative Ethnic Conflict. A taught course in the concepts of identity, nature of ethnicity, and the politics of culture will provide me with the academic background needed to pursue my career of service to the Latino community. Most of all I believe my life in Belfast will force me to internalize the history and conflict that once consumed Belfast and Northern Ireland. I would find the experience extraordinarily rewarding.

I am also interested in the National University of Ireland in Galway for an L.L.M. in Human Rights. With future aspirations as an advocate for minority rights, I believe the L.L.M will set a firm foundation in the pursuit of my goals. The Equality Studies Program in the University College Dublin also offers a unique opportunity to explore my interests in minority groups. These programs are specific to my interests and will propel me into the field of public policy and advocacy for Latino issues.

More personally, I have never explored Western Europe and I am eager to take a step beyond my travel to Latin America and Asia. I am thirsty to branch out to another culture. The opportunities in Ireland will provide me with a broad understanding of ethnic minority struggles around the world and contribute to my personal growth as a world student and future political activist.

The spirit of the Mitchell Scholarship is fitting to my experience as an advocate for marginalized voices. Through my commitment to minority group's equal representation and protection of rights in political systems, my goal is to help ease future tensions within and beyond American society. Following the efforts of Senator George J. Mitchell, I hope to further Latino issues in the greater American society and support policies to improve the conditions of Latinos as a way to prevent rising tensions among citizens of the United States.

The Gates Cambridge Scholarship

The Gates Cambridge Scholarship program, created by the Bill and Melinda Gates Foundation, offers various scholarships funding between one and four years of study at Cambridge University in England. Areas of funded study are graduate, affiliated (a second undergraduate degree), clinical, and MBA, and the scholarships are competed for internationally. Students apply directly to Cambridge through the usual procedures, with the scholarship award decision heavily driven by the target Cambridge department. About 500 US students per year apply for the scholarships, with approximately one-fourth of them being offered a follow-up interview. Nearly 100 scholarships are awarded per year, and about one-third of those awarded scholarships typically go to US applicants.

The Gates Cambridge Scholarship Selection Criteria
Gates Cambridge Scholarship applicants are evaluated by the following criteria:
- exceptional academic achievement and scholarly promise;
- aptitude for research, analysis, and analytical thinking;
- appropriate fit between candidate's plans and Cambridge offerings, as revealed through the applicant's written application and interview.

Gates Cambridge scholars will become leaders who address such global concerns as social equity, health, and technological advances. Obviously, evidence of an applicant's ability to have such an impact leads to a more favorable outcome.

Preparing the Gates Cambridge Scholarship Application
Gates Cambridge application questions vary slightly based on the area of funded study, but commonalities are questions related to your intended course of study and a 500-word personal statement. When answering these and other narrative questions, detail should be given about how your past activities reflect both leadership and service, and for how a particular course of study at Cambridge will serve to help you attain your goals. A useful exercise is to browse through a copy of a recent yearbook of Gates Cambridge scholars (available on-line). The yearbook gives profiles of those who have received the scholarship, outlining examples of their leadership, service, and long-term goals. For instance, from the 2004 yearbook, one scholar notes the value of her volunteer work in Ecuador. Discussing research and future plans, one scholar describes his plan to work on neuron regeneration at the Brain Repair Centre in Cambridge, while another summarizes his long-term goal to serve in Pakistan as a financial advisor.

Obviously, familiarizing yourself with these current scholars will help you decide how to present yourself so that you can stand tall among them.

Evaluation of Two Sets of Sample Gates Scholarship Application Essays

The two sample excerpts from Gates Cambridge applications show the depth and diversity of students who apply for this scholarship. The first student, studying colon cancer, shows interests in everything from Renaissance painting to technical writing, while the second, studying speech technology, discusses interests ranging from computer security to swing dancing. Both of these students were awarded a Gates Cambridge Scholarship.

The first writer uses her short statement of research proposal to demonstrate her thorough awareness of the program at the center where she aims to conduct research at Cambridge. In her accompanying 500-word essay, she strikes a bold and creative tone by representing herself as something of a modern "Renaissance woman" (she even explores her creativity by "reproducing an intricate Renaissance painting" at the age of 13)—one who sees the study of science as an outlet for her creative mind, and one who takes the initiative to co-found and edit a health journal as well as teach science to students in state custody. Her theme of creativity as the "driving force" in her development and eventually leading her to science is both rhetorically persuasive and stylistically elegant.

The second writer discusses the specific course of study he would like to complete at Cambridge, followed by research which he hopes would make computer technology available to a wider audience, "including those suffering from physical disabilities." His passion for working in this area becomes further articulated in his 500-word essay, where he expresses concerns about sensitivity of personal information and "the safety and stability of the global economic community." Like the writer in the first example, he sees education as an important vehicle for change, and he has taught computer literacy classes to the elderly as well as studied abroad during his junior year at Oxford University. He ends his essay affirming his desire to "take action to improve the condition of humanity."

> More information on the Gates Cambridge Scholarship is located at
> http://www.gates.scholarships.cam.ac.uk/

SAMPLE RESPONSES TO SELECT QUESTIONS ON THE GATES CAMBRIDGE SCHOLARSHIP APPLICATION

Statement of Research Proposal.

Molecular staging of colon cancer, or the correlation between phenotype and the discrete genetic mutations present at a particular pre-malignant stage, will lead to more accurate prognosis, therapeutic intervention, and treatment targeted for a precise genetic profile. With these theories in mind, I plan to pursue my MSc at Cambridge University and to focus my efforts on elucidating the genetic profiles of colon cancer. I would be honored to work under the direction of Dr. Carlos Caldas of the Hutchinson/MRC Research Centre, whose laboratory is engaged in characterizing the molecular profiles of colon cancers and elucidating prognostic indicators in the onset of cancer. I have chosen to pursue graduate studies at Cambridge because of its unrivaled reputation for scientific achievement. I am confident that the intellectual development I would be afforded at Cambridge, through a rigorous and largely independent training program, would be unmatched by most other institutions. Furthermore, Dr. Caldas' laboratory is concerned with the biological behavior of cancer at the genetic level and uses this understanding to guide therapy; the partnership between basic science and its clinical counterpart are integral to my future career as a medical scientist.

In not more than 500 words, please describe below how your interests and achievements, both academic and extra-curricular, demonstrate a capacity for leadership, commitment to using your knowledge to serve your community and to applying your talents to improve the lives of others. Please also explain how your proposed studies in Cambridge will help you with the aims of your future career.

At thirteen, I wanted to explore creativity through reproducing an intricate Renaissance painting. Using dozens of blues and greens, I emulated the brush strokes and shading. And after much toil, I felt confident that museum curators would have a hard time distinguishing between mine and the original.

In receiving a first place award at a local art competition for my rendition of Tintoretto's *Christ at the Sea of Galilee*, I experienced only partial satisfaction. My painting was merely a great reproduction. My arts classes stressed imitation, and I realized that applying creativity would not occur until much later. Thus, I set aside my study of art, and continued my pursuit of creativity.

At the time, my interest in science was also begging for exploration. I had my first experience with research in eighth grade—"Are There Really Any Differences Between Commercial Hand Lotions?" While engaged in devising a method to test the antibacterial effectiveness of hand lotions, I found an immediate outlet for originality. The creativity in science proved to be both objective and self-perpetuating; the means of uncovering new data is an indisputably creative endeavor and a single question often gives rise to many more. Thus, I found creativity responsible for both initiating and driving the scientific process.

Years later, I find that the accumulation of complex genetic mutations responsible for the evolution of cancer leaves much for my creative mind to ponder. A single pathway for any given cancer doesn't seem to exist, but several genetic permutations often lead to the same end. My fascination with contributing to an understanding of these "creative" processes lies in their potential for development of chemopreventative strategies that may halt pre-malignancy as well as for treatments individualized to fit a precise genetic profile of cancer.

I find the processes associated with the study of rhetoric complementary to processes that propel science. In both fields, hypotheses look to evidence for support and a meaningful conclusion leads to a refined question. In addition to the science of writing, I have developed an appreciation for the writing of science. I co-founded and edit the Journal for Pre-Health Affiliated Students (JPHAS). I expanded JPHAS from an initial pre-medical only publication because I recognized the increasing interrelatedness of health careers and that an awareness of healthcare options may yield more satisfying results for students.

I have extended the scientific process to my service within the larger community. In the past, I received enormous fulfillment working with boys in state custody, teaching them science in hopes they will acquire useful academic knowledge and a sense of accomplishment. I currently take part in a weekly seminar, "Youth and Science: Possibilities and Challenges." Recently, I helped initiate a program aimed toward the girls housed in a shelter. Finding that the same science lessons didn't accomplish the same goals, I combined my old passion, art, with my new vocation, science, to generate more relevance and interest. The newly developed ten sessions include "Genetic Gems," where the central dogma of biology lends itself to deciphering girls' names (amino acid sequence) into double-stranded jewelry (DNA codons). While the immediate goal of the program is to spark the girls' interest in biology, I hope the program will have a longer lasting impact on their sense of intellectual capacity.

Creativity has been the driving force in my development, and science provides the most promising pathway for me to explore the full potential of my creativity. In pursuing an MSc in Molecular Oncology at University of Cambridge, I will establish the ideal foundation for my future role as researcher, medical practitioner, and academic pursuing a deeper public consciousness of the cancer problem.

SAMPLE RESPONSES TO SELECT QUESTIONS ON THE GATES CAMBRIDGE SCHOLARSHIP APPLICATION

Statement of your research degree proposal, or reason for wanting to undertake a taught course.

Studying Computer Speech, Text, and Internet Technology at Cambridge will provide me with the necessary background to pursue my future career. Upon completion of this course, I intend to work on the development of new methods of interacting with computers and accessing web-based technology. This work would serve to make technology accessible to a much wider audience, including those suffering from physical disabilities, and also by improving the exchange of information both nationally and internationally. As technology plays an ever more prevalent role in our society it is critical that it remains accessible and understandable to all and that it serves to break down barriers between people rather than constructing them anew. Technological advancements must be developed in accordance with these ideas, or else there is potential for a division between those to whom technology is accessible and those to whom it is not. By completing this course at Cambridge, I will be prepared to fulfill my personal and career objectives as I work to improve international communication and understanding by developing new internet technologies.

In not more than 500 words, please describe below how your interests and achievements, both academic and extra-curricular, demonstrate a capacity for leadership, commitment to using your knowledge to serve your community and to applying your talents to improve the lives of others. Please also explain how your proposed studies in Cambridge will help you with the aims of your future career.

I strongly feel that working to better society in a manner that utilizes one's strengths for maximal effect is of the highest importance. As technology has grown ever more prevalent in our society, computer security has become critical to the safety of the international community. This digital security is necessary both to ensure the physical safety of society, by protecting sensitive information from unauthorized individuals, and also to ensure the safety and stability of the global economic community by preventing attacks upon business, which can result in devastating financial losses. By performing this research I will be working to improve the security of the global community through a role in which I can be most effective. My research will make vulnerabilities in current security protocols easier to detect and correct and those in future protocols easier to prevent. Having completed this research, I will be prepared to continue working to create a safer society as I perform further research or provide security consultation to the public and private sectors.

Throughout my academic career I have pursued this goal of improving the lives of others by using my personal strengths. During my first two years at Mythic University, much of my time was devoted to the University Swing Dancing Club, in which I served as both

Secretary and President. This organization of more than 700 members promotes the sport of swing dancing and provides a valuable social, creative, and cultural outlet to the university community—both faculty and students—through regular dances and lessons. In this leadership role I taught lessons, organized dances, petitioned the university for funding, and negotiated contracts with nationally recognized bands and instructors. I also organized and oversaw committees delegated to specific tasks such as fund raising. As President of the club, I was also involved with a philanthropic dance marathon benefiting children with leukemia, which helped to raise over 2 million dollars for research. Again I was able to help others by using my individual abilities and by working with others towards a common goal.

In my home community, I have taught a series of computer literacy classes for the elderly, hoping to open to them new avenues of communication and a wealth of information as well as ease their anxiety about daily interaction with an increasingly high-tech society. At the same time I helped a local museum gain greater exposure and share its information with a wider audience by designing its website. While studying at Oxford University my junior year I was a member of the Union Society and regularly attended lectures and debates, which addressed topics such as fair trade. This transformative experience help me to stay informed on current issues that impact the international community.

It is critical as members of a global society that we remain cognizant of the challenges that plague our fellow citizens, but this is not enough. We must take action to improve the condition of humanity through whatever skills we have available. My past experience demonstrates my desire to fulfill this goal, and through education and research at Cambridge I will be able to continue this pursuit to greater effect.

The Cooke Scholarship

The Jack Kent Cooke Foundation was established by the businessman and philanthropist Jack Kent Cooke, and supports both undergraduate and graduate scholarships for students of strong academic achievement (at least a 3.5 GPA), impressive character, and financial need. The Foundation awards student scholarships through several different programs, including a scholarship for those transferring to four-year programs from community colleges. Each award covers educational and living expenses, and the amount of the award varies based on costs and length of program. Students are nominated for the scholarships by designated faculty representatives at their schools, and each institution may nominate up to two students. Scholarship nominees are not required to be US citizens, and there are no age restrictions.

The Jack Kent Cooke Scholarship Selection Criteria

Cooke Scholarship applicants are evaluated by criteria including the following:

- academic achievement, leadership, public service, and appreciation for the arts and humanities;
- drive to succeed and ability to think critically as evidenced in the application materials;
- unmet financial need.

In some areas, including visual art, dance, industrial design, and music, students are encouraged to submit recordings or portfolios of their work for consideration.

Preparing the Jack Kent Cooke Scholarship Application

In preparing a Cooke Scholarship application, one of the best ways to begin the process is to read through the biographies of past winners on the website. This will give you an idea of both the schools from which scholars applied as well as the value of each winner's personal background. Here you will find stories of a self-proclaimed "computer music geek," a woman who continued her education despite being stricken with MS, single parents, and people who returned to school after decades of work. At the same time, there are just as many students who went the traditional educational route straight through school and earned the scholarship. Thus, one gets an uplifting sense that there truly is no "typical" Cooke Scholar. Browsing through these biographies, you will also find wording similar to that used by students as they answered their application questions.

The Cooke application includes questions to be answered with short narratives as well as an extensive essay for the undergraduate scholarship and a narrative autobiography and resume for the graduate scholarship. Given the nature of the scholarship and weight of the questions, you must make it a point to respond with genuineness. Among the questions, you're invited to discuss a work of art, project a decade ahead in your life, write about an important event from history, discuss a recurring literary theme, and describe yourself as a competitor. In answering such challenging prompts, smart writers speak from the heart while still keeping an academic focus appropriate to a scholarship of such importance.

Evaluation of Sample Jack Kent Cooke Scholarship Materials

The following pages contain excerpts from the applications of previous Cooke Scholarship winners, with a sample from an undergraduate transfer, a student entering graduate school, and a sample resume.

In her short answers, the undergraduate transfer student describes herself confidently as a "Renaissance woman" aiming for a law career to benefit the underserved population in her home city. We find these two themes of diverse interests and commitment to law throughout her answers, as she describes student government work, appreciation for local architecture, a concern for children, and a desire to teach a future course at her local community college. In her essay on a historical event, she chooses the Holocaust, focusing in particular on her knowledge of the novel *Fateless*, by Holocaust survivor Imre Kertesz.

The sample graduate scholarship application and resume come from a cancer survivor and former sales and marketing director who re-started her adult life by leaving her job and attending an all-women's college, where she thrived and began a journey toward becoming a professor, writer, and activist. Her essays are as richly detailed as her narrative autobiography, drawing on best-selling authors, scholarly references, Christian traditions, and metaphor. She summarizes the chancy move she made in life when returning to school by paraphrasing Tennyson: "It is better to have lived and lost, than never lived at all." The overriding message to readers should be clear: She has lived and *won*.

> More information on the Jack Kent Cooke Scholarship is available at
> http://www.jackkentcookefoundation.org

SAMPLE RESPONSES TO SELECT QUESTIONS ON THE JACK KENT COOKE UNDERGRADUATE TRANSFER SCHOLARSHIP APPLICATION

Question #5. List the degree and area of concentration you will pursue if awarded a Jack Kent Cooke Foundation Undergraduate Transfer Scholarship. Explain the reason for your study and career choice.

I pride myself in being one of a handful of "Renaissance Women" able to balance course combinations like Philosophy and Fiction, Drawing and Database Management, and Anatomy and Accounting in a true liberal arts fashion. Not only has my background been a source of self-fulfillment and interesting dinner party conversation, the unique realm of versatility I have developed has made me an asset in numerous work and volunteer situations. I expect my background and future educational experiences to continue this trend. With the Jack Kent Cooke Scholarship, I will pursue a bachelor's degree in English/Pre-law and, if my portfolio is accepted, I will minor in Studio Art at Mythic University. Not only have I developed a love for the law from a Business Law course and United States District Court grand jury duties, I discovered a talent for drawing after participating in two student art shows on my community college campus. After obtaining a bachelor's degree and a Juris Doctor Degree, my primary career will encompass civil law, with part of my practice dedicated to the poor and underserved population in my hometown of Mythic City. I also plan to teach paralegal courses part-time at my current community college, and I plan to write and illustrate at least one book in my lifetime.

Question #6. Describe a recent experience in which you made a difference. Explain what was accomplished, your role, and what you learned and/or would do differently.

This past fall, Student Government Treasurer Janet Student and I worked together to pilot a campus recycling program. While several people saw the need for campus recycling, when Janet presented her idea last spring Student Government did not have the funds to support it. Plus, with our campus maintenance staff being unionized, recycling at that time would have brought forth questions of how to coordinate the emptying of containers until union contracts could be re-discussed. Even starting a student organization focused on recycling was not feasible since Student Government could not afford to fund the organization as they had funded all the other student organizations on campus.

Fortunately, Janet established herself at the college that spring and was elected as Student Government Treasurer, and I was elected as President. Janet and I spearheaded the project, established outside contacts with other groups who recycle, researched prices on containers and other materials we would need to facilitate the venture, and succeeded in starting a pilot program.

While both of us felt great that we were helping the environment, the true realization that recycling is making a difference on campus is the positive feedback offered by our students and staff. We have received verbal comments, emails, several students asking about joining Student Government, and, as time passes, fewer and fewer recyclable materials are ending up in our rubbish containers. My only regret is that Student Government did not have the funds to start something like this sooner, because it has had such a positive impact on campus life.

Question #7. Discuss a piece, or pieces, of art, literature. music, or film. Why has it been meaningful to you? What have you learned?

Several months ago, I researched Second Empire architecture for my Art Appreciation course and selected a neighborhood bed and breakfast inn for discussion. The inn I selected is a two-story French Victorian brick structure erected in 1872. Its design touts the characteristic steep, boxy mansard roof (named after Francois Mansard, who developed the technique in the 1600s) and dormer windows. In the United States, buildings of this nature are found primarily in the Northeast and the Midwest because these were regions of high economic activity in the era when the style was most popular. According to the inn's website, the house has been recognized as an outstanding example of Second Empire architecture by the Indiana Historic Site Preservation Committee.

Because I worked at a bed and breakfast inn for several years, and because I currently live in a historic district of downtown Mythic City, I have a genuine love for old houses. Plus, I find architecture to be an especially intriguing type of art because it offers a permanent fixture of form and function. My specific attraction to this inn had to do with its oddness amidst its surroundings: the beautiful building towers over nearby mansions, trees, and other cityscape; and it almost seems a bit uncomfortable squeezed into the corner lot of a bustling business district. But through my research, I was better able to picture the inn in its historical 19th century glory. I came to see that the original owners not only had the funds to supplement such a grand venture, but also the desire to create a work of art that would testify for centuries to the greatness of the European influence and the history of the American Midwest.

Question #8. Write about an experience that has changed your perspective on or your attitude towards a personal, social, or political issue.

I recently heard on the radio that the Federal Communications Commission (FCC) is discussing a change in law that would impose monetary penalties on radio disk jockeys (particularly the "shock jocks" who purposely use rude language to shock listeners) for each instance of inappropriate word usage, as opposed to the current regulations that only allow a set financial sanction no matter what or how much inappropriate language is used in a show. Usually I advocate freedom of speech as long as it does not infringe on the constitutional rights of others and, in fact, if I find a show on television or the radio to be offensive, I utilize my freedom to change the channel to something better suited for my taste. In this particular case, however, I have allied myself with the FCC. I worry about the parent driving a van full of children to or from school who inadvertently stumbles upon a Howard Stern-type show. Perhaps if the FCC cannot advance a new penalty for inappropriate language, an advocacy group would promote a V-Chip option, similar to what is in many televisions today, in car and home stereos.

Question #9. A decade or more from now you are a "successful" person, by your own definition. What year is it? Why are you successful? How did you get there?

On Wednesday January 29, 20xx, I am gazing out of a window in my law office, wondering if the snow will let up well before the class I am teaching this evening. The medical malpractice chapter I'll be teaching from always sparks some lively discussion, and I hope to stick to the syllabus as much as possible. I have been teaching part-time at Mythic Community College since I had received my Juris Doctor degree five years ago: one Business Law course on Wednesday evenings and one Introduction to Paralegal Studies course delivered via the Internet. I have received some stellar student evaluations from both courses, and everyone seems to enjoy the PowerPoint presentations I create for each week's lessons and my easily navigable faculty website. Without my Associate's Degree in computers, my supplemental Web Design training, and all of the experience from my previous jobs and public relations roles, I would not be able to integrate my teaching with my legal career so seamlessly.

I turn my attention back to my desk and the six manila files still waiting to be perused. With my supervisor's permission, I devoted my entire day to representing matters for the poor and underserved. Fortunately all the cases thus far have been misdemeanors and easily resolved; but by the looks on my clients' faces and their exclamations of "Thank you," "Bless you," and "You have saved our family," it appeared as if I had the power to perform miracles before their very eyes. I enjoy even my difficult cases because I love my job, but a day such as this is unquestionable reassurance that the career I have chosen is the best one for me.

Question #10. **Essay:** *Write an essay on* **one** *of the following topics. Check the box below to indicate the topic you are answering:*

- ▢ *We live in a time of great and controversial issues—local, national, and global. Create a newspaper headline regarding an important issue. Explain why you chose the topic; how you think it can be resolved; and your role, if any, toward its resolution.*

- ▢ *Identify one event from history that has a relevant lesson for our times. Describe how you would apply that lesson to a situation today.*

I believe that the Holocaust is a very relevant event in our world's history. I became fascinated with Holocaust events during a conference in Washington D.C. about a year ago: the interest in the Holocaust museum exhibit was phenomenal, and if the depicted events did not speak to the citizens of our times, a lack of patronage would have been a definite sign.

Prior to my visit to D.C., the information I had about the Holocaust was vague, at best. Somehow each of my English teachers had neglected to assign Anne Frank's infamous diary, and with my personal schedule I never managed to locate it on the library shelf when I had the time and desire to read it. Fortunately, one of my community college instructors introduced me to *Fateless* by Imre Kertesz. Not only did my eyes engulf each page of words in a matter of days, I utilized the library and the Internet to integrate several supplemental works about the Holocaust into my final paper.

A popular saying about history is that those who do not have knowledge of the past are condemned to repeat it. This lesson can be applied to everything from politics to one's own personal life. While a noted mass murder of an entire race has not happened recently, racial and religious tensions fuel daily attacks around the world. The possibility of a dictatorship in current times has already been manifested with people like Saddam Hussein. Therefore, a dictator commanding a Holocaust-like event such as Adolf Hitler did could also be a close possibility. Kertesz, a Holocaust survivor, values the past as a way to prevent such horrible events from repeating themselves in the future: "The Holocaust is a value because it has led to immeasurable knowledge through immeasurable suffering, thus creating an immeasurable moral resource" (1997). Kertesz has openly condemned the suppressing of Holocaust stories by members of his generation. Instead, he urges every person to embrace the incident as a valuable learning tool. Kertesz's devotion to educating others about the Holocaust, and his desire to prevent its replication, led to him to share the story of his own imprisonment at Auschwitz in the novel *Fateless*.

One lesson that can be learned from the Holocaust is the importance of resilience in the face of adversity. While most of us would hope that no human would have to suffer such an extreme form as torture, survivors such as Imre Kertesz are valuable to us not only because they are human beings, but because they are teachers. These teachers can pass on learning that can only be gathered from experience, and these teachers can help prevent the same mistakes from being repeated. In *Fateless*, Kertesz's narrator (who is telling Kertesz's own story) utilizes numerous coping techniques to deal with what is going on around him. Sometimes we attribute his rationale to his young age, or to his naïveté when our experiences would have us act differently, but the fact that the narrator tries to cope is to be admired and learned from. Readers can also gather lessons of how racism and discrimination are wrong, even in a transaction as minimal as overcharging someone for a loaf of bread because he or she is Jewish.

At the same time, while we are feeling sorry for the Jews, we are also questioning their reactions. In a *Newsweek* interview, Kertesz shared, "They [the Germans] forced a person to choose in a way we were never forced to choose before: to become either a victim or a perpetrator. Even surviving involved collaboration, compromises you had to make if you wanted to bring a bigger piece of bread home to your family." Imre Kertesz also stated that he felt lucky to have been at Auschwitz. "I experienced my most radical moments of happiness in the concentration camp. You cannot imagine what it's like to be allowed to lie in the camp's hospital, or to have a 10-minute break from indescribable labor. To be very close to death is also a kind of happiness. Just surviving becomes the greatest freedom of all."

When Kertesz mentions freedom in relation to a concentration camp, a prison, the reference seems odd and out of place. But what people in the United States today can gather from that definition of freedom is an appreciation and understanding for the freedom they themselves are blessed with: dictates such as The Patriot Act seem like minor inconveniences when considering how Auschwitz prisoners were constantly watched and often did not have access to or knowledge of loved ones, and the problems of the ever-criticized United States government pale in comparison to the consequences of a marked dictatorship.

In *Fateless*, Imre Kertesz teaches readers about the value of the human experience. With all of the lessons we could take from the Holocaust and apply to modern times, the most important lesson of all is not to repeat the past by our actions. In honor of Kertesz and those who have given us books, memorials, and exhibits about the Holocaust, we should utilize these resources to face the past, and then look forward to and work for a brighter future.

SAMPLE RESPONSES TO SELECT QUESTIONS ON THE JACK KENT COOKE GRADUATE SCHOLARSHIP APPLICATION

Question # 4. List the graduate degree and area of concentration you will pursue if awarded a Cooke scholarship. Explain the reason for your study and career choice.

My graduate studies will be the zenith of thirty years of looking at the world through the lens called "religion." I have applied to Ph.D. programs in Religion (or Religious Studies) departments with a concentration in American religious history. My graduate studies will allow me to explore modern and popular religious movements in America as responses to the tensions in contemporary society. Modern television programming and movies about goddesses, witches, otherworldly creatures and monsters, and powers or miracles "from beyond" proliferate. Best-selling authors like Deepak Chopra (*Seven Spiritual Laws of Success*, etc.) or Neale Donald Walsch (*Conversations with God* series), or movements with religious/spiritual components like Alcoholics Anonymous or *A Course in Miracles* prove that alternative, non-institutional religious expressions have captured the imagination of millions of Americans. I am interested in how participants define spiritual intention and authority. Are these movements successful in creating community, fostering healing, and achieving social justice or do they foster little more than a heightened sense of self-importance—sanctifying individualism? Some programs encourage participants to be in touch with nature or the messages from their own bodies. These goals may be indicators of either a new ecological theology; or, the careful manipulation of popular concepts to appropriate moral authority. I want to evaluate and understand these new religious/spiritual expressions as part of my preparation to become a professor of religion, a writer, and an activist. As a professor of religion, I want to teach my students about the past to help them make appropriate ethical choices for their future. As a writer and activist, my work in religious studies will be synergistic, influencing my own work for social justice.

Question # 5. What are your long-term career plans?

I want to be a college professor, writer, and activist. As a professor of religion, I would engage my students in discussions about the sacred texts from the great religious traditions and ask them to look for connections (or conflicts) between teachings and actions. I would help them evaluate their own personal ethical choices in comparison with other religious or spiritual frameworks. Scholars should be informed by the past but encouraged to move into the future, creating a new response to contemporary challenges. This kind of scholarship is best fostered within a collaborative community that encourages dialogue across disciplines and participation in issues of social justice. The dynamics within the academic community should instruct and inspire. For those who are within the religion department, the challenge is to find ways to celebrate the diversity of religious and spiritual traditions without claiming supremacy for any specific doctrine. As a writer, I plan to write books both for the academic community as well as for a popular market exploring the intersection between religious thought in modern America and ethical action. I want to inspire readers to operate from within their respective framework of religious/spiritual beliefs as a springboard into personal activism. As an activist, I plan to continue to engage with my family, community, and global community within a context of compassionate commitment. I want there to be synergy between my academic work and my work in the community. I would like to continue the kind of work that I am doing now through the Mythic Leadership Center. It is very important for people to learn not only to ask the right questions, but also to transform their answers—however tentative—into plans for action. I want to be part of that process—as a professor, a writer, and an activist.

Question # 6. Describe a recent experience in which you made a difference. Explain what was accomplished, your role, and what you learned and/or would do differently.

As a peer mentor in the Mythic Leadership Center, I work with students who want help expressing their ideas. I recently worked with a second-year international student who wanted to apply for a study abroad program. In her statement of purpose, she was to describe her goals and objectives. She initially complained that she didn't have any—she had no idea what she was doing or where she was going in her life. When encouraged on, she explained that she hadn't made any friends and felt lonely and disconnected from campus life. These feelings of isolation seemed to be making her feel unfocused academically as well. We spent the appointment talking about her favorite courses and her country. As she described her interest in ecology and economics, she became animated and passionate. At the same time, she spoke eloquently about the ecological problems in her country. I helped her see the connections between her coursework and her country's problems. When she brought back her rough draft the next visit, she had explained how her coursework at her selected study abroad institution intersected with her newly defined interests in ecological economics. Since her selected school was in the same part of the world as her native country, she argued that it had the faculty and resources germane to her country's specific issues. Her enthusiasm for her area of investigation was evident and her argument was persuasive.

I believe my sessions helped her connect to larger issues and concerns. She felt like she could make a difference in changing things in her country. Perhaps her feelings of passionate engagement will affect her social relationships too. My sessions with her remind me that I cannot always start with the specifics of a paper or a presentation without taking time to understand the author. Sometimes there are other issues or obstacles that need to be resolved before the real work can begin.

Question # 7. Identify a recurring theme in classic and current literature, and discuss the relevance of the theme to your life.

The theme of sacrifice is imbedded within the literature of most religions (*Bible, Ramayana, Qur'an,* etc.), Greek literature (including the plays of Euripides, *Aeneid* by Virgil, *Odyssey* by Homer) and echoed within popular literature. It is difficult to find literature that does not require a character to question how much s/he is willing to give up for God or the common good or for love or to lose twenty pounds. The American Dream is predicated on the idea that anyone can achieve the good life in exchange for some form of personal sacrifice. Consequently, this theme is not only relevant to my life, but also unavoidable. How do I determine the priorities of my life in order to balance my personal goals with the good of the greater community? I will need to give up something on behalf of something else that I think is more important. Or will I? I do not choose to see my life as an endless sequence of personal compromises and deprivations, beating my breast in righteous indignation over the sacrifices I am called to make! Rather, I choose to view my life as a series of choices that creates greater alignment and resonance with my ideals. I make choices that create more harmony. Perhaps sacrifice and harmony are the opposite sides of the same coin, but differences in mindset are profound. Therefore, to reach my personal goals, I do not sacrifice going to the movies so I can spend more time on my homework. I choose to express myself as an excellent student, taking the time that I need to do my work to my satisfaction. To contribute to my vision of the global community, I do not sacrifice my free time to work as a volunteer helping to promote leadership initiatives and programs for women in my community. Rather, I choose to participate. I am free to volunteer or stay home. There is no sacrifice in my choice. I find joy and fulfillment in my choice to participate. In the final analysis, I do not find that choices need to be embedded in the language and imagery of sacrifice. For me, it is no sacrifice to live an ethical life—it is harmony.

Question # 8. There seems to be a conflict between land development and ecological concerns. What solutions would you suggest that would satisfy both?

The conflict between land development and ecological concerns reflects the conflict between individual rights and community/global rights. Land development concerns often include the idea of profit that can be oppositional to ecological concerns. Economic growth is predicated on increasing production while lowering costs. This places tremendous pressure on utilizing underdeveloped natural resources, conflicting with ecological goals of preservation. Without a shift in emphasis from individual rights to community and global goals, the respective goals of land development and ecology are irreconcilable. Solutions that would satisfy the conflict between land development and ecological concerns must be situated within a commitment that resources are for the benefit of every living being. In addition to people, a community includes animals and plants, and those resources that provide life for the community (including water, air, and earth). Those who claim ownership rights need to rethink their claim in terms of "stewardship." If land were developed under guidelines that preserved community standards of well-being, development would be more likely to provide sustainable benefits to a broader population. Enlightened developers recognize that a sustainable future has more value than monetary and momentary profits. Examples of this can be found within the category of agricultural land development that includes farming techniques, pesticide use, and water use. A broader view that encompasses ecological concerns has became necessary to alleviate crisis situations (toxic food, saltwater intrusion, toxic water or depleted water sources, dustbowl scenarios, etc.). From this example, we can learn that it is possible and advantageous to reconcile the needs of the community with land development. A shift in core values that encourages cooperation and community over individual rights will lead to progress in reconciling ecological concerns with other categories of land development.

Question # 9. What do you value most? Explain why.

When I first thought about answers for this question, my answers were around ideals like "love," or "truth," or "freedom." Yet, as I continued to think, I realized that there was only one answer for me: I value my body the most. Without my body and my senses, I would be unable to experience the world around me. "Love," "truth," and "freedom" have value because I can embody those concepts or express them in this physical world. I rely on my body to know how I feel. The nerves and muscles and organs of my body mediate emotions like love, joy, pain, and sorrow. I rely on my ability to read the body language of others to help me determine how they are feeling. If I see someone smiling and waving her hand, the message is clear, "I'm glad to see you!" I also need my body to perform my intentions. No matter how clearly I can present an idea in my head, the idea is nothing until I can share it. I can use my mouth and breath to create words to describe my idea or I can use my hands to build or create my idea. For instance, I use my body to plant and care for a garden. My hands, arms, feet, and legs work together with tools and dirt to bring my vision to fruition. In time, I can pick the herbs and vegetables, smelling the damp earth and feeling the sun on my face. I can make soup with my vegetables and herbs and share that soup with my neighbors or carry a bowl to a sick friend so she can taste some sunshine. My body allows me to comfort another by holding her in my arms or to help another by sharing her tasks. Like-minded individuals use their hands and heads and hearts to "body forth" common goals and ideals—creating and fostering communities. I cannot think of any ideal or philosophy that has any meaning without an expression in or through a body. Even in the Christian tradition, the "Word" was made flesh. While I often take my body for granted, I am very grateful that I have a healthy and effective body. My world would not exist without it.